AN ILLUSTRATED HISTORY OF
RUGBY REBELS, ROLE MODELS AND GIANT KILLERS

AN ILLUSTRATED HISTORY OF
RUGBY REBELS, ROLE MODELS AND GIANT KILLERS

THE PLAYERS, PEOPLE, TEAMS AND IDEAS
THAT CHANGED RUGBY FOREVER

JAMES STAFFORD

Illustrated by Raluca Moldovan

POLARIS
PUBLISHING

This edition first published in 2023 by

POLARIS PUBLISHING LTD
c/o Aberdein Considine
2nd Floor, Elder House
Multrees Walk
Edinburgh
EH1 3DX

www.polarispublishing.com

ISBN: 9781915359094
eBook ISBN: 9781915359100

British Library Cataloguing-in-Publication Data
A catalogue record for this book is available on request from the British Library.

Designed and typeset by Polaris Publishing, Edinburgh
Printed in Great Britain by CPI Group (UK) Ltd, Croydon, CR0 4YY

To my incredible mother, for always being there for me.

'I think it's worth all the suffering and hardship if one person's life is changed from hearing about my story.'
Jillion Potter, US Rugby Olympian

CONTENTS

INTRODUCTION

There's an old cliché, almost as old as the sport itself, that says rugby is a game for people of all shapes and sizes. And it's true. But it's often overlooked that it's also a sport for all types of personalities and backgrounds as well.

For too long the perception of rugby outside the rugby community – and even sometimes to its shame within it – is that it is a sport for men of a certain background, a distinct character and of a particular class. It's an understandable charge and one that far too many reactionary grey committee members in old school ties have unfortunately done their best to uphold for most of the game's long and storied history.

This book was written to help shine a light on the broad range of personalities and people that give the sport its greatness. It aims to tell of those who changed the game with their footwork and brains, rather than just their size and power; of those who walked out of lonely dressing rooms into the wide open exposed playing fields of the world, despite the roars and curses of those in the stands who hated them for their skin colour; of those who rose to the top as thousands of others were wishing (and hoping) them to fail because they were women, not men; of those who overcame cancer and broken necks to pull on their national shirt; and of those who saw a new way of playing or even watching a sport that no one had seen before them.

Many in these pages will be familiar faces to some readers, but I do not believe many will be familiar or aware of every face or team that features. This book looks to celebrate rugby in both the countries that are famed for it and the ones where often even the residents of that nation have little knowledge of the sport. After all, a story is no less interesting or human because it occurs away from the gaze of the lands that make up the Six Nations or Rugby Championship.

I hope that young and old will be inspired by the pages that follow. The stories you are about to read aren't just entertaining or fascinating parts of rugby history, but offer plenty for people looking for motivation both in sport and in the game of life. Rugby is a game that can inspire people of all shapes, sizes, personalities and background.

IAN McKINLEY

*'You'd be in the middle of Twickenham and Vunipola
was running at you and you might only see one leg and
you'd go for that leg.'*
Ian McKinley

**The rugby player who overcame the loss of his eye to play Test
rugby and helped open up the game to others who had been
prevented from playing due to eye injuries or medical issues.**

Main teams: UCD, Leinster, Viadana, Zebre Parma, Benetton,
Barbarians, Ireland U20s, Italy
Position: Outside-half, centre
International caps: 9 (2017–19)
Points: 3 (1 penalty)

On 16 January, 2010, Ian McKinley was playing centre for
University College Dublin (UCD) against Lansdowne in the
All Ireland League Division Two. He was just out of his teens
and part of the famed Leinster Academy system and had a
promising future ahead of him as either a centre or outside-
half, having already played a few games for the senior Leinster
side. His world was to change completely within five minutes
of kick-off.

Lying on his back in a ruck, a stray boot from a member of
his own team caught him in the face and seriously injured his
left eye. McKinley was rushed to hospital with a burst eyeball.

Over the coming months, the unlucky Irishman spent a long and difficult time having complex and risky operations to try and save his eye. When he wasn't in hospital, he had to religiously follow strict medical advice on how to best help his eye recover.

One major consequence of McKinley's injury was that his depth perception was affected. During his early days in hospital, he broke a glass of water when he completely misjudged its distance when he tried to pick it up. He effectively had to learn to recalibrate the way he perceived the world around him and it was three months before his vision had improved enough that his injured eye was able to see how many fingers his doctor was holding up during his frequent examinations.

It was another month again before McKinley was allowed to begin doing some light training. Before then there had been a major concern that too much movement or physical exercise could damage his retina. It's fair to assume most people would have retired from rugby after such a terrible injury, but by the start of the 2010/11 season, with his left eye now having around 50 per cent vision, he began pre-season training with Leinster.

The first comeback

His condition didn't stop some opponents from trying to take advantage or putting his sight at risk. In one game for Dublin club St Mary's, McKinley prevented a player from taking a quick penalty and a scuffle broke out. Another opponent came from behind and dug his finger into McKinley's good right eye. If that wasn't bad enough, the thug admitted that he knew McKinley had a severely damaged left eye and that was why he had done it.

In February 2011, McKinley was back playing for Leinster and even picked up a player of the match award and scored a try in a game against Benetton. By May he had done enough to be offered his first senior professional contract and had regained about 70 per cent vision in his injured eye. But then, disaster struck. Playing for Leinster A, McKinley had to leave the match as his vision began to rapidly deteriorate. It turned out he had developed a complicated cataract and needed surgery.

Worse news was to follow: not long after this incident, his retina became detached and he needed yet another emergency operation. It was not a success. Doctors told McKinley that the damage was too great and his eye could not be saved.

At the age of 21, McKinley announced his retirement from the sport. He had played six times for Leinster and been capped for the Ireland U20s, even captaining the latter in a game in the 2009 Junior World Championship. At such a young age his rugby dreams seemed to be over.

Yet, unbelievably, his elite career had actually barely even started. Not only would he lace his boots up again, he would be part of a campaign that would change rugby forever.

The second comeback
In 2013, McKinley got an unexpected offer that would alter the course of his life. He had begun coaching in Dublin after hanging up his boots and was also studying sports management at university. Out of the blue, he got a phone call asking if he would be interested in moving to Italy to become technical director of Leonorso Rugby Udine, overseeing teams in the under-6 to under-20s age range. He quickly accepted the challenge.

But while the move abroad and winning a job within the sport he loved initially helped McKinley, he eventually had to admit he had not coped well mentally with his enforced retirement from playing. Things got so bad, he broke down in front of his brother, Philip, and admitted he was in a bad place mentally as he still wanted to play rugby but was not able to.

Philip decided to help and contacted some people he knew to try and see if there was any way that his brother could play again through the use of special protective goggles. In his autobiography, *Second Sight*, Ian wrote that, within a week, Philip sent him an email which said: 'I've been reflecting a great deal since last week, about our conversation about your ambition to play again. I keep coming back though to two things: Risk and Limitation.'

The email discussed the concept of trying to find a way to use modern technology to create special eye protection that would permit him to play again. It continued: 'You are down and desperately frustrated at being unable to play. So, it's a lose/lose situation from whatever way you look at it. However, if you were to return, you would reverse all that. You would be an inspiration to tens of thousands of young people, you would be able to deliver on the skills and development invested in you and you would no longer feel the frustration you do. It would become win/win . . . at the end of the day, it's the love of mud, scraped knees and sticking to diets that you miss the most. So your desire and request are not selfish or egotistical, it is in fact good, heart-warming pure love for the sport, which any rugby fan or authority should respond most openly and positively towards.'

With Philip leading the charge, the pair began researching everything from eyewear technology to changes in international rugby laws and regulations to see if they could find a way. They also contacted the mechanical engineering department at UCD, Ian's old university, and the technical department at World Rugby (then the International Rugby Board) to begin exploring how they could make working prototypes of protective goggles. As it happened, World Rugby was also in the very early stages of looking into whether it was possible to create goggles for rugby players who had a medical condition that meant they needed to protect their eyes.

It was to be the beginning of a long, difficult, inspiring and ultimately successful journey. By early 2014, World Rugby had agreed that a trial of goggles in rugby could take place and McKinley had a working prototype made from an incredibly strong polycarbonate material to try out. They weren't perfect and there were plenty of issues to iron out, but it was a start. After successfully training with them at Leonorso, McKinley was selected to play in a match for the club against Oderzo. The teams played in division three of the Italian leagues and the standard and facilities were a world away from what he had previously known in Ireland. But none of that mattered. All that mattered was whether the goggles worked.

They did. Despite an early hiccup when his goggles came off in contact, the Leonorso debutant bagged 28 points in a 65–5 win. McKinley was able to feed back on the good and bad things he had experienced with the goggles and the technicians working on them could begin to refine things such as the way they fogged up or how insecure they were. It was later discovered that up to 10 degrees of vision on McKinley's left side was obscured by the goggles and it would be a long time before this problem was rectified.

The Irishman was soon signed on a professional contract for the 2014/15 season by Rugby Viadana, another Italian club, but one which sat at the top table of the domestic game.

Mai Mular (Never give up)

The more McKinley played, the more attention was drawn to the goggles and the potential they had to help others. In a twist of fate, McKinley discovered that Florian Cazenave – a former French opponent of his from his days with Ireland U20s – had also suffered the loss of an eye and was not allowed to play in his native France. He too came to play in Italy and used goggles to protect his sight. The pair even met in a pre-season friendly.

In 2014 McKinley was invited to play for the prestigious Barbarians invitational side – becoming the first player to do so of course while wearing eye protection. By the 2015/16 season, McKinley had also begun playing for Rugby Zebre on permit, helping out when their top players were away on international duty. It was another significant sign of his progress and the first time goggles had been worn at this level of rugby.

For all the technological and technical improvements made to his eyewear though, McKinley still had to relearn how to do many of the things on the field that would have been second nature to him before his injury. As a left-footed kicker, for instance, he had to adapt the way his body was positioned when he kicked as he no longer had a clear view of the ball as it dropped onto his foot.

Rain of course was another problem for a player wearing equipment over his eyes, as were scratches and smudges. It meant it was important that a second or third pair were always on hand to replace a suddenly unusable set.

While his depth perception had improved since his initial sight loss, McKinley admits now that this issue was a particular problem in night games under floodlights. In one match, he even had to deal with an angry mosquito that had somehow worked its way inside his goggles. The creature made its presence known during play and he had to wait until a break in play to free the thing!

In spite of all this, McKinley continued to defy the odds and rise up the ranks.

Roadblocks at home

McKinley wasn't just having to fight the medical odds though. He was also forced to fight for the right to play. In 2015, the unions of England, France and Ireland did not permit players to wear goggles and had not signed up to be part of the World Rugby trials. When he wasn't training, playing or working with experts to improve his eyewear, McKinley was helping lead a strategic campaign to get these unions to change their minds; engaging with them personally and professionally and bringing to them the weight of expert advice and direct examples of his own personal experience.

Their refusal to allow goggles on the field meant that while the former Leinster star could wear his goggles when playing at home for his team against an Irish side, he was unable to play in the same fixture in the land of his birth. As his club was playing in the Pro12, which included four Irish teams, this was a major problem. It also meant he was unable to play in European competitions on English and French soil.

In his autobiography, McKinley gave powerful examples of what this ban meant for people with eye issues: 'A number of Irish underage players suddenly began to be blocked or prevented from playing rugby . . . in August 2015, seven-year-old Ryan Totten was told he couldn't play rugby anymore . . . In October, the same situation arose and his father launched a petition to lobby the IRFU on behalf of his son. In November, a referee prevented two players for Portarlington Under-13s in County Laois from playing at the start of a match.'

In late 2015, the Irish Rugby Football Union (IRFU) confirmed they would not allow McKinley to wear his goggles on Irish soil, meaning he could not play for Zebre in an away match against Connacht. This prompted him, with the support of his family and friends, to go public and launch the 'Let Ian Play' campaign. He focused on the following points:

- It was a breach of McKinley's freedom of travel to provide services pursuant to EU law.
- It was a breach of the European Charter of Fundamental Rights.
- The IRFU's position breached his rights under the Irish Constitution and the European Convention of Human Rights law regarding disability.

McKinley also said the IRFU's stance 'contradicted the 'Spirit of Rugby' slogan that all unions aspire to achieve'.

The campaign caught the imagination of the sporting public and soon gained support across the world and generated massive amounts of media attention. Tens of thousands of people signed up to a petition supporting his cause and countless people wrote letters to the IRFU and politicians expressing support.

The refusal of the IRFU to allow McKinley to play also threatened his prospect of signing for Zebre as cover during the Six Nations when their top stars were away. If he couldn't play in certain away games, it didn't make economic sense for the club to bring him into their squad. The IRFU meanwhile stepped up their communications around why goggles were not permitted and wrote to every club in Ireland confirming why they would not allow players to wear them. They were then immediately embarrassed when the Association of Optometrists of Ireland made their support of McKinley's goggles public.

During all this fuss, the IRFU had written to McKinley saying he could play without the goggles, which, of course, was a far riskier proposition. Quite frankly, it was nonsense.

Thankfully, by mid-December, after a personal presentation by McKinley to the board, the IRFU caved in to common sense and public pressure and agreed to join the global goggles trial. McKinley made sure that Ryan Totten, the young boy who had been prevented from playing in Ireland, got a pair to play in. Not long after this breakthrough, McKinley signed with Benetton Treviso.

Alongside his actions in his homeland, he also campaigned to encourage the national unions in England and France to sign up to the global goggle trials. While the English union decided to run with their own trials, rather than be part of the World Rugby one, they did give him permission to play in international competitions with the goggles when he was in England.

The French Federation (FFR) held out even longer than the RFU and the IRFU when it came to allowing McKinley and others to play in goggles. In fact, the FFR even ignored a letter from him on the subject. But it ultimately seemed to be the president of the FFR at the time, Pierre Camou, who had an issue with the trials and when he left office the incoming Bernard Laporte confirmed France would join up to the trial in his acceptance speech! This allowed McKinley's U20 opponent Florian Cazenave to finally play in his homeland again too.

In the spring of 2019, five years after the trial had begun, World Rugby officially permitted the use of the goggles pioneered by McKinley. His courage and persistence had helped change the accessibility of rugby union and inspired people around the world in all sports. He played a part in opening the door to thousands who otherwise would never have been able to play.

Italy calling

If McKinley overcoming his injury to play rugby again and then helping to develop and legalise the use of goggles in rugby wasn't inspiring enough, there was more to come. In 2017, six years after his injury, he was selected to win his first cap for his adopted country. McKinley came off the bench in the 60th minute to kick a penalty and help steer Italy to a 19–10 win over Fiji in Catania.

In his book, McKinley wrote proudly of celebrating afterwards with his family:

'Everything that we had all fought for as a family was for this day and it felt so, so satisfying. I wasn't just happy for myself but for my whole family. This monumental achievement was due to everyone's contribution. What I was particularly grateful for, and always will be, was that they all pulled together with their resources as best they could for me.'

McKinley won nine caps in all, including three against Ireland. He remains forever grateful for the opportunity Italy offered him: 'Adopting me represented the fighting attitude in Italian rugby. They did everything in their power to help facilitate me as a player and that also trickles down to the clubs that I played for, whether it was Leonorso, Viadana, Zebre or Benetton. During the prolonged campaign to have the goggles approved, the Federation even provided me with special insurance for one of the games. They didn't need to do that, but they wanted to help me and that is why I am so attached to them.'

McKinley's bravery and persistence has helped make rugby a more inclusive and better sport.

MAGGIE ALPHONSI

'We are measured on the impact we have on others.'
Maggie Alphonsi

Maggie Alphonsi overcame a tough childhood and being born with a club foot to win a World Cup and become one of England's greatest players.

Main teams: Saracens, England
Position: Flanker, centre
International caps: 74 (2003–14)
Points: 140 (28 tries)
Honours: 2014 World Cup winner; Six Nations (six Grand Slams, seven titles); captain of Saracens for 2015 league and cup double; International Rugby Board Player of the Year (2006); Sunday Times' Sportswoman of the Year (2010); first female player to win the Pat Marshall Award voted for by the Rugby Union Writers' Club; MBE.

When Maggie Alphonsi was a young toddler growing up in Lewisham, south London, few would have seen a future in elite sport for her. She had been born with a club foot (a condition in which an infant's foot is twisted or turned inward) and had to undergo many operations growing up to try and improve the foot. While she ultimately overcame the problem to succeed in rugby, it would cause her many severe complications throughout her career.

Alphonsi grew up in a single-parent family on a council estate where life could be very tough and social conditions unforgiving. Yet she overcame these early challenges to become a Hall of Fame rugby player and one of the greatest stars in the history of the England team. Looking back on her career in 2019, she reflected on just how critical her mother had been to her later success on and off the field: 'Opportunities were low. My mum was a single parent and an amazing woman, she had two jobs so I could have a life.'

Her mother 'drummed' into her that if she wanted to succeed, she had to put in the hard work. But despite these sensible words, Alphonsi didn't immediately put the wisdom into action. She admits that in her early school years she was far from an ideal student and preferred socialising to studying. Getting a telling-off from her teachers was almost a daily event at one point and it wasn't beyond the realms of possibility that she would end up getting expelled. Then, aged 13, an incident took place that would change her life and, ultimately, help change the future of England rugby.

One of her female teachers came to school one day sporting a black eye. Curious, Alphonsi asked how it had happened. The teacher said she had received it playing rugby for Wales. The holder of the shiner was none other than Liza Burgess, former Wales captain and Hall of Fame player; she was one of the most important players in the foundation of the women's game in the UK and is still a key administrator today. Burgess suggested to a sceptical Alphonsi that she should give rugby a try; arguing that it could be a way to channel her energy. Writing in the *Telegraph* in 2019, Alphonsi laid out her initial reaction to the idea:

'At first I thought she was mad. I had grown up in a single-parent family on a football-obsessed council estate in Edmonton. I had been born with a club foot and walked with a limp. I was a girl. I was black. There simply weren't many people like me who played rugby, or any top-level sport at all.

'Liza didn't care about my excuses. She told me to get the W6 bus to Saracens, my local club, and ask to play. For a few weeks I ignored her advice. I didn't want to go on my own to play a sport I didn't know or understand with people who I thought would judge me. Instead, I played my guitar and got into more trouble until there were really very few options left. So, I made what to me seemed a very brave choice. I got the bus to Saracens and asked if I could take part in training. I discovered I was actually quite good, and that neither my gender nor ethnic origin mattered. For the first time in my life I felt completely free. I had made a choice that transformed my life.'

The beginning

Alphonsi may have hesitated about dipping her toes into rugby's waters, but she was soon in at the deep end and swimming like a natural. During her very first session with Saracens she immediately knew she had found a sport that fitted her personality and strengths. The girl from Edmonton loved the contact and aggression, particularly the tackling.

The honours quickly piled up, including her being selected to captain the under-16 Great Britain touch rugby team on a tour to Australia. While she excelled in the non-contact version of the sport, her heart and body loved nothing more than tackling. She relished defending not only in matches, but in training too, where she would happily be the main tackler in defensive drills where players were forced to 'run the gauntlet'.

After turning 18, she was chosen to be part of the England academy, before being selected to win her first cap for England A. As well as winning international honours, Alphonsi was succeeding in the domestic game too, being named player of the year for Saracens in the 2001/02 season.

After turning 19, Alphonsi was hopeful of retaining her place in the England A set-up for a summer tour to South Africa. Instead, she was named to be part of the senior squad that was travelling to Canada with coach and former Australian international Geoff Richards.

Her first cap in an England shirt was in the centre, not at seven and she marked her debut with a critical try as the Red Roses won 10–5. But the high was followed by a low as a serious ankle injury ruled her out of the Six Nations in 2004.

Yet her performances had brought her to national attention and a year after her debut *The Times* was running features highlighting Alphonsi's rising star: 'Maggie Alphonsi has proved, if you are good enough, you are old enough.'

Graham Smith, who coached with England from 2003 to 2015, said that the first time he saw Alphonsi play she was in the centre. While he was immediately impressed, he thought she had all the attributes that would make her a flanker.

'I was struck by her awareness of where the ball was at all times and her ferocity in defence, tackle and in competing for the turnover,' explained Smith when asked for this book to reflect on her career. 'I had an instinct that she was a seven, not a 12. And to make that transition, she had to drop out of the elite England squad of 44 players so she could learn about her new position. She had the will and the desire to do it. We spent hours working on the change and she worked incredibly hard on everything from turnover techniques to positional play. She also toiled away in the gym to build up her strength.'

What struck Smith and the other coaches who worked with Alphonsi, was her willingness to be coached and to learn. That, and her iron will and commitment to be the best she could possibly be. Gary Street, who was head coach of England and with the national side from 2007 to 2014, tells of how when he first met Maggie when she was aged 14, she was already asking what she needed to do to play for the national side.

'She became a great player at seven,' says Smith. 'With her ferocity in the tackle situation, she could punch above her weight in contact. It made oppositions aware of her and they saw her as a threat when they had the ball. Her exceptional fitness, which saw her nicknamed the "Machine", allowed her to maintain her pace and power for 80 minutes in a way few other players were capable of.'

Not only did Alphonsi adapt to being an openside flanker, she excelled. Smith reflected on her ability to do similar things to players like Richie McCaw, saying: 'Maggie could do things so quickly that the referee would miss the first action. She had this ability and she was hard to put to ground and could stay so low and look like she was on her feet. People would struggle to put her down. In the tackle and jackal situation, players like Richie McCaw, David Pocock and George Smith were always accused of cheating. Were they? Arguably, yes. But that's what great back rowers do. Maggie had that ability to get her hands on the ball and be a real pain for opponents.

'Another thing that marks out great players like Maggie is how coachable they are. They listen and learn and then there comes a point they are almost coaching themselves and you are just putting questions to them about why they did things and how they can get better. And they will contact you with thoughts and ideas on how to improve.'

It was as a seven that Alphonsi would see out the rest of her career for England and she soon became one of the first names on the team sheet, playing in both the 2006 and 2010 World Cup finals. Sadly for the 'Machine', she was on the losing side in both finals. Her performances in the latter tournament really helped establish her as one of the most high-profile names in rugby. Yet it wasn't enough. She wanted to win a World Cup above all.

In 2010 the *Sunday Times* crowned her Sportswoman of the Year and within two years her impact on the sport was recognised with an MBE.

Amid all this success, it is worth remembering that Alphonsi was always having to overcome issues related to her club foot. The condition put certain strains on her body that made her have to train a certain way and increased her propensity to suffer injury; her hamstrings in particular were unreliable and she also had to endure related knee and back pain.

While Alphonsi was building her early rugby career she was always either studying or working full-time. She studied sports and exercise science at De Montfort University, earned a masters in sports and exercise from Roehampton and also attained a BTEC National Diploma in leisure studies from Hertford Regional College.

Alphonsi also had to work multiple jobs to support her dream. Unlike her full-time male peers, the flanker needed to make sure she could cover everything from her training gear to her medical expenses and travel costs. She eventually benefited from the UK's National Lottery funding scheme for athletes, but she always had to ensure she made the most of what were relatively limited financial resources.

As an international she was part of an incredible seven successive Six Nations titles with England, helping her nation to Grand Slams in six of those championships.

Third time's the charm

The 2014 World Cup was Alphonsi's last chance at global glory. It had been 20 years since England had last lifted the coveted cup, having lost in the finals three times on the trot (2002, 2006, 2010). Aged 30, and having been part of two of those runner-up campaigns, Alphonsi knew 2014 was her final shot at winning the big one.

The year hadn't gone exactly as the Red Roses had planned. A below-par display away to France in the opening game of the Six Nations ultimately cost them the title. England won their other four games, but France claimed the Grand Slam. With the World

Cup itself taking place on French soil, this wasn't the greatest of omens. Many in the press and rugby community wondered if it signalled England would once again fall short.

In spite of the setback, England were not worried. Alphonsi, in an interview with ESPN, spoke of how well head coach Gary Street and assistants Simon Middleton and Graham Smith had meticulously planned and prepared the team throughout the year so that they peaked physically and mentally by the time the World Cup came along.

'They covered every detail,' she explained. 'They empowered the players to take a lead and they challenged us all to get better each day.'

The group also spent more time in training camp than they had ever done before any previous tournament. The players and management were going to do everything possible to reach their goal. Yet Alphonsi almost didn't get to compete in the 2014 World Cup. She had undergone major knee surgery before the tournament and some feared she wouldn't even make it or wouldn't be able to reach the standard she was known for.

As it turned out, she made it and arrived in great physical shape. And on 1 August, England, wearing unfamiliar red and white hoops, kicked off their World Cup bid in ferocious form, swatting Samoa aside 65–3 in a ten-try battering. Next up, Spain were swiftly swept aside 45–5, despite lots of the big guns, including Alphonsi, being rested.

The next and final pool contest was against Canada and was a different beast entirely. The result had major implications for what happened next in the tournament. The North Americans had also efficiently dispatched both Samoa and Spain, but hadn't racked up quite as many points (winning 31–5 against Spain and 42–7 over Samoa). Whichever side won would win the pool and, in theory, get an easier draw in the semi-final.

As it turned out, England were arguably somewhat fortunate in a 13–13 draw. Canada scored two tries to England's one in an incredibly tight encounter. The Red Roses' outside centre Emily Scarratt kicked all three of her place kicks (two penalties and a conversion) to help stave off defeat. With ten minutes remaining, Canada powered over from a driving maul and felt they had scored. The referee didn't have a good enough view to award the try and the television match official was not consulted. It was a lucky escape.

England didn't let Canada get another sniff and the match finished in a draw, meaning England won the group on points difference. As a result, England faced Ireland in the semi-finals and Canada had to square up to the hosts and reigning Grand Slam champions, France.

Ireland had seen off the challenge of New Zealand in the groups and had run England close in the Six Nations earlier in the year, going down 17–10 at Twickenham after putting up a strong fight. As expected, the Irish came out all guns blazing and even opened the scoring through a powerful try from a driving maul after 15 minutes. For the first quarter of the match, everything seemed to be going right for the team in green and, briefly, it seemed possible Ireland were going to follow up their shock win over the Black Ferns with another major scalp.

It wasn't to be. By half time England were 18–7 up, with Scarratt again to the fore both with boot and in open play. Ireland were clinically put to the sword as normal service was resumed and, with Alphonsi key as always in the forward battles for the Red Roses, another final was secured. Reflecting on her team's 40–7 triumph Alphonsi said England had 'clicked… nothing could go wrong and we all felt in the zone'.

Their next opponents, it turned out, were not to be tournament hosts and Grand Slam champions France, but the team that had frustrated England in their pool: Canada. The North Americans had squeaked home 18–16 to set up an intriguing final.

Alphonsi knew this was her last chance to get her hand on a world title. She has spoken since of how the previous two final losses had driven her to succeed in the 2014 World Cup. Indeed, England had 11 survivors from the 2010 final in their match-day squad, all of them determined to lay some ghosts to rest and claim their nation's first women's World Cup since 1994.

On 14 August, 2014, England and Canada met at the Stade Jean-Bouin in Paris to fight for the World Cup. England were considered favourites, but Canada were not to be dismissed lightly. Not only had they held England to a draw in the pool stages, they had also twice defeated England in the 2013 Nations Cup in the USA. While that Red Roses side was an experimental one, it did mean Canada knew what it felt like to beat them and held no fear of the famous white shirt.

Alphonsi got herself in the mood ahead of the game by blasting out Linkin' Park music. England, led by captain and fly-half Katy McLean, started the stronger of the two sides and led 6–0 after 25 minutes thanks to two penalties from Scarratt.

Alphonsi of course played her part in putting England on course for glory. A well-coordinated team attack, originally launched from within their own half, saw England stretching Canada back and forth across the pitch. With the Canadian defence in trouble, England put width on the ball from an offensive manoeuvre launched just over 30 metres out. Alphonsi positioned herself in midfield and ran a support line to second row Tamara Taylor, who beat her first opponent with a dummy, and then passed on to Alphonsi as she took contact. The flanker took the ball just inside the Canadian 22, drew in the opposing full-back, Julianne Zussman, and at speed, and with perfect timing, delivered a beautiful pass to full-back Danielle Waterman who sped over from 15 metres out to give the Red Roses a commanding lead.

England went into the interval 11–3 up. Canada pulled it back in the second-half with two further penalties to make things interesting, but a late try from scoring machine Scarratt (who bagged 16 points in all) sealed a 21–9 victory. Alphonsi and co finally had their hands on the trophy they had worked so hard for.

'To become a world champion was all I had ever wanted,' said Alphonsi, 'and it is all I had been talking about for 11 years. To finally do it was a dream come true. We had finally achieved the thing that I had set out to accomplish and I was truly happy.'

After global glory

Alphonsi retired from Test rugby after the World Cup, to focus on playing with Saracens. Now a World Cup winner, she felt it was the perfect time to call time on her England career. After announcing the decision, she revealed that one of the things she would miss the most from the international arena was singing the national anthem and having the crowd singing it back.

The Machine also signed off her club career in style. Her final game for the Saracens saw her claim a try as she helped her team seal a Premiership title with a 30–0 over Wasps.

With her victory flags planted firmly on the playing fields of her life, Alphonsi set about building new goals and reaching new heights off the field. Just as Alphonsi was a trailblazer on the rugby field, she became one off it too. The combination of her rugby experience, sporting intelligence and profile within the women's game opened up opportunities for her in front of the camera as a rugby pundit. But unlike other ex-players in the women's game who had only worked within the women's game, the former flanker broke down doors of opportunity with her microphone too.

During the 2015 men's Rugby World Cup, she became the first female pundit to cover a men's Test match in an international tournament. Her success in the role inspired others and helped shift attitudes to female pundits in rugby union and within a few years it became increasingly common to have more women in the commentary box, at pitch side and in the studio.

Hanging up her boots didn't put her sporting ambitions to rest either. Even before she had retired, she was in training to represent Great Britain at the Rio Olympics in 2016 in the shot put. Remarkably, the head coach of Great Britain's Paralympic team had – on account of Alphonsi's club foot – looked to see if she could be classified to compete in the Paralympics. She addressed this in an interview in 2015, saying: 'My right foot is turned all the way in, but I've trained so well on it I probably wouldn't be classified as a paralympic athlete any more.'

In her youth, Alphonsi had represented her borough at discus and shot put and when the chance to compete in the Olympics came up, she said: 'Why not? Why not give it a go?'

Ultimately Alphonsi didn't make Rio, but the fact she came within touching distance told you everything you needed to know about her will and athletic ability.

Graham Smith is not remotely surprised by Alphonsi's success off the field, saying: 'If you look at what she's doing after rugby, you can see she puts the same into that as she does on the field and that's why she is a success.'

Alongside her broadcasting career, Alphonsi has served as a national member of the RFU Council and has a successful career as a motivational speaker and brand ambassador. Her insight and expertise have earned her a place on elite World Rugby voting panels, helping to choose winners of awards such as World Rugby Team of the Year, Coach of the Year and Player of the Year.

Alphonsi is hugely (and rightly) proud of what she has achieved in life and also grateful for what her chosen sport has given her. 'Rugby has allowed me to be the person that I am today and it's given me so many memories that I can look back and say I was proud to be a part of that. And now I hope that through this sport I will go on to inspire others and go on to change the lives of many other people.'

GIANT KILLERS
JAPAN (2015)

*'Japan can only play one way, we've got a little team,
so we have to move the ball around and cause problems.'*
Eddie Jones, Japan coach for the 2015 Rugby World Cup

The story of the 'Miracle in Brighton' and the greatest upset in rugby history.

South Africa 32 Japan 34
(Brighton Community Stadium, Brighton)

19 September, 2015 – Pool B, Rugby World Cup

It's possible to make the case that the defeat of South Africa by Japan isn't just the greatest upset in Rugby World Cup history, or even the greatest in rugby history, but that it is the greatest in the history of any single match in team sports.

It wasn't just what Japan achieved that glorious day in Brighton in 2015, it was the manner of how they achieved it. They combined planning and preparation with strategy and tactics. They threw in courage and confidence, with analysis and cool-headed thinking. They brought incredible physical conditioning with extraordinary technical skills. Most of all, when the chance for a famous draw was a simple kick away in the dying seconds, they put it all on the line and risked agonising defeat for the glory of victory. And they did all this against one of the greatest rugby nations of all time.

It was all so dramatic that as soon as the final whistle was blown, people began saying they should make a movie about it. And, well, they did. It was that incredible.

A humble history of defeat

Rugby in Japan can trace its roots back as far as 1866 when the game was played in ports, but these contests were between foreign sailors and workers, rather than locals. In his wonderful *A Game For Hooligans: The History of Rugby Union*, Huw Richards tells of how in 1899, two Cambridge graduates, Ginnosuke Tanaka and Edward Clarke introduced rugby into Keio University.

Thirty-three years later, in 1932, Japan played their first official Test match, beating Canada 9–8. It was a long while before Japan began to play the major nations and it was the 1973 tour of England, Wales and France that finally brought the Brave Blossoms to the attention of European fans.

It was in this period Japan began to form a reputation for technical expertise, speed and tactical innovation – while lacking the physical punch needed to take them to the next level. Japan won just two of their nine games against Test, regional and club opposition, with wins against Western Counties (Wales) and a French Regional XV. Caps were not awarded in the contests against Wales (a 62–14 loss) and France (a 30–18 defeat). The team were popular with fans, but treated somewhat as a novelty and even inspired songs that were intended to show affection but were packed with crude racial stereotypes.

Yet, there was no getting away from the fact that traditionally the Japanese international team was often physically overmatched by the established nations. The positive side of this was it led to the creation of a rugby culture that welcomed innovation and was fanatical about perfecting technical skills. Japanese sides had to make every piece of possession count against the top teams, and any edge they could find had to be exploited. Clever back moves, the use of speed and width in attack and an unorthodox approach to set-piece play were deployed to try and counter the power of their larger rivals. But courage and street smarts will only get you so far. It's not by chance that rugby is a sport with relatively few genuine upsets. The mantra 'a good big 'un will always beat a good little 'un' could have been coined for rugby. The attrition of a full 80 minutes was usually too much for Japan in the big Tests.

Failing on the world stage

Nothing illustrates just how amazing the win over the Springboks in the 2015 World Cup was more than a glance at the history of Japan in the global jamboree. The Brave Blossoms have taken part in every single edition of the tournament, allowing us to easily put into context just how much they beat expectations in Brighton. Here is their World Cup record ahead of the 2015 edition.

1987: *Played three, lost three.*
- Japan 18 USA 21
- Japan 7 England 60
- Japan 23 Australia 42

1991: *Played three, won one, lost two.*
- Japan 9 Scotland 47
- Japan 16 Ireland 32
- Japan 52 Zimbabwe 8

1995: *Played three, lost three.*
- Japan 10 Wales 57
- Japan 28 Ireland 50
- Japan 17 New Zealand 145

1999: *Played three, lost three.*
- Japan 9 Samoa 43
- Japan 15 Wales 64
- Japan 12 Argentina 33

2003: *Played four, lost four.*
- Japan 11 Scotland 32
- Japan 29 France 51
- Japan 13 Fiji 41
- Japan 26 United States 39

2007: *Played four, drew one, lost three.*
- Japan 3 Australia 91
- Japan 31 Fiji 35
- Japan 18 Wales 72
- Japan 12 Canada 12

2011: *Played four, drew one, lost three.*
- Japan 21 France 47
- Japan 7 New Zealand 83
- Japan 18 Tonga 31
- Japan 23 Canada 23

Played: *24*
Won: *1*
Drawn: *2*
Lost: *21*
Points for: *428*
Points against: *1,159*

The single win that breaks up the dismal Japanese World Cup record between 1987 and 2011 came against lowly Zimbabwe, a side that have only ever made it to two World Cups. Both of the draws came against Canada, a side that is sadly a pale imitation of what it used to be. The barely comprehensible 145–17 defeat to New Zealand in 1995 is made worse by the fact it was essentially a second-string All Black XV. In contrast, South Africa, Japan's 2015 opponents, had won two of the five tournaments they had appeared in (they were not invited to the 1987 and 1991 editions due to apartheid, see page 150). As New Zealand at that point had won two tournaments from seven attempts, it meant percentage wise, the Boks were the most successful World Cup team ever.

The rant that changed Japan

In 2012, the Japan Rugby Football Union (JRFU) made a move that would change the future of the national team forever and take the nation to the top table of the global game. Australian Eddie Jones was named as head coach after former All Black John Kirwan resigned from the position. Jones was the perfect fit to turn around the fortunes of the Japanese. Not only did the former New South Wales hooker come with an excellent coaching pedigree (including the Brumbies, Australia and Saracens), his mother was a Japanese American, meaning he had strong national and cultural ties with the nation. He had coached at Tokai University, Suntory Sungoliath and had been an assistant coach with Japan in 1996.

Jones understood the challenges faced by Japan on the rugby field, as well as the potential waiting to be unlocked. And to get his team to play to their best, he was not prepared to make any compromises or take any prisoners.

In the professional era, Japan had increasingly brought in overseas players who would later qualify on residency grounds for the national side. Jones looked to limit this. He also wanted Japan to stop trying to ape the style of other nations. Kirwan and his predecessors had, he felt, tried too hard to imitate others, rather than being their own team. Quite rightly, Jones believes that teams that copy others are always behind the curve. Even if they ever manage to master the strategy and tactics they seek to emulate, the top teams will have by then moved on again. It was a flawed approach. Better to be true to yourselves and forge your own identity.

Jones openly stated that Japan should sit among the top ten sides in the world. They were sat in the 16th spot when he set this goal. He has also admitted in recent years that he used to consider Japan a 'joke' rugby team, claiming their average score against Tier One nations was an 85–0 loss.

The former Wallaby coach also hated the team nickname of 'The Brave Blossoms'. He believed it was 'absurd' and felt it patronised them by encouraging a mentality of 'you go out there boys and try your best and as long you do that and score a few points at the end of the game everyone will be happy'.

Jones's reign got off to a shaky start in 2012. In his first Pacific Nations Cup, Japan lost all their games against Fiji, Samoa and Tonga. Later that year, Jones was part of an extraordinary press conference that showed the world just how ruthless he could be in his desire to win. After a poor loss to the French Barbarians, Jones was facing the press pack with his captain Toshiaki Hirose. At one point, after Jones fumed about the poor performance and had apologised for the display, Hirose let out a nervous smile as he prepared to speak. His coach responded with fury, glaring at his skipper, before going on to deliver one of the most epic rants in rugby folklore: 'It's not funny. It's not funny. That's the problem with Japanese rugby, seriously. We're not serious about winning. If we want to win, we've got to go out and physically smash people. And we didn't do it. We knew how the French Barbarians were gonna play.

'I think I should probably leave. In reality, some players today will never play for Japan again unless they change. That's the reality . . . there are players that didn't want to make tackles. They are never going to play for Japan again. Unless they change.

You know, we've got to grow up . . . What are we going to do with Japanese rugby? Do we want to grow up? We've only got three years to the World Cup.

'Do you want me to resign now [in response to a press question]? I'm happy to. I take full responsibility for the defeat and the performance. So who would you select? I pick six New Zealanders in there and we win the game. Do you want me to do that? So, before when Kirwan was coach everyone complained about the number of foreigners. Now we are trying to develop Japanese players and you are complaining about it. Which way do you want it? I've got to find players that want to fight.'

Jones was asked about why Japan had performed better in the second half of the loss. He responded: 'Historically all [the] big games Japan has played, they get beaten in the first half and then try in the second half. We need to change the mindset of the players. The French players are grabbing us and stopping us defending and we are letting them do it. We've just got to want to win more.'

Jones then waved away the JRFU media officer who seemingly wanted to end the press conference, stating he was happy to continue. After again offering to resign if that's what people wanted, he responded to another question with: 'It was disgusting today. There's no other way of looking at it. We had 15 players out there today that did not put their bodies on the line and that's my fault as a coach. We've got a real problem in Japanese rugby unless we change things considerably, and that's why I'm being so aggressive about how we played today. Because we can't accept it. Because nothing is going to change otherwise. The players have got to understand that. They have to take responsibility. I'm taking responsibility and the players come in and say, "Ah, well, we didn't do this, we didn't do that." That's a load of rubbish. What we didn't do is play with any sort of spirit and any sort of physicality tonight. Why have we got at the end of the game, players rushing out of the line wanting to make tackles? Why weren't they doing that at the start of the game? Because they are frightened. We've got to change that mindset. We go out and all we want to do is compete.'

The press conference was a pivotal moment. Jones believes it was the 'best thing' he could have done and that it helped transform the national team as the players became aware that it was no longer acceptable to be content with an 'heroic defeat'.

The plan

From then on, things began to change. Jones steered his team to some respectable wins including a triumph over Romania in Bucharest, the team's first Test win in Europe. Most notably, Japan beat Wales for the first time. Admittedly, Wales's touring party was weakened by the call-ups to that summer's British and Irish Lions tour, but it was still a much-needed scalp of a major nation.

Two years out from the World Cup – at the start of a period in which Japan would beat Italy, the USA and Canada and reach ninth in the global rankings – Jones launched his plan to shock South Africa. With captain Michael Leitch at the steering wheel, Jones devised an intense training programme geared towards the opening clash with the two-times World Champion Springboks. Amazingly, the Japanese squad was still not fully comprised of full-time professionals at this point. Nonetheless, Jones believed that with focus, brutal training, the optimum strategy and the forging of a unique Japanese playing style, they could humble the Boks.

The head coach cleared out the dead wood, the players he felt were not up to Test rugby or simply didn't have the right attitude. He placed the team under constant pressure, presenting them with high-stress situations. In one game, he told his players they could not kick the ball unless they were near their own tryline. They had to find another way to make ground and successfully attack. Of course, once the opposition realised what was happening, this only made things tougher.

Jones also decided to transform the way Japan thought about their size. He wanted to make their relative lack of stature an advantage. Why not create a style that moved giant teams (and they don't come any bigger than South Africa) around the field and wear them down? A key moment came when he appointed former French hooker Marc Dal Maso as scrum coach. Dal Maso actually welcomed the fact Japanese players were smaller, believing it helped give them an advantage and suppleness the bigger packs lacked.

Steve Borthwick, the former England lock, was also brought in to work with the forwards and cleverly redesigned the way they approached things like line-outs so that their lack of size wouldn't hamper them.

Jones labelled the team's arduous training regime for the 2015 World Cup as 'Beat the Boks'. Training, which often started at five in the morning (especially helping the part-time players), pushed them to their physical limits. But it also incorporated drills which drastically improved their ability to read and understand a game and enhanced their ability to communicate on field. Every aspect of how Japan approached their games was continually refined to make them a better side. Slowly, but surely, the players began to think they could turn the rugby world upside down. But outside of the Japanese camp, anyone who seriously thought Japan could beat South Africa would have been considered to have lost their minds. That kind of stuff only happened in movies.

The miracle

The greatest match in World Cup history took place in Brighton on a glorious day. South Africa arrived with an understandable confidence and lined up with a starting XV boasting 851 caps, making it the most experienced Springbok side of all time.

From the kick-off, Japan looked sharp and composed. Full-back Ayumu Goromaru, who had been brought back into the fold by Eddie Jones after falling out with previous coach John Kirwan, kicked a penalty to give his side a 3–0 lead after just seven minutes. It was an impressive start. But at the time, those watching saw it simply as the Boks taking a while to get into their stride and as a classic example of the unfancied minnows opening the fighting with the usual heart of a yapping and determined underdog. Everyone knew it couldn't last. Underdogs almost always had more bark than bite.

And, sure enough, it didn't last. When South Africa powered over for a try after 17 minutes through flanker Francois Louw driving over from a typically powerful Bok line-out maul, it was no more than was expected. With the score now 7–3, everyone watching assumed it was business as usual. Except, it wasn't. Just before the 30-minute mark, Japan hit back when captain and flanker Michael Leitch capped off a period of forward dominance in the South Africa 22 with a line-out try of his own.

The South African television commentators openly expressed their surprise at the ability of the Japanese to push the Bok pack around. This was not part of the script. Japan added the extras through Goromaru to lead 10–7.

Japan's defence was tough and smart. Designed to combat the exceptional power of the larger South Africans, the Brave Blossoms favoured chop tackles, over big physical hits. It was high risk, but they executed their task so well the underdogs usually got the reward they wanted.

In the 33rd minute the Boks, unable to make much headway in the open areas of the field, resorted to type with another driving maul try from a line-out. This time hooker Bismarck du Plessis earned the five points.

This seemed to put things back on script and most knowledgeable rugby viewers would have felt a growing sense of inevitably about it all. Sure, Japan were taking it to the scary Goliaths. But whenever the going got tough, South Africa could steamroller them. The minnows would tire, as has happened thousands of times in Test rugby, and the favourites would ultimately cruise home comfortably. What's more, the pace at which Japan were playing, while admirable, only seemed to be leading them down a path of total exhaustion. How could they keep this up?

The half-time score was 12–10 to the Boks. During the interval, pundits and fans across social media and on television praised Japan, but almost no one would have changed their prediction of a comfortable win for the side in green and gold.

The second half

The second half was only three minutes old when Japan's Goromaru kicked another penalty. They were back in the lead. 13–12. Interesting. But no cause for alarm for the former two-time world champions. Especially as, just a minute later, Japan missed a tackle and South Africa's second row Lood de Jager charged over from 30 metres to score. It was the kind of try Tier Two nations always seemed to cough up eventually. With the conversion kicked by Pat Lambie, it was 19–13 to South Africa. Surely, fans thought, this really was the beginning of the end of any romantic dreams that history was in the air?

But Eddie Jones and Japan hadn't worked this hard for so long to panic now. This was the new Japan. A heroic defeat wasn't going to cut it. They kept coming in waves at the Springboks and within ten minutes Goromaru had taken advantage of the penalties the Japanese pressure had won and kicked six more points. It was 19–19. Now it really did feel like something special might be looming on the horizon. The South Africans could never have expected anything like this.

A further exchange of points from the boot of each team's kicker made it 22–22 after 60 minutes. Then, disaster struck for Eddie Jones's men, once more seeming to spell the end of the budding fairytale. South African replacement hooker Adriaan Strauss took a routine crash ball on the edge of the Japanese

22, looking to set up a new platform for attack. The Blossoms' defence failed: the first-up defender was bounced off, the second one was unable to act in time and the last man, winger Kotaro Matsushima, was completely wrong-footed. Try. With the extras it was 29–22 to the Boks.

After all their toil, was this what would kill Japan's hope? From the kick-off, the South Africans gained a penalty and cleared to the Japanese 22. It felt like a massive momentum shift. After 65 minutes Japan had made 103 tackles to South Africa's 62. Even if the minds of the men in red and white were willing, it looked as if the bodies would start giving out. The Boks kept coming at them, looking for the fatal sting. In the 66th minute the favourites declined a penalty to go for the corner. Yet an attempted deceptive set move from the line-out was repelled. Japan cleared their lines.

Boom! In the 68th minute, Japan's Goromaru scored as intricate and as inspiring a team try as you will ever see. From a line-out five metres outside their opponent's 22, on the left-hand side, Japan attacked from quick front ball. Replacement scrum-half Atsushi Hiwasa rifled out a lightning pass to inside centre Harumichi Tatekawa. Taking it at pace, and cleverly using a dummy runner to disguise his next move, he gave a short ball to fly-half Kosei Ono who, taking two men out and only taking three steps, sent a short inside pass back to Matsushima who exploded onto the ball. The pacy winger accelerated through the gap that had opened up, beat three defenders and, just after crossing the threshold of the Bok 22, he delivered the ball out of contact to Goromaru who finished in the right-hand corner what had been a move of beauty and impeccable timing. It was Hollywood-level stuff. The dream was back on . . . again! Television cameras captured the look of spectators who were half elated and half in utter shock. The Japanese players embraced each other in ecstasy. With the conversion it was 29–29 with ten minutes left.

The drama came thick and fast and two minutes later South Africa came within inches of the line on several occasions. Even the referee fell over (with no one near him) in all the thrills. Japan clung on through sheer force of will it seemed (yet, of course, the discipline and structure had to be there first). The Springboks left the 22 with the reward of a successful penalty though and with seven minutes left, the score was 32–29 to the men in green. However, every time the cameras fixed on the crowd, their supporters looked nervous

The call

Japan simply refused to die and came at their opponents again and again as time slowly ticked away. It was not just their determination that inspired the crowd into a frenzy, it was the skilful attacks they employed to try and find a weakness. The rugby was, simply, beautiful. As the clock hit 78.19, Japan's flanker Michael Broadhurst dived for the line with defenders clinging on. He was held up somehow and his side emerged with a penalty and Springbok prop Coenie Oosthuizen was sin-binned. Japan had a chance to kick a penalty and claim a famous draw. It's what everyone expected them to do. Michael Leitch thought otherwise. He opted to go for the corner and the win.

The subsequent attacking maul seemed to work and Japan drove over the line and both teams collapsed in a heap. Try? Was the ball grounded? Referee Jerome Garces went to the television match official. The crowd, with eyes covered, nails being chewed and hair being pulled, waited. And waited.

No try. Scrum five to Japan. 35 seconds left.

After South Africa were forced to reshuffle their pack due to their prop having been carded, Japan won a penalty from the scrum. Again, Leitch declined a kickable penalty and opted for the scrum. Even the Japan coaches wanted him to kick the points. But he believed. He felt something was on.

Furious, Eddie Jones smashed his walkie talkie into the ground in anger. He was sure his side had thrown away the chance to draw the game.

The clock ticked into the red. The scrum got reset . . . and reset. Finally, play went ahead as the clock hit 83.00. It was a terrible scrum for the attacking team and the ball squirted out the back but, somehow, Japan recovered the awkward bouncing ball and stayed alive. Then they attacked the blindside through their captain. South Africa held them five metres out. Japan started working through the phases. No one shied away from responsibility. They moved their way into the centre of the field, then went wide right through more phases. Leitch carried again and was four metres short this time.

Then, it happened. With 83.47 on the clock, the Brave Blossoms switched the attack from their position on the far right to go left, moving the ball quickly through the hands. A miss pass from Tatekawa skipped past two attackers and found replacement back row Amanaki Lelei Mafi who had been pointing to an opportunity and weakness he saw in the defence. It was clear to all watching the Bok defence was stretched, exhausted, desperate. The crowd noise swelled to unimaginable levels. Mafi, who found his space instantly shut down, moved the ball into his left hand and stiff-armed Jesse Kriel who was shoved back. He accelerated on, drew another defender and threw his own miss pass to replacement wing Karne Hesketh who, pushed on seemingly by a cacophony of screams and yells from the rabid crowd, ran the final seven metres into the left-hand corner and into rugby and sporting folklore. The try turned the sporting world upside down.

The players hugged and screamed and roared, all arms entangled in joy. The cameras cut to crying fans . . . shell-shocked fans . . . disbelieving fans . . . players from both sides collapsed on the floor in extremes of joy and sorrow. The conversion was irrelevant and its subsequent failure meant nothing. It was 34–32. It was history. Japan had followed up their 1991 win over Zimbabwe by scalping the head of the Springboks 24 years later. This was the stuff they make movies out of. Which, they subsequently did. The scenes that played out were everything that is good about sport.

In his post-match interview, Eddie Jones said: 'If you are a child in Japan you will watch this and you will want to play rugby for Japan.'

One South African pundit, Jon Cardinelli, said: 'Japan competed like wolverines on Red Bull.' Heyneke Meyer, the defeated South African coach, admitted they had let a proud rugby nation down.

The two sides had never met before. Which meant that Japan could now boast a 100 per cent record against the southern hemisphere powerhouse. The result led to a huge wave of interest in rugby in Japan and was perfect timing and one in the eye for those old rugby heads who had been sceptical of the decision to award them the 2019 World Cup hosting rights. There was no doubt now. This felt like destiny.

Cruelly, Japan's status as a Tier Two nation would contribute to their undoing. They had just four days to recover and face a fresh Scotland who, being a Tier One nation, had a far more favourable schedule. Japan fell 45–10. They recovered to beat Samoa (25–6) and the USA (28–18). This was an extraordinary set of results for a team who had gone into the tournament with just one win from 24 World Cup games. Yet, they missed out on the quarter-finals on points difference and became the first team ever to win three pool games and not emerge from the group stages.

As long as rugby is played, though, this match, quite rightly, will never be forgotten.

MATCH DETAILS

Japan: Ayumu Goromaru; Akihito Yamada, Male Sau, Harumichi Tatekawa, Kotaro Matsushima; Kosei Ono, Fumiaki Tanaka; Masataka Mikami, Shota Horie, Kensuke Hatakeyama, Luke Thompson, Hitoshi Ono, Michael Leitch (captain), Hendrik Tui, Michael Broadhurst.

Replacements: Takeshi Kazu, Keita Inagaki, Hiroshi Yamashita, Shinya Makabe, Amanaki Mafi, Atsushi Hiwasa, Yu Tamura, Karne Hesketh.

Tries: Leitch, Goromaru, Hesketh
Conversions: Goromaru (2)
Penalties: Goromaru (5)

South Africa: Zane Kirchner; Bryan Habana, Jesse Kriel, Jean de Villiers (captain), Lwazi Mvovo; Pat Lambie, Ruan Pienaar; Tendai Mtawarira, Bismarck du Plessis, Jannie du Plessis, Lood de Jager, Victor Matfield, Francois Louw, Schalk Burger, Pieter-Steph du Toit.

Replacements: Adriaan Strauss, Trevor Nyakane, Coenie Oosthuizen, Eben Etzebeth, Siya Kolisi, Fourie du Preez, Handre Pollard, JP Pietersen.

Tries: Lowe, B. Du Plesis, De Jager, Strauss
Conversions: Lambie (2), Pollard (1)
Penalties: Lambie, Pollard
Yellow card: Oosthuizen

DODDIE WEIR

'Ah, well. It's been a good old time hasn't it?'
Doddie Weir after Marius Bosman intentionally
injured the Scot's knee and ended his Lions tour.

**On the field, Doddie Weir was one of the most popular
Scottish internationals of the modern era. His bravery and
determination when it came to tackling motor neurone
disease after his retirement, won the admiration of the
sporting world.**

Main teams: Stewart's Melville RFC, Melrose, Newcastle
Falcons, Border Reivers, Barbarians, Scotland, British and Irish
Lions
Position: Second row, number eight
International caps: 61 (1990–2000)
Points: 19 (4 tries)

George Wilson Weir was born in Edinburgh in the summer of
1970. Known affectionately as 'Doddie', he was the eldest of
four children and grew up on a farm in the Scottish Borders.

At his prime, Doddie towered over fellow Scot players at 1.98
metres (6ft 6in). Some match programmes listed him an inch

taller, but he claimed he was happy being listed at the shorter height as otherwise he was put in the 'freak zone'.

Doddie was highly celebrated as a player during his career, winning 61 caps for Scotland and touring with the British and Irish Lions. But he occupies a special place in rugby folklore that was only partially earned by his impressive achievements on the playing paddock. He tragically died aged just 52 from motor neurone disease (MND) and spent the last few years of his life heroically fighting the disease and raising millions of pounds in the search for a cure through his foundation.

Horses and giraffes

Doddie's route to rugby was a slightly unusual one. As a youngster with an agricultural upbringing, he was drawn to horse riding. Along with his sister he would compete in equestrian events and he was good enough to represent Scotland. During a session at his local pony club one day, he met a coach from Melrose Under 14s who persuaded him to come down and have a game of rugby with Melrose. Doddie was at the time playing a bit of rugby with Stewarts' Melville RFC. However, they played on Saturday which didn't suit him and Melrose played on Sundays which was far better.

In later life, Doddie would say that his early experience in horse riding gave him a strong core, something that helped him get high in line-outs and adjust and compete while in the air. He added that his ability to study and learn show jumping courses and dressage tests came in handy when memorising complicated line-out calls too.

Doddie's lanky physique didn't always serve him well when it came to making an impression. In a national trial match in 1992, after he had already won multiple caps, one newspaper stated he simply didn't carry enough weight to 'tangle' with his far larger English counterparts. But these weight concerns were not new to Doddie. After his one and only cap for Scotland B in

1989 (although he would later play for Scotland A), journalist Brian Meek praised the second row's skills, but commented that he 'still looks like he should eat more porridge'.

His appearance always drew comments. His fellow countryman, and legendary rugby commentator, Bill McLaren, once memorably described the way he ran and carried the ball as resembling a 'mad giraffe'. Throughout his career, no matter how many honours he won (both in the 15-a-side code and the sevens format), Doddie always harboured grave doubts about his ability and admitted that physically he was 'skinny as a rake'. Thankfully, others were far better judges of just how good a player he was.

In 1990 he was part of the Melrose team that won the Scottish league title. Jim Telfer, the coach at the time, said that the win was more important to him than the Scottish Grand Slam that same year.

Telfer wasn't always impressed with Doddie's approach to rugby though. Stories are legion of Doddie doing whatever he could to skip brutal early training sessions on a Sunday morning. Nonetheless, his natural athleticism and line-out brilliance kept him in the first XV. Telfer later summed up what Doddie could be like to coach in the player's autobiography:

'He's the village idiot, loud very loud – gregarious, doing daft things like nudging you when you're off balance, or grabbing you and sticking his finger in your ear. But when that switch was on, as a rugby player, whether with club or country, Doddie was a completely different animal: focused, concentrated, confident, a huge presence, ferociously proud and committed, and immensely physical.'

In the summer of 1990, still only 19, Doddie was selected for Scotland's tour of New Zealand. This was a strong Scottish side that was fresh off a Five Nations Grand Slam. He played and impressed in the wins against Poverty Bay-East Coast, Nelson Bays-Marlborough, Southland and Manawatu. While he didn't make the Test side, understandable at his young age, he so impressed the-hard-to-impress locals that he was approached by Waikato to stay on and play for them. Just a few months later Doddie would get his call-up to the national side.

Scotland comes calling

Doddie's debut for his country came in November 1990 against Argentina at Murrayfield. Packing down in the second row, he helped his nation to a 49–3 victory. By the 1991 World Cup he had established himself as a regular in the pack and remained first choice for most of the next decade. Telfer was thrilled that Scotland finally had a line-out jumper who 'jumped up, not down'.

Doddie was a lock for his first 14 appearances, before appearing at number eight for nine of his next ten caps (the other cap was at replacement lock), and then returning to the second row for the remainder of his Test career. He was part of the Scotland side that made the semi-final of the 1991 World Cup, narrowly losing to England 9–6 in Edinburgh after the infamous missed penalty from Gavin Hastings. He had played in the wins over Japan, Zimbabwe, Ireland and Samoa to get Scotland within touching distance of a final appearance.

Doddie's two tries against the All Blacks in the 1995 edition of the World Cup made him the first player to have ever scored two tries for Scotland in one game against New Zealand. The *Rugby Union Who's Who* annual lamented that this would have given him status as a national hero had the Kiwis not won 48–30.

In the twilight of his Scotland career he did play a part, albeit a small one, in helping his nation to their first Five Nations win since 1990. In a season plagued by injury, he turned out against Wales in the 33–20 win at Murrayfield, making him part of the 1999 championship winning side. It remains, at the time of writing, the last time Scotland have won the championship.

Doddie won the final one of his 61 international caps against France at Murrayfield in 2000. Despite two yellow cards for the visitors, Doddie and his team tasted a 28–16 defeat.

In 2001 he would win a cap for Scotland A, offering him a chance to pass on his vast experience to younger players.

Living with Lions and Falcons

During his years at the top, Doddie played for several clubs. Not long after professionalism came into rugby in 1995, the 'Lamp-post of the Line-out' joined Newcastle Falcons (then still Newcastle Gosforth) which was considered 'the first professional club in the world'. The club at the time was backed by Sir John Hall and England fly-half Rob Andrew had been appointed director of rugby. Andrew himself personally recruited Doddie.

Interviewed later on his decision to move, Doddie said: 'Loyalty's important, but in the end, it was an easy decision to make. I'd been at Melrose for seven years and we'd won the title five times. Money was not a major issue. I found the north-east very hospitable, everybody says hello and you get value for money. You don't want to pay too much for a pint.'

The club soon got promoted to the top-flight of English rugby after finishing second in the league. The following season Newcastle claimed the Premiership title, pipping Saracens by a single point (there were no play-offs back then). To this day Newcastle are the only side to have won the top league of English rugby in the first year after promotion.

After joining Newcastle, Doddie's career went from strength to strength. In 1997, by now his country's most-capped forward, he was named Scotland's best player of the Five Nations. His performances saw him named in the inaugural professional British and Irish Lions squad for the legendary 1997 trip to South Africa. Part of the reason for his success at this time was he had taken a more professional approach to conditioning, even getting serious about weight training. He had been inspired by the legendary fitness coach Steve Black who worked with Newcastle at the time.

With the game now professional and revenue being crucial to success, cameras were allowed behind the scenes to create a documentary on the trip. The subsequent *Living with Lions* VHS became a cult piece of rugby film as fans lapped up the first-ever opportunity to get a decent glimpse of what exactly went on away from the actual matches. Doddie's charisma, positivity and humour shone through in the video and made him a firm fan favourite.

Doddie didn't just perform off the field either, his performances in the red shirt were strong enough that he started three of the first four games. Then disaster struck and, sadly, it was no accident. During the Lions' 64–14 win over Mpumalanga, Doddie suffered a knee ligament injury thanks to the cowardly act of opposing second row Marius Bosman. The home player, unable to compete equally on ability and talent, decided to be a thug and cruelly stamped on Doddie's knee, taking out his victim's medial ligament as the knee hyper-extended.

The clip of Doddie responding to the news of his tour being over is one of the most poignant sporting clips you will ever see. Half smiling and half grimacing through the pain, he simply says: 'Ah, well. It's been a good old time, hasn't it?'

In his autobiography, Doddie wrote of his continuing anger about the incident: 'I thought I held it together quite well, on the outside. Inside, my stomach churned and I really wanted to scream, not in agony, not at the news – injuries will always be part and parcel of rugby – but at the way I'd been booted out of the tour.'

Bosman was not even banned for the incident, merely fined. On his return home, Doddie named the metal boot cleaner he had outside his house 'Marius' so he could take pleasure in cleaning his boots upon it.

Doddie would go on to captain Newcastle. He led his team, containing stars such as Jonny Wilkinson and Va'aiga Tuigamala, to a 30–27 win over Harlequins at Twickenham to win the 2001 Tetley's Bitter Cup.

Doddie finished his club career with Border Reivers and retired in 2005 (Reivers was a Scottish professional side that formed in 1996 and disbanded in 2007).

The 'Mad Giraffe' also once had the honour to captain the Barbarians – although he claims his decision to opt to kick a late penalty in one match (which the kicker subsequently missed) ended his career in the famous black and white shirt.

After hanging up the boots

Looking back on his career, Doddie was grateful to have played in an era when the social side of rugby was still a major part of a player's life. He believed a few drinks were the best way to bring a team together and never felt the same love for the professional game as he did its amateur father.

Once retired, the charismatic Doddie had no problem becoming a popular speaker in rugby's after-dinner circuit and a regular pundit for the BBC. He also moved to a farm not far from where he spent his childhood and worked there and in a waste management company.

Tragically, in late 2016 he was diagnosed with motor neurone disease (known as ASL or Lou Gehrig's disease in the USA). MND is a terminal condition which attacks the nerves, meaning messages sent from the brain to the body's muscles stop working properly. It increases in severity over time and there is no way to predict how quickly the symptoms will worsen. Eventually the sufferer is unable to eat, drink properly and, ultimately, unable to breathe.

Doddie first suspected something was wrong when he injured a hand working on the farm and noticed that it didn't heal as expected. Over time, he gradually began losing strength. He was initially told by doctors that in all probability he would be in a wheelchair within 12 months. Doddie defied these predictions, but as time passed he lost a great deal of strength in his arms and hands and soon he was needing help with dressing himself. With the support of his wife, Kathy, and his three sons Hamish, Angus and Ben, he did everything he could to fight the disease – from intensive physio and exercise to setting up the My Name'5 Doddie Foundation to raise awareness about MND. His foundation would have a huge impact not just in generating vital research funds, but in giving the public a better understanding of what MND is. Within a year of setting it up, Doddie and his team had raised £1 million.

Doddie continued to provide for his family while all this was happening, working on both the farm and in his waste management role. He believed he was lucky to have jobs he could still work in, despite his declining physical condition. Throughout his illness, he received wonderful practical support from ex-teammates such as Gary Armstrong, Scott Hastings, Gavin Hastings, Will Greenwood, and Rob Wainwright. Several years after he had been diagnosed, Doddie joked that they had originally signed up to help him as they thought he would only last six months and instead he hung on for several more years!

In 2018, the Welsh and Scottish Rugby Unions announced that games between Wales and Scotland would now be played for the Doddie Weir Cup. Doddie and his family brought the new trophy onto the pitch and the big man said after that: 'Normally you get a cup named after you when you are not here, so I thoroughly enjoyed it.' Ever the joker, Doddie remarked the silversmiths had made the trophy's handles look like his 'massive ears'.

Speaking to the *Guardian* in 2019, Doddie spoke of his frustration around the lack of progress in treatment for the disease: 'In Scotland there's only one drug for it. One drug that came out 22 years ago. Basically, you've got a death sentence. So, my crusade at the moment is to try to get options for people who have this, so they have a chance. It might be a minimal chance but at least a better chance than they have now.'

In his effort to fight the hold the disease had on him, Weir travelled several times to the US to get access to a drug that was unavailable in the UK.

In 2019, Doddie almost died while on holiday, choking on a small piece of toast. His wife saved him, but he still had to spend several days in hospital due to the pain from the after effects. The incident showed just how fragile life had become, with even the smallest thing potentially putting his life at risk. As the disease's cruel effects grew stronger, he also suffered several serious falls, some of which required hospital treatment or medical aid. That same year he received the Helen Rollason Award for Outstanding Achievement in the Face of Adversity at the BBC Sports Personality of the Year Awards.

Towards the end of his extraordinary life, Doddie was getting around in a mobility scooter or wheelchair and using a voice app, controlled by his eyes, to communicate. Even at this stage he continued to have a flutter with the online bookies – using an app to help him place bets. Sadly for him, his wife Kathy refused to top up his gambling account when his funds fell down to a measly 38 pence.

Doddie's success in raising awareness and millions of pounds for his noble cause led to all sorts of recognition, including an honorary degree from Abertay University. True to his flamboyant character, he accepted the reward in an extravagant tartan suit. In his acceptance speech he said:

'I've got a wedding anniversary on Monday and I never thought for one moment I'd be here to celebrate that so I'm doing very well and still enjoying quite a lot of Guinness. But I have to admit, I got Covid back in February and it knocked me back on the red wine a little bit but I'm trying very hard to get the taste back and fighting very strongly to get a cure for this horrific issue. When people are diagnosed with MND, they are told they have one or two years to live, so for me to still be here six years in is quite unbelievable.'

In the same month, Doddie was awarded an OBE in the Queen's honours, further helping him raise vital awareness, support and funds. Even medical experts were surprised by just how much money Doddie raised and how much his work in raising the profile of MND had done to push forward the research. His foundation had genuinely made a difference.

In November 2022, Doddie made his final public appearance at Murrayfield, ahead of Scotland's meeting with New Zealand. Entering the field in a wheelchair with the aid of his three sons and loving wife, Doddie presented the match ball to Scotland captain Jamie Ritchie and All Black leader Sam Whitelock. The packed Murrayfield loudly and clearly showed their love and admiration in what was one of the most touching pre-match scenes ever witnessed on a rugby field. Doddie, clad in his trademark blue and yellow tartan, was clearly in an advanced stage of suffering and almost unrecognisable from the young man who once scored two tries in one game against the team that was about to do battle with Scotland.

In a fitting tribute, Scotland wore blue and yellow tartan numbers to support Doddie's foundation.

Doddie was just 52 years old when he died on 26 November, 2022. Until the end, he never complained. He once said: 'I have never, ever thought "Why me?" It was "Right, let's get this sorted" . . . it's like with rugby. if you don't get in the team, do you give up your jersey or do you fight?'

Doddie had survived six years with the condition, defying the predictions the disease may take him after a year. In those six years he achieved extraordinary things and did so much to raise awareness of MND and to collect vital money to fight it. It's no exaggeration to say that millions more people have an understanding of this cruel condition than before he went public with his illness.

Doddie may be gone, but his spirit lives on through his family, friends and his foundation. Quite simply, he was one of the greatest characters in rugby.

A legacy of love and hope

The My Name'5 Doddie Foundation continues to campaign and raise money. For more information on how the foundation can be supported, visit www.myname5doddie.co.uk. The foundation has donated to research at King's College London, Oxford University and Edinburgh University.

SARA COX

'Yeah, I'm going to get stung a couple of times,
but I know that what I leave behind me will
make life so much easier for the next generation.'
Sara Cox

In 2016, Sara Cox became rugby's first female full-time professional referee. Her remarkable rise to the top has helped transform attitudes to women in rugby and shown future generations a whole new world of opportunity and possibilities.

Career highlights: First ever full-time professional referee, officiated at Test matches (men's and women's), three World Cups, Olympic Games, Premiership Rugby (men's and women's), RFU Championship, Army v Navy.

The laws of rugby are among the most complex in any professional sport and rely so much on interpretation that even the most learned students of the game will find plenty to disagree on when presented with an identical scenario.

As a result, those who referee at the elite level have to be made of stern stuff. To climb from litter-strewn park pitches to the flawless fields of Test stadiums requires expertise, tenacity, fitness and skin as thick as that of a rhino wearing kevlar. For elite referees, the pressure comes not only from players and coaches, but print journalists, broadcast pundits, commentators, tens of thousands of screaming fans and, most cruelly of all, the teeming millions on social media. And while without officials blowing whistles there is no game, it often seems the bile of the 'wronged' rugby community does all it can to discourage fresh refereeing blood.

If reaching the top of the refereeing tree wasn't daunting enough, Sara Cox had it twice as hard on her way there. Before her, no other woman had ever become a full-time professional referee. In a sport that, for the vast majority of two centuries, has been primarily an all-male closed shop, it takes a special personality and determination to succeed. Let's not forget, the first two editions of the Women's World Cup were not even sanctioned by World Rugby as far too many men in positions of power – who would happily wax lyrical about 'rugby values' whenever they had the chance – did all they could to block, slow down or even outwardly denigrate women playing the game. Even today, with women's rugby now part of the mainstream, there are still loud and vocal chauvinistic pockets polluting the game with outdated language and attitudes when it comes to female rugby.

Yet Cox has overcome all that. She's swatted away the usual insults referees face – as well as the additional ones that come coated in an extra layer of bitterness and ignorance due to her gender. Proudly, she has reached the top of the game and made history as she has done so. Most importantly, she's blazed a trail for others.

A life on the greens . . . almost
Sara Cox was born in Exeter in 1990. She hails from a rugby family, with her dad playing for both the police force and Cullompton RFC in Devon. When she wasn't watching him play and helpfully kicking the ball back to the players when it came off the field, she was accompanying her father to cheer on Exeter.

But despite the family rugby connections, Cox's early sporting obsession and success came in an altogether different sport: golf. Encouraged by her golf-loving grandparents, who had once provided her with a child-sized club, hacked down from full size, Cox took a serious stab at a golfing career. Possessing both a natural talent and the will to succeed, she won a scholarship at a local golf club before she had even become a teenager.

As a member of the English Women's Golf Association (now part of England Golf), Cox took her first steps on the path to a possible professional career. Constantly playing in tournaments and training relentlessly, she had to balance her sport with her studies. It wasn't always easy.

'I had to make a decision,' says Cox looking back. 'I either had to look at US colleges and start pushing hard to get an offer from one, or I had to focus on my GCSEs. It was tough working it out at that age. I was spending all my weekends playing golf and putting hundreds and hundreds of golf balls in my front room on the days I wasn't on a real green. I got to a point where I thought, "I don't want to do this anymore, I just want to be happy and spend time with my friends, and I wanted golf to be a hobby."'

The decision disappointed her father, but he supported her. 'My dad, bless him,' recalled Cox, 'his heart sank. But my parents, they always said that if you stop enjoying something just tell us and we'll stop. There was no pressure. But they said you have to be comfortable with the decision so you don't look back on it in 20 years and regret it. I had to decide on getting qualifications or pursuing professional sport. I had struggled academically. I got diagnosed in primary school with dyslexia. It wasn't life-changing, but it made school harder for me than for many others. It also meant that I couldn't realistically do both sport and school. I made the decision to do my GCSEs. I still look back now and say it was one of the best decisions I made.'

Cox, showing the determination that would serve her so well later in rugby, cracked on with her studies and came away with what she calls 'pretty decent grades'.

Rugby comes calling

After walking away from the golf dream, Cox found herself a little unsure what to do. She tried all sorts of sports, including basketball, before deciding to have a proper go at rugby. The problem was, she was at an age where she was too old to compete with boys and there were no junior girls' teams near enough for her to join.

One of the teachers at Cox's school was Ian Brown, who played for Exeter Chiefs. Cox asked him why she couldn't play rugby at school. Brown offered to help out and suggested she gather up other like-minded girls and promised to give up his lunchtime to train them.

Cox had previously played a bit of rugby with the boys at the school, but that came to a nasty end when she broke her collarbone thanks to her being at the end of a somewhat unorthodox tackle – it involved a knee – that stopped her scoring a try and sent her flying.

While Cox could only recruit two other girls willing to join her on the rugby field during lunch, Brown still gave them training sessions – even if their options were limited in what they could actually do.

'I owe a lot to him,' recalls Cox. 'Even if I didn't realise it at the time.' Eventually, Cox joined up with Cullompton RFC, where a player from the senior women's XV suggested she try and put together a team. Again, only a handful of players could be found at Cox's age group, but the club helped them practise. More determined than ever, Cox refused to give up and looked around other local clubs to recruit like-minded girls who were searching for a youth team. Eventually a team was formed at Exeter Saracens that gave Cox and friends a place to play (they created the first U14s and U18s women's teams). Indeed, the sides still thrive today and Exeter Saracens can proudly cite internationals such as Abbie Brown as having come through their ranks.

Trying for England

After trying multiple positions around the field (including sticking her head in the scrum), Cox soon settled down as a utility back, with wing her most frequent role. A natural sportsperson, Cox, unsurprisingly, soon got noticed by national selectors and had several England age-grade trials (these covered U19s, U20s and U21s as England rugby changed its setup and structure).

Ironically, in light of her later career choice, Cox could be a bit of a handful for referees. 'I was a bloody nightmare,' she admits. 'I think a lot of it was I did know the laws, even if some would argue these days I don't. I used to spend a lot of time watching the game and I understood from observing the top levels of men's rugby what was happening and so I picked up on those kinds of things. I'm quite a visual learner. So I'd get on a rugby pitch and be like, "That's not how they do it on the telly" and "I don't get why you are penalising this". A lot came from knowledge, and a lot from being a player and my personality.'

A nasty injury during another England age-group trial was to bring on the beginning of the end of Cox's playing days. A hard knee into the sternum in a tackle situation led to the winger laying on the ground, in agony, asking herself: 'Why am I here?'

She now sees the moment as a catalyst to change in her life. The injury caused short-term problems, but would not have prevented her playing on. 'Looking back as an adult my heart wasn't in it,' says Cox. 'It wasn't that the injury stopped me playing, but it was a trigger point. It refocused me a little bit and forced me to think about what I wanted. And I eventually realised that being an elite rugby player wasn't it.'

For a time, Cox tried various things, including playing and refereeing basketball. But she kept finding herself drawn back to the rugby field, just not as a player anymore.

'For whatever reason I kept coming back to rugby,' says Cox. 'I'm not sure why. I think I just enjoyed rugby so much. I never went in with a clear pathway to say right you will do this and this and become a referee. In all honesty, I looked into how I can give back to the game and I thought that, well, if as a player I had been willing to stand there and tell a referee they were getting something wrong and I've never refereed, then it's about time I stood in their shoes and had a go myself.'

Cox took a refereeing course and made her first tentative steps with whistle in hand, later saying: 'For whatever reason, it just stuck. I had never stuck with football, basketball or golf, but with rugby it felt a bit like I was completing the puzzle.'

Early success

Cox got a major sign that she was on the right path when she returned to England age-group trials again, but this time as a referee. After she had officiated a trial game, one of the coaches approached her. When Cox had been a player, the coach in question always felt Cox wasn't quite giving management what they needed. But after seeing her with the whistle, the coach remarked: 'This is you. This is where you are most comfortable. Just keep going.'

'I never looked back after that,' says Cox. Aged 17, she refereed a boys' under-15 game in Tavistock. Not long after, with a proud and supportive mother on the sideline in the freezing cold, she nervously took charge of her first proper adult game (not including a local friendly Boxing Day run-out she had overseen a few weeks before). Shortly after kick-off, Cox started getting abuse from a man on the sideline. It was so obnoxious and so constant, the novice referee had to do something. And she did.

'I stopped the game and walked over to him,' says Cox. 'I told him that as an adult he was here to set an example and that he currently wasn't. I told him the boys were here to play rugby and he was shouting at me telling me something different. I asked him to please be quiet. My mum, bless her, stood watching all this. And then I got on with the game.'

Not only did the spectator remain quiet, he even approached Cox afterwards and apologised and told her no referee had ever done that to him before and that he didn't even know why he had been shouting as her officiating had been fine.

After this baptism of fire, Cox progressed further and further up the food chain. Soon she got her first senior men's game: Sidmouth Seconds v Brixham Thirds. She had been expecting to run the line, but referee and mentor Simon Lane surprised her by suggesting she control the game herself. After initially saying she couldn't do it, she took on the challenge.

'It was a great test and a wonderful environment,' says Cox. 'Simon had been there to step in if anything had gone wrong, which helped give me the confidence to do it. I still have the newspaper cutting of the match, which has a photo of me laughing with one of the players. It made the back page of a local paper as it was, of course, an unusual story.'

It wasn't all plain sailing. Cox had to overcome the usual pressures referees come under, but with the added pressures of her gender which led to more scrutiny and, inevitably, comments and complaints from sexist dinosaurs.

'Yeah, I had it all,' says Cox. 'I had had a lot of it as a player too, all the old fuddy duddies saying: "Women shouldn't be doing this and should be in the kitchen."

'It was the same with reffing. I've heard it all. Times have moved on now thankfully, and the female comments have died down a bit. But when I first started I was one of only two women on the refereeing circuit. I think I'm part of a rare breed, possibly the last, in the women's elite panel, that has gone from the very bottom to the top. Which teaches you so much. Quite simply, I was not going to let people ruin something I enjoyed just because they were uneducated in what they were doing. If you want to shout at me, come and put yourself in my shoes first. If

I had given up, I would have become another number that had bowed down to ignorance.'

Onwards and upwards to history

Not only did Cox persevere through the tough early times, she excelled, rising up first through the Devon Referees Society and then the South West regional group. Next came international honours both on the World Sevens Series and in 15s. In 2014, she was named as an assistant referee for the 2014 Women's World Cup. At every level she improved and continued to develop as an official, putting in every hour she could and frequently taking unpaid leave from work to follow her passion.

Then in 2016, she made history. The RFU, impressed by what they had seen so far, offered Cox a full-time professional contract. Amazingly, this was not actually what Cox had been planning for. While ambitious, she was also working hard in her day job in a recycling business in Exeter and seeing plenty of success. Suddenly, she had a choice to make.

'I had to make a decision about the balance between my refereeing and my career,' says Cox. 'I just couldn't keep going. It just happened I'd had a few chats and the RFU put a contract in front of me. So I went to my managing director at work and I sat down with him and said I was aware I had spent so much time out of the office. I'd had 75 days unpaid leave one year and I knew I was a problem for their budget. But I was invested in the company and wanted to stay. However, I told them about the contract offer from the RFU and asked what they thought. They were turning over £18 million a year and now probably do triple that. So, this was a great place to be working and building a career. My boss said "Coxy, you can't look back on this in ten years' time and say you gave this up to come on a journey with us. You'll kick yourself for not trying. Take the contract. I know how important this is. If you don't, then I'm going to fire you anyway".

'And that was the conversation we had and the next day I signed the contract and handed in my notice.'

In her inaugural year as a professional referee, Cox became the first woman to take charge of a Women's Premiership final as Richmond beat Saracens for the title. She also went to Rio to officiate at the 2016 Olympic Rugby Sevens.

As Cox continually rose to the challenges put in front of her, the RFU renewed her initial one-year contract and each season seemed to bring further honours. In 2017 Cox became the first female referee for a National League One match and she also refereed in the Challenge Cup and the Women's World Cup. In 2018 she became the first female to referee an RFU Championship match (Cornish Pirates v Doncaster); officiated at the Commonwealth Games; became the first female referee of a game between two Premiership men's sides in a non-league game (Northampton v Wasps), and was assistant referee to two men's Test matches (Hong Kong v Germany and Kenya v Germany).

In 2020, Cox was assistant referee to Wayne Barnes in a Premiership match between Bath and Wasps. In 2021 she refereed the gold medal match in the women's sevens final in the Tokyo Olympics as New Zealand beat France. For all the buzz of taking charge of such a match, there were downsides. In particular, the social media abuse came thick and fast. 'You name it, they complained about it,' recalls Cox.

Then, in September 2021, came the match which truly propelled her into the global rugby spotlight. In September 2021, aged 31, Cox became the first 'woman in the middle' of a men's Premiership match overseeing a Harlequins win over Worcester at the Stoop.

'If I could bottle that feeling that day I'd be a very rich person,' Cox told the press afterwards, reflecting not just on the match, but also the positive reaction of the crowd. 'It is something I don't think I will ever replicate. People could say what they liked on social media, they were never going to take that unique moment away from me.'

The moment was all the sweeter as she had first been due to referee a Premiership game in June, but Covid intervened and the match was cancelled. Furthermore, in summer 2021, Cox had a personal health issue she feared was breast cancer. She told the *Guardian*: 'I found a lump in a place I wasn't expecting to find one. Everything else suddenly doesn't matter anymore. Your whole world stops spinning. You stand there and think "Now what?" Unfortunately, there is cancer in my family: my grandmother had it and my mum had a scare as well. You forget about being out on a rugby pitch and all the things that come with that.'

Fortunately, Cox got the all clear on the health front and she was able to continue forging ahead on the field, whistle in hand.

In recent years, more female referees have begun emerging in elite rugby and their relative rarity in the men's pro game does lead to some amusing moments. Unlike many sports, rugby has a culture where match officials are frequently referred to by players as 'Sir'. Force of habit means Cox is addressed by this salutation hundreds of times a season. 'They stand there almost like young schoolboys,' laughs Cox. 'Often, they then start mumbling as they try to figure out what to call me. I don't mind at all. By the time they've tried to come up with an alternative such as 'Ref' or 'Ma'am', they've often forgotten the point they were trying to make anyway.'

There was further history made in 2022 when, along with Hollie Davidson of Scotland, France's Aurélie Groizeleau and England's Claire Hodnett, Cox formed the first-ever all-female officiating team for a men's international. The quartet took charge of Italy's 38–31 win over Portugal in Lisbon.

First through the door

Whatever Cox goes on to achieve in her career, she has earned her place as a key figure in the evolution of the sport and will serve as inspiration to countless others within and without rugby. Like all those who are 'first through the door', she has had to battle prejudices and overcome obstacles that had never been challenged or beaten before. Cox told the *Guardian* in 2021: 'It's like walking through a patch of stinging nettles. If you're the first one to do it, you're going to get stung. If you're the next person behind me, I've already created the path for you. You just need to walk . . . Sometimes the easiest part of your job is being on that field. You're free of the peripheral noise . . . you go out and feel at home. In your mind you're thinking: "This is what makes me happy." I will love this opportunity as a first but what I would really love is for women referees to become the norm. With the number now involved, it can only inspire others. I want to grow interest, motivate others, while doing my job, which is to be out there in the middle of a rugby pitch. Yeah, I'm going to get stung a couple of times but I know that what I leave behind me will make life so much easier for the next generation. I think we've got people in the Rugby Football Union who are willing to look at the future of the game and have a genuine desire for it to be all inclusive, no matter your background, your sex or how you identify.'

While many will see Cox as offering inspiration to future female rugby referees, she is keen to highlight that her story can inspire beyond the sport she has chosen. 'I don't think it is about going into refereeing,' says Cox. 'I think it is about a life lesson. My mother taught me early on, if someone offers you an opportunity, do it. Or you may look back and wish you'd done it. There isn't much I passed up on. There may be some things I wish I had not done, but there are very few opportunities I passed up as I knew they may never come around again.

'During Covid, two people I knew dropped dead suddenly. Life is so fragile and you have to take those opportunities and just go. I chose refereeing, it's not for everyone. Some choose playing, that's not for everyone. Have a go at everything, find out the stuff you fancy doing, run with it and don't let anyone stop you.'

FRANK HANCOCK

*'He was a man of outstanding character and leadership,
quite a brilliant three-quarter and noted for his dodging,
and corkscrew running. Idolised by his team he inspired
them to achieve some of the most remarkable performances,
based on team work and unselfishness.'*
D.E. Davies

**The 'extra' three-quarter who spurned kicking and changed
the way teams lined up forever.**

Main teams: Wiveliscombe, Cardiff, Somerset, Wales
Position: Centre
International caps: 4 (1884–86)

Few players have played so little top-flight rugby yet had such
a monumental impact on the sport as Frank Hancock. He was
an Englishman who captained Cardiff and Wales; passionately
hated teams kicking at goal; believed in the 'passing game'; and
was at the heart of the creation of the modern three-quarter
system still in use today. Hancock's story is short, but is one
of the most remarkable in the game and a must-study for any
students of the sport's rich history.

A rugby revolutionary

This rugby radical was born in Wiveliscombe in Somerset in 1859. His family were in the beer brewing industry and he too would go on to work in this area as an adult. Frank was one of nine brothers and three sisters. Several of his brothers played first-class rugby and one even went on to play for England.

When Hancock began playing, the standard formation for a rugby union team was nine forwards and six backs (some teams, however, even favoured just five backs!). The standard formation of six backs lined up with two "half backs", one centre, two wings and a full-back. At the time, forwards didn't specialise in the way they do now and would pack down in the scrummage pretty much in the order they arrived. Even scrummaging formations could vary between clubs and countries, with differing numbers in each row depending on the preferences and strengths of individual players and teams.

Hancock was a centre of exceptional ability who combined agility and speed with power. He was an elusive runner with an ability to make deadly 'corkscrew runs'. His 176.53cm (5ft 9.5in) and 79.4 kg (12 st 7lb) physical stats may not seem much by modern standards, but it was hefty enough for a three-quarter of the day and made him a tough opponent. He possessed a knack for setting other players free and putting them into space. In the often stifling and claustrophobic playing fields of the 19th century – with balls that could be like a bar of soap in the dry, let alone the wet – his talent for offloading, passing and producing scoring chances made him a dangerous attacker.

Hancock was not only a natural talent, but a natural leader of men. By the age of 17 he was captaining his home team Wiveliscombe – at the time this was a significant club in an area of England in which rugby union flourished. His performances as both player and captain earned him the honour of leading his county, Somerset, on many occasions.

Cardiff calling

Hancock moved to Cardiff in 1883 to work at the family brewery, which at one point oversaw 77 pubs and eight breweries across Wales. Cardiff was an up-and-coming industrial town at the time with a rapidly expanding population and plenty of thirsty workers willing to hand over their hard-earned cash to sample the Hancock family's beer. Thanks to its docks being an ideal location to export Welsh coal, which was in demand around the British Empire, Cardiff's population expanded by almost 80 per cent every ten years between 1840 and 1870. The town became a focal point for Irish and English migrants. In the 1840s around a quarter of Cardiff's population hailed from England and 10 per cent from Ireland. By the 1880s Cardiff was the largest town in Wales.

While he may have had to leave Wiveliscombe behind, Hancock was still desperate to play rugby and immediately joined Cardiff RFC (today known as Cardiff Rugby). The club had been formed in 1876 and was already establishing itself as one of the most powerful teams in Wales. Still only 23, Hancock progressed from the second XV to the firsts in a short space of time.

His debut for the senior side came on a drizzly and dreary day in February 1884 away to Cheltenham College. Most history books list his debut as being due to the first-choice centre being unavailable. However, a news report for the match claims half the first team didn't turn up due to the rain and several players from the seconds, who were travelling on the same train for their own away game, were suddenly promoted.

Despite the late changes, Cardiff earned a good win against a highly-respected opponent. The *Western Mail* said that Hancock 'distinguished himself by a couple of good sprints' and while several history books list him as scoring two tries, the *Mail* does not record this feat. Either way, so impressive was his debut in the famous blue and black of Cardiff, the selection committee did not feel they could drop the Englishman for the next match. However, they also did not wish to deprive the usual starter of his place. A compromise was reached: Cardiff would retain Hancock and recall the usual centre, leading to Cardiff deploying an 'extra' three-quarter.

From such indecision and politeness came a sporting revolution. Cardiff, who had a solid enough pack to offset the loss of a ninth forward, soon found this additional back opened up all sorts of attacking possibilities and in Hancock they had a skilful and visionary enough player to exploit the new opportunities that a second centre offered.

In April 1884, after only a handful of games for Cardiff, Hancock was selected for Wales. Although he had only arrived in Wales the year before, there was little controversy about his selection for his newly adopted nation. In the early days of international sport there were no firm rules on eligibility and for many people it made perfect sense that Hancock would represent the nation he lived in and the country of the club he played for. His brother, Froude, would play for England and if it had not been for an injury to Frank in 1886 they may well have met on the Test field. All of this may come as a surprise to those who think international eligibility is far too lax today and falsely believe things used to be much stricter.

Almost perfect
In the 1884/85 season, Cardiff continued to refine their new three-quarter system with Hancock at the heart of its development. The season brought 15 wins, two draws and just seven losses in a fixture list full of solid teams. The results helped cement the club's reputation as one of the strongest teams in South Wales.

But the best was yet to come. Hancock, now 26, was appointed captain for the 1885/86 campaign. It was an inspired choice as he was admired by his fellow players as a player, a leader and a man. His reputation and exceptional playing and leadership abilities allowed him to set out his stall as captain. It was like nothing seen before or since in rugby.

Hancock was so fanatical about teamwork, the passing game and the importance of scoring tries, he told his players quite firmly they would not be allowed to attempt drop goals under his captaincy and the pursuit of the try was all. The only kicks he permitted were conversions and, it seems, goals from mark (an old and relatively rare method of scoring that existed until 1977).

This is far more revolutionary than it appears. Until the late 1880s there was no point-scoring system in rugby. Due to the way the sport had developed, the main method of 'scoring' was tallying up converted tries, known as 'goals', drop goals and goals from mark. The try is named so as it allowed teams to have a 'try' at kicking for goal. One converted try, drop goal or goal from mark would beat any number of unconverted tries (penalty goals came in later that year, but were not immediately adopted in all countries or competitions). If teams were level on goals, only then was try count considered. Therefore, kicking drop goals was a key tactic for any team.

It wasn't like Cardiff hadn't been stung in recent times by these laws either. In the 1884/85 season, Cardiff lost away to Moseley in the dying minutes due to a 'magnificent' late drop goal. They had been winning by three tries to nil just moments before. A similar three tries to one drop goal loss had also occurred that season away to detested local rivals Newport.

With Hancock's anti-kicking mantra in place, Cardiff embarked on one of rugby's most remarkable seasons. For the first eight games they did not concede a single score, not even a drop goal. In contrast, they helped themselves to an incredible 30 converted tries and 22 unconverted tries. The first side to score against them was Moseley in game eight, but Cardiff's one converted try and one unconverted try was enough to see them to another road victory.

In the 27 fixtures that season, Cardiff blasted their way to 131 tries, 70 of which were converted by Hugh 'Sawdust' Hughes – an impressive amount in an era with heavy leather balls, poor pitches and no kicking tees (a team mate would hold the ball in place for the kicker). Cardiff's positive mindset, talented players and their exploitation of the four-man three-quarter system made them all but unstoppable in Wales and England that season. The press raved about Cardiff's handling and playing style, claiming nothing before had been equal to it.

In the end, only two sides managed to score against Cardiff all season: Moseley (three tries in two games) and Gloucester (one try). This meant Cardiff finished with a plus-127 try difference! Not a single Welsh side managed to score against Hancock's men, not even with a drop goal from distance. The captain had an incredible season, missing only one game and helping himself to 19 tries (some sources list his tally as 18).

There is a lovely tale which shows just how committed Hancock was to the passing game. In one match one of his teammates had the audacity to attempt a drop goal. The Cardiff captain was furious and lambasted his colleague and made it clear that if any of his players tried such a thing again he would be removed from the game.

After winning their first 26 games, Cardiff had one final hurdle left to complete the perfect season: Moseley at home. As Cardiff had already beaten the Midlanders away, they could be forgiven for being confident in repeating the feat in the familiar surroundings of Cardiff Arms Park. Preparations were made for suitable celebrations of the 'Invincibles' after the match and supporters of the club had, for weeks, been raising funds so the players could be given suitable mementoes to mark their achievement.

It was not to be. As one journalist put it: 'At the eleventh hour the fates turned against them.' Hancock's revolutionaries fell at the final hurdle as Moseley scored two converted tries to Cardiff's solitary try. History has made this shock defeat even more bitter in hindsight as the club has never yet managed to go an entire season unbeaten (even worse, in the 1905/06 season, only a late, freak loss to the great All Blacks prevented an unbeaten season for the Blue and Blacks).

Nonetheless, in spite of the final-day disappointment, Hancock's Cardiff were celebrated and praised by all and had earned their place in rugby folklore. Shortly after the Moseley game the *South Wales Echo* wrote: '[Hancock] was captain of the team and something more. He was their tutor. To him is due the credit of initiating and perfecting his followers in that passing game which so often baffled and non-plussed their opponents.'

Cardiff rugby historian D.E. Davies called Hancock a 'Messiah'. At the club's end of season dinner, a special song was composed and sung to the tune of a well-known ditty that contained the words:

> *'Skipper Hancock he has been the mainspring of the Cardiff team,*
> *Tidy man, but O! by Jingo! Don't we like his rare old Stingo . . .*
> *'Tis because he runs a brewery that his runs are so corkscrewery.*
> *At three-quarter he is warm, and he does keep up his form.'*

The Welsh experiment succeeds . . . eventually

Hancock won four caps for Wales in total. In the 1886 fixture against Scotland at the Arms Park the Welsh selectors made Hancock captain and opted to try Cardiff's four-man three-quarter system. It was the first time it had been deployed at international level by any team. Sadly, the game was a disaster for Wales. The Welsh pack were unsuited (or unable) to play the type of game needed for this strategy and failed to cope with the strong Scottish pack and their extra numbers. Hancock had to abandon the plan, switch Welsh superstar and fellow centre Arthur 'Monkey' Gould from the centre to full-back, and move the original full-back, Harry Bowen, to the pack. By then, however, the damage was done. Scotland eased home by two goals and one try to nil.

Some of the post-match reaction to the Welsh selection and philosophy was brutal. The *Guardian* wrote that the four-man three-quarter system had been a disaster and had been implemented to 'please Cardiff'. Others, however, defended Wales's vision, if not their execution. Journalist 'Old Stager' in the *South Wales Echo* wrote that the mistake was not in playing four three-quarters, but in abandoning it and moving Bowen into the pack. He argued: 'The four three-quarter game, if I may so call it, is principally objected to because it gives you a man less in the scrimmage, and it is pointed out that unless you can hold the scrimmage, the finest backs in the world are useless. Well, my impression of Saturday's game is that in the tight packs our men quite held their own. It was in the loose they were beaten.'

The selectors lost their nerve. Wales would not adopt the system again until 1888 in a match against the New Zealand Natives. This time, the hoped-for fruit finally came forth and as Wales and Welsh clubs showed its value time and time again, it was eventually adopted by all countries and clubs until it became the standard formation we know today.

The four-man three-quarter system – and the passing game it was so well suited to – helped lay a major part of the foundations for the Golden Era that Wales would enjoy between 1900 and 1911.

The light that burns twice as bright . . .

Having shone as both captain of Wales and Cardiff, it seemed Hancock had the rugby world at his feet. Yet, incredibly, the 1885/86 season was to be his last. Still only 26 years old, he hung up his boots.

At Cardiff's annual meeting in August 1886, he confirmed that the earlier indications he had given on retiring were true. Hancock was reported as stating that 'owing to circumstances, and mainly to the fact that he was about to be married, he should be obliged to resign his position as captain of the team. He would always take a deep interest in the club, and though he would not actually play, he would be happy to serve them in whatever capacity they chose.'

In the amateur era, many players, even at the top level, could not always balance the demands of business and family with that of their sport – especially a rough and physical one like rugby. With Hancock taking on increasing responsibility in the family brewery, he simply felt it was time to move on.

Hancock may have left the playing fields with years still left on the clock, but his legacy has stood the test of time. The Cardiff legend died in his native Wiveliscombe aged 84 in 1943. In 2011 he was placed in the World Rugby Hall of Fame for his 'outstanding contribution to the game'. At the same event his beloved Cardiff RFC became only the second club to be placed in the Hall as well. He would no doubt have been proud.

GIANT KILLERS
SWANSEA RFC

*'Tell them back home we lost, but, please, don't
tell them we were beaten by a pair of schoolboys.'*
Jack Manchester, New Zealand captain

**Swansea RFC in Wales were the first club team to beat all
three of the big southern hemisphere nations.**

Founded: 1872
Nickname: The Whites/All Whites
Giants brought down: Australia (1908 and 1992), South Africa
(1912), New Zealand (1935)

Swansea RFC are one of the great clubs in British and European
rugby. Founding members of the Welsh Rugby Union in 1881,
the club has a long and distinguished history including three
Welsh Cup titles (the tournament was launched in 1972) and
four Welsh league titles since leagues were founded in 1990.
Until the reorganisation of Welsh club rugby in 2003, when
Swansea Rugby Football Club Ltd and Neath RFC formed the
Ospreys, Swansea were one of the titans of the UK game.

Like the other traditional big-four clubs of Welsh rugby,
Cardiff, Scarlets (formerly known as Llanelli) and Newport,
Swansea have taken the scalp of major southern hemisphere

touring sides. Until the dawn of professionalism, South Africa, New Zealand and Australia would visit Europe on mammoth tours, playing multiple Test matches as well as games against clubs, universities, county and regional teams. The most famous of these touring sides were the 1905 All Blacks, who won 34 of their 35 matches across Great Britain, Ireland, France and North America. Their solitary loss was to Wales in Cardiff.

What makes Swansea special when it comes to giant-killing is they were the first to bring down all of the big three of South Africa, New Zealand and Australia. Cardiff and Newport have also beaten all three sides (with Cardiff having beaten Australia six times), but Swansea had claimed their touring Triple Crown by 1935, just three decades after the visit from the First All Blacks.

The Wallabies are scalped
1908 – Swansea 6 Australia 0 (St Helen's, Swansea)

Australia's first major overseas tour was an epic one. In total, 39 games were played across Australia, Wales, England, USA and Canada. An additional Test match in France was cancelled due to a waterlogged pitch. The team assembled on 8 August, 1908, had their first game two days later in Melbourne and played their final match in Victoria, Canada, the following February.

The 'First Wallabies' even played against Cornwall in the final of the 1908 Olympics Games during this expedition. Yes, you read that right. Australia and Cornwall (representing Great Britain) competed for a gold medal and the Wallabies cantered to a 32–8 win. If that isn't strange enough, no other nations entered the event.

Outside of the Test matches with Wales (a 9–6 loss) and England (a 9–3 win), all other matches were against club, university or county/regional teams. Swansea were the Wallabies' 30th opponents and the contest took place on Boxing Day. By this point the visitors had fallen to Llanelli, Wales and a Midlands Combined XV. While not as dominant as their fierce All Black predecessors of 1905, or the Springboks of 1906, they were still a strong team. The UK press initially dubbed the visitors the 'Rabbits', but this was not to the taste of the tourists and they promoted the use of the Wallabies nickname which endures to this day.

Newspaper reports put the crowd that flocked to St. Helen's to see this game was as high as 40,000. It was a dark grey afternoon, but the usual wet Swansea weather held off. The Wallabies, as was their custom for this tour, opened with a war dance. It was a shambolic, crass affair that had been created to copy the popular haka of the 1905 All Blacks and the Zulu dance of the 1906 Springboks. Tour captain and forward Herbert Moran detested the dance, writing years later: 'The memory of that war cry provokes anger in me even after all these years . . . We were expected to leap up in the air and make foolish gestures which somebody thought Australian natives might have used in similar circumstances and we were given meaningless words which we were to utter savagely during the pantomime . . . I refused to lead the wretched caricature of a native corroboree and regularly hid myself among the team, a conscientious objector.'

Swansea were confident they could follow in the footsteps of Wales and rivals Llanelli and beat the Wallabies. They were led by the legendary Billy Trew (able to play fly-half, centre and wing). Trew was an exceptionally tough little man, weighing just 67kg (10st 7lb). Despite constant injuries in his career, which many blamed on his lack of stature, he won 29 caps over 13 years. This is an incredible number for an era in which Wales sometimes played just three games in a season. He had led Wales for most of their first three Grand Slams, so was the perfect man to take on a Test team with a mere club side.

The Whites started 'on the Mumbles side' of the ground with the wind to their backs. Within five minutes, legendary Swansea and Wales full-back Jack Bancroft put the home side up with a penalty.

Later in the first half, Swansea doubled their lead with a try (then worth three points) from British Isles (now the Lions) forward Edgar Morgan after an unstoppable 'rush' by the pack. Excellent and committed defence from the All Whites meant that there would be no further scoring in a game in which the two sets of forwards competed intensely to come out on top. Australia's Tom Griffen suffered the 'humiliation' of being ordered off for 'rough play'. The first of many famous tourist wins was in the bag for the west Wales side.

Australia lost five of their 39 matches in total, with the other defeats coming to Llanelli, Cardiff, Wales and a Midlands Combined XV.

Swansea would again beat the Wallabies in 1992. The reigning world champions fell on a wet day by a convincing 21–6 scoreline, with the points coming from tries by Scott Gibbs and Garin Jenkins and the rest of the tally coming from the boot of Aled Williams.

Swansea: J. Bancroft, P. Hopkins, W.J. Trew (captain), H. Thomas, H. Toft; R. Jones, R.M. Owen; D.J. Thomas, H. Hunt, I. Morgan, E. Morgan, G. Hayward, I. Williams, D. Griffiths, D. Davies.

Australia: P. Carmichael, C. Russell, J. Hickey, E.S. Mandible, A. McCabe; C.C. McKivatt, F. Woods; C. McMurtie, J.T. Barnett, T.S. Griffen, N.E. Row, C.C. Hammond, S. Middleton, P. McCue, T. R. Richards.

The Springboks are tamed
1912 – Swansea 3 South Africa 0 (St Helen's)

The second Springboks to tour Europe played 27 matches, of which five were Tests against the Home Unions and France. They won all of their international matches, but lost three of their non-Test encounters. Their vanquishers were Newport, London Counties and, of course, Swansea.

Once again, the Welsh side faced a touring side on Boxing Day. The two teams had not met before, but the Boks had won in Swansea over Wales 11–0 in 1906, in what some saw as an unofficial world championship game. In 1912, 35,000 spectators jammed themselves into St. Helen's hoping to witness their side do what Wales had not been able to do in either 1906 or just a few weeks prior at Cardiff, where the tourists had won 3–0. As is so often the case in Swansea rugby, rain and water played a starring role. A Biblical downpour almost saw the game cancelled and ground staff were forced to carve out drains across the field to aid the release of water from the playing area. The fixture went ahead, according to *The Times*, in 'conditions that could not have been more unfavourable for football or more decidedly against the South Africans. The ground was everywhere a sea of mud, and was under water in many places.'

It was suggested that the match would have been deemed unplayable for a normal club fixture. Its prestige saved the day. While the rain wouldn't have hurt the home team's chances, it wasn't anything the South Africans hadn't dealt with before in Wales. With their huge backs and fiercely aggressive and strong forwards, they could certainly cope with an arm wrestle in west Walian mud. Swansea went into the match undefeated thus far that season and were once again captained by Billy Trew. Never was a skipper more put to the test than he was that day and, boy, did he pass with flying colours.

As against the Wallabies, Swansea played with the wind in the first half. Understandably, in light of the rain, the backs saw little ball and gradually Swansea seemed to gain the upper hand in the loose. The home pack were, as most top Welsh sides of the time were, adept at dribbling the ball en masse downfield. Working in concert they constantly caused the Boks all sorts of problems. Eventually their dominance paid off and forward David Thomas claimed what would turn out to be the only score of the game. The Boks thought they had grabbed an equaliser later in the contest, but the referee did not believe the try to be legitimate as he felt a Swansea player had grounded the ball first.

In the second half, Swansea lost winger Howell Lewis to injury with 20 minutes remaining. In those days no replacements were allowed, so they had to batten down the hatches and hold on. This is where Trew showed his rugby brain. He took out not one, but two forwards and placed them in the backs, leaving Swansea with just five forwards to hold the fort. From his reading of the game that had so far unfolded, and in light of the conditions, he felt this was the best way to cling on to the lead. Which is exactly what they did.

Swansea had now defeated two of the big three tourists. It was only New Zealand that remained for a clean sweep.

Swansea: D. Williams; H. Lewis, W.J. Trew (captain), T. Williams, F. Williams; S. Jerram, O. Jenkins; D.J. Thomas, T. Morgan, E. Morgan, B. Williams, B. Hollingdale, G. Hayward, H. Moulton, G. Evans.

South Africa: P.G. Morkel; E.E. McHardy, J. Stegman, R.R. Luyt, J. Morkel; F. J. Dobbin, F.J. Luyt; D.F.T Morkel, G. Thompson, A.S. Knight, W. H. Morkel, S.H. Leger, J.A.J. Francis, W.A. Millar (captain), J. D. Luyt.

The All Whites (and some schoolboys) beat the All Blacks 1935 – Swansea 11 New Zealand 3 (St Helen's)

This remains one of the greatest results in Welsh club history. By beating the All Blacks at the third time of trying, Swansea became the first non-international side to beat New Zealand and the first side to beat them in Europe since Wales in 1905.

When Swansea had met them back on that original tour, they had led 3–0 against Dave Gallaher's men at the halfway stage. The lead came thanks to a try from forward Fred Scrine. Sadly for the home side, they conceded a second-half drop goal and, with drop goals worth four points back then, it meant a 4–3 defeat.

In 1924, Cliff Porter's Second All Blacks won all 32 matches on their tour, securing rugby immortality through means of their invincibility. Swansea were swept away by a crushing scoreline of 39–3, conceding nine tries. In the era of three-point tries and relatively inaccurate goal-kicking, this was a major thrashing.

Ahead of the contest against Jack Manchester's Third All Blacks of 1935, both teams were forced to announce line-ups with key players missing. *The Times,* in its match preview wrote: 'The Swansea pack cannot hope to equal the All Blacks in weight whatever they may achieve in cunning and enthusiasm.'

Swansea, captained on this historic occasion by flanker Edgar Long, were not afraid to put their faith in youthful talent, and famously selected two schoolboy cousins from Gowerton grammar school at half-back: Haydn Tanner and Willie Davies. The sixth formers were aged just 18 and 19 respectively.

The occasion did not daunt the whippersnappers, who would be key to the most splendid day in club history. The All Whites blitzed the visitors in the opening half, bagging all their 11 points in that period. Despite the predictions of the London-based press, the home pack more than held their own both in the legitimate aspects of the game and the fisticuffs that continually broke out. The backs, led by the sixth-formers, 'fairly and squarely' outplayed the All Blacks.

Tanner and Davies, *The Times* wrote, 'bamboozled' their opponents and were 'ably supported' by the centres Ron Williams and Claude Davey. Swansea's first try came from Dennis Hunt, who crashed over after gathering a loose ball at the Mumbles End, which came about from a Willie Davies kick. The remaining two tries came from Davey.

The first of these was described by the newsreel of the day (these were shown in cinemas as part of the entertainment before films in the pre-television age) as 'the finest try you ever saw'. Swansea launched an attack from a loose ball on the half-way line, about ten metres to the right of centre pitch. Willie Davies started his run by offering a dummy, which the All Black defender only half bought. But it was enough, combined with a shuffle of the hips and a step, for him to beat his man. Davies then accelerated like a walking Welsh half-back cliche and beat four more defenders and drew a fifth, before passing to Davey, who was right on his left shoulder, as he took contact. From about ten metres outside the 22, the centre burnt two covering Kiwis to score under the sticks. The conversion was added by Wilf Harris. Davies had a hand in the second try too, combining with Dai White and Ron Williams to put Davey over.

Winger Nelson Ball pulled a try back for the All Blacks, but that was all they would ultimately manage. Being in Swansea, rain, of course, played a part in the match. Light drizzle before the interval became a downpour after the break, further frustrating the Kiwis who had to try and open up to chase the game.

Swansea's defence was solid all second-half and, to the thrill of the 40,000 crowd, they held on to become only the second team after the British and Irish Lions to defeat the trio of New Zealand, South Africa and Australia.

After the match, All Black captain Jack Manchester, famously said: 'Tell them back home we lost, but, please, don't tell them we were beaten by a pair of schoolboys.'

Tanner, who wasn't even legally old enough to drink at the time, would go on to make his debut as part of the Welsh team that beat New Zealand later that month. Four other Swansea heroes joined him: Idwal Rees, Harry Payne, Don Tarr and Claude Davey.

Tanner's gym mistress accompanied him to Cardiff to ensure he did not get lost on his way from Penclawdd. The win means he is one of only a handful of Welshmen to have played in two winning matches against the All Blacks. Tanner would play for Wales for 14 years, never being dropped on his way to 25 caps.

The 1935 All Blacks lost three games of their 30-match tour. They suffered defeats to Swansea, Wales and England and were held to a 3–3 draw with Ulster.

Swansea: E. Jones; G. Davies, E.C. Davey, R. Williams, G. Griffiths; W.T.H. Davies, H. Tanner; E. Long (captain), W.E. Harries, D. White, J. White, D. Hunt, H. Payne, D.J. Tarr, G.H. Taylor.

New Zealand: D. Solomon; N.A. Mitchell. G. Gilbert, N.J. Ball; E.W. Tindill, T.H.C. Caughey; M.M.N. Corner; H.F. McLean, J.G. Wynyard, R.R. King, W.R. Collins, J.E. Manchester (captain), G.T. Adkins, A. Lambourne, C. Pepper.

JAMES PETERS

*'It is quite possible however that for sentimental reasons
which need not be detailed, the selection committee
have preferred not to select Peters, especially as the
opponents of the England team will be South Africans.'*
Yorkshire Post, 24 November, 1906

**James Peters was the first black player to represent England,
overcoming a difficult childhood, racial prejudice and physical
injury to prove himself as a top club and international player.**

Main teams (rugby union): Dings Crusaders, Knowle RFC,
Bristol, Plymouth RFC, Somerset, Devon, England
Main teams (rugby league): Barrow RLFC, St Helens
Position: Outside-half
International caps: 5 (1906–08)
Points: 6 (2 tries)

'Jimmy' Peters' life is one of the most enthralling in the history
of British rugby. He was the first black player to win a cap for
England, a remarkable achievement in light of the prejudice he
had to overcome and the difficult childhood he lived through.

Peters was born in Salford, Lancashire, in 1879 to an English mother and a Jamaican father. Both parents were part of a travelling circus. Whilst Peters was still a young boy, his father died a 'shocking death in a lion's cage'. If this wasn't tragedy enough, the loss of his father's income meant his mother was unable to support him and the unfortunate boy had to join another circus where he was to train to become a bareback horse rider.

Aged just 11, he broke his arm badly and, unable to ride, was no longer deemed useful by his circus employers and ended up in Southwark, London, living in an orphanage. Later he would move to another orphanage in Greenwich. Once his arm had healed, Peters soon demonstrated a natural talent for sports and excelled at rugby, cricket and athletics.

J.C.W. Fegan, who ran the orphanage in Southwark, wrote the following on Peters: 'Jimmy Peters is the champion athlete. He seems constructed differently to other humans – all joints and springs inside – resilient as India-rubber in some parts, hard as ebony (and nearly as black) in others. At cricket or football Jimmy is admittedly the non-pareil captain. But it was on a Roll of Honour Day last March when we had our Athletic Sports at the London Athlete Club ground at Stamford Bridge, that Jimmy revealed an acuteness that astonished us all. For some days before hand, the excitement rose to fever point, for the interest in athletics is very keen, and knots and mites were discussing their chances for this or that event. I understand Jimmy "lay low" and wore an inscrutable, Sphinx-like face-but when the day arrived, he just swept the board. The 100 yards, mile, long jump, high jump, walking race, kicking the football, and throwing the cricket ball.

> 'Now and then it seemed the chain of success would be broken, but at the pinch Jimmy could always do "the little bit extra" to win. But Jimmy's best performance that day we all felt was when he gallantly gave up one of his own prizes to another fellow who had been his close rival.'

Peters trained as a carpenter and printer and, while still a young man, his work led him to move to Bristol. Playing as a half-back, he first joined Dings Crusaders, a club formed in 1897 and which had its roots in the slum area of the city. It was founded as part of the Dings Boys Club, an organisation which used sport to help inspire young people who, outside of work and school, would usually have had few creative or athletic opportunities. These clubs provided an outlet where young men could stay healthy through sport, burn up pent-up energy and, crucially, stay away from public houses and avoid the temptation of associated 'immoral' activities. After also playing and impressing for Knowle, Peters was invited to join Bristol. The selection of a black player for the club was by no means without controversy. Upon joining the club, one committeeman resigned in anger at the selection of a non-white player and others protested openly. A local journalist wrote that Peters, who he referred to in a derogatory manner, was keeping a white player out of the team.

Today, the ESPN rugby database on international players lists him under his supposed nickname 'Darkie Peters'. However, Tom Weir of De Montfort University, who has carried out some excellent research on the player's life, questions if this was a name used much during Peters' career.

Peters joined Plymouth in 1902 and also represented both Somerset (1900-03) and Devon (1900-09) at county level. He helped guide Devon to the county championship in 1906 and, no doubt in large part due to that achievement, Peters was selected for England. Being picked to play for the national team is an exceptional achievement for any rugby player, but it must be remarked how extraordinary it was for Peters to do this in the early years of the 20th century. Rugby has always been primarily a middle-class sport in England and to succeed not just as a working man, but a black working man in the conservative Edwardian era, is no mean feat. There is no doubt he would have been subject to prejudice on and off the field. Sporting history is sadly littered with examples of non-white players who have had to work twice as hard or be twice as good as their fellow white players to be considered for selection. Despite all this, Peters got the call up for England to face Scotland in the 1906 Home Championship (today's Six Nations).

Inevitably, there was outrage among many in the status quo and papers like the *Yorkshire Post* wrote that his 'selection is by no means popular on racial grounds'.

A winning debut
England triumphed at Inverleith by 9–3 (three tries to one). This was a good win for the English who were in the midst of a dismal few years and on a seven-game losing streak. In contrast, Scotland were, along with Wales, the strongest Home Union side during this era. *The Sportsman* newspaper wrote that the 'dusky Plymouth man did many good things, especially in passing'. Another paper made note of how his 'dazzling passing' helped create two tries.

Peters retained his place for the trip to Paris five days later, scoring a try as he helped England to a 35–8 win. France were newcomers to the international rugby arena and this fixture, the first time the sides had ever met, was not a part of the Championship. Nonetheless, with two wins from two games, Peters had enjoyed a wonderful start to his England career.

One step forward, two steps back?

In the context of British society at the time, it could be argued that England selectors had been what we would now call 'progressive' by picking Peters. Sadly, the following season, it appears they may well have caved in to the wishes of the touring South Africans who were making their first appearance in Europe.

Rugby journalist E.H.D. Sewell wrote that the Springboks 'preferred not to play against a coloured man' on their tour. It has been claimed that when Peters was named in the Devon side to face the Springboks early on in the tour, the tourists initially refused to play the match and it took an intervention from the South African high commissioner to ensure that the game went ahead. However, the truth of this story is disputed by some.

Nonetheless, by not even selecting Peters for the two trial games before the England international, it appears the RFU may well have shamefully danced along willingly with the racist views of their guests. When he was not named in the Test side, several newspapers accused the RFU of excluding Peters from the England team due to his race and the possible upset it may cause to the Springboks. The refusal of Percy Coles, the RFU secretary, to comment on the matter was seen by many as effectively confirming the theory.

Peters would not appear in an England shirt again until the 1907 Home Championship match with Ireland. In total he would win five caps for England.

He remained a highly popular figure back in Plymouth and a local paper named him 'man of the year' in 1907, writing: 'Although not of our complexion Peters may accept the compliment that we regard him as a 'white man', in a land where to be regarded as a 'white man' confers a dignity to which a great many white men do not attain.'

Rugby values again fall short

Three years after his final England cap, Peters lost three fingers in a working accident. To aid their player at a difficult time, Plymouth arranged a testimonial match to help raise funds for him as his ability to work and support his family was likely severely impacted (and for a period he was unable to play too). Pathetically, due to the strict amateur laws of the day, this 'payment' led to the RFU classing him as a professional and he was banned from the sport for life.

Peters turned professional by playing rugby league with Barrow and St Helens before retiring in 1914. Despite his extraordinary life, his death in 1954 was almost unmarked in the national newspapers. It wasn't until 1988 that another black player, Chris Oti, lined up in an England team.

DID YOU KNOW?

The first non-white international rugby player was Scotland's Alfred Clunies-Ross who played in the inaugural rugby Test match in 1871. He was born around 1851 (no exact date is known) in the Cocos Islands, which sits in the Indian Ocean between Sri Lanka and Australia. His grandfather, John Clunies-Ross, was from the Shetlands and had laid claim to the uninhabited Cocos Islands in the 1820s after having travelled through them on a whaling ship. The islands stayed in the family for generations and the head of the family was often lauded (perhaps a little mockingly) as 'King of the Cocos Islands'.

Alfred had been sent to Scotland to attend university and study medicine, where he soon showed an aptitude for sports such as rugby and cricket. A full-back, his clubs included London Wasps, Edinburgh Wanderers and St George's Hospital.

The first ever international involved 20 players per side and was won by Scotland by one goal (a converted try) and two tries to nil. It was Clunies-Ross's only international appearance.

SHANE WILLIAMS

'I am forever contemplating how I got myself into such a position and am thankful for the fact that I did. It gives me goosebumps.'
Shane Williams

Diminutive winger Shane Williams is today regarded as one of the greatest wingers to have played elite rugby. At the start of his career though, many doubted he had the physique to compete at the highest level.

Main teams: Amman United, Neath, Ospreys, Barbarians, Wales, British and Irish Lions
Position: Wing, scrum-half
Wales caps: 87 (2000–11)
Points: 290 (58 tries)
Lions caps: 4
Points: 10 (2 tries)

In 1999, Graham Henry coached Wales to an extraordinary run of 11 consecutive Test wins. It equalled the nation's previous best winning run which had occurred between 1907 and 1910. One of the key elements of Henry's teams was the selection of big wingers. Regular players picked for Wales in this period on the flanks included Gareth Thomas and Dafydd James. Both were former centres and both were big men.

Modern diets, developments in conditioning programmes and the trends of professional rugby have all combined to make rugby players bigger and stronger than they were in the amateur era. As the millennium approached, it seemed the days of dancing, side-stepping, pocket Welsh wizards were well and truly in the past.

There were many raised eyebrows across Wales when, for the opening match of the Six Nations in 2000, Henry selected former scrum-half Shane Williams in his matchday squad to face France in Cardiff. Shane stood at just 1.70m (5ft 7in) and weighed around 70kg (11st).

A dreamer drifting

Williams was born in Morriston, Swansea. By the time he was 11, he would think nothing of turning up to play with his local under-14s side. But despite his obvious natural skills, pace and athleticism, he didn't gain any county or regional honours as a youngster. Williams also loved to play football and take part in gymnastics; sports which ultimately served him well and helped to make him a more complete player and athlete in his later life. Williams was a more than useful footballer and caught the attention of a few scouts.

In his teens, he would, to the frustration of both sides, switch between playing football for Cwmamman United one week and Amman United RFC the next. He even skipped a soccer cup final once to play in a 'meaningless' league game of rugby which he knew would be fast and open and give him a chance to run and rack up some tries. He was just happy to be running around with a ball.

Eventually Williams opted to focus more on rugby and joined Neath – the temptation of a rusty old car and just over £100 a week being a key factor in his decision. Still only semi-professional at this stage, Williams played at scrum-half. His size seemed to dictate that this was realistically the only position that suited him.

Williams had to be a tough cookie to succeed in the rough and tumble of Welsh club rugby. In his first full league match with Neath, he had his nose broken the first time he received the ball thanks to a high tackle by Pontypridd's giant Dale McIntosh.

In spite of the success he would ultimately attain in rugby, Williams admits his ambitions were fairly limited in his early days. He was content to play for Neath (whose coach Lyn Jones converted him into a winger) and didn't really believe he would ever be good enough for Test match rugby anyway, so he thought he may as well enjoy himself.

Not ready to step up

Williams quickly began winning over fans with his acceleration, side-step and deadly eye for the tryline. His try tally was soon totting up and he was seemingly always making plays that were worthy of the highlights reel. Supporters loved seeing him outwit or outmanoeuvre the muscle-bound behemoths he would face and he rapidly gained a cult following.

Within 18 months of signing his first contract with Neath, romantically-inclined fans began shouting for Williams to get a call-up for Wales. Yet, Williams had not even won any age-grade honours at national level. More cynical fans felt that while the jinking wonder was great box office, he simply didn't have the size or strength for international rugby.

Which is why Williams was as shocked as anyone when he was informed by his grandmother, who had just read the news in the paper, that he had been selected to play in the Probables team against the Possibles in a Welsh trial in Swansea.

The young winger had a decent outing in the trial, but admitted afterwards that he only expected to make the Wales A team when it came to selection. When his name wasn't read out by Henry as part of the Wales A squad, Williams, disappointed, switched off and stopped listening. So when he was named in the squad for the Six Nations, he missed it! It was only when his teammates began congratulating him afterwards, Williams realised he was in.

While future World Cup-winning coach Graham Henry, one of the best brains in the game, may have believed in him, Williams had serious doubts about his right to be mixing with the national squad. He said it came as a relief when he was named as a substitute for the opening match with France as he felt he wouldn't have to face the pressure of being a starter.

When Williams was told to get ready and warm-up so he could come on in the game itself, the 22-year-old froze. Instead of ripping off his tracksuit and bursting into the Cardiff cauldron, he pretended not to hear the instruction to get ready. He was simply too nervous and didn't want to go on. In his 2009 autobiography, Williams wrote: 'I can honestly say that I didn't want to go on and make my debut for Wales. At that stage, we were about 20 points behind. I was in such a daze that I wasn't even aware of the score, but I knew it was turning sour for us, and now these people wanted to put me on in direct opposition to Émile Ntamack, France's talisman at the time. He was one of the best wingers who had ever played for France, and there I was being sent into the lion's den to face him. My heart just sank.'

Williams claims in his autobiography, written with Delme Parfitt, he got 25 minutes in the match, but in fact a simple check of the match video or game reports show he actually came on in the 72nd minute. Looking as white as a ghost and wearing the oversize cotton shirt of the era, he almost looks like a ball boy that has wandered onto the pitch for a dare. Indeed, Jonathan Davies, the ex-Wales star sat in the commentary box, joked Williams only looked about 12.

Williams' second touch saw him take a ball from his full-back Shane Howarth just inside his own ten-metre line, and in the middle of the park. With plenty of space, Williams set off, looking to inspire Wales with some late magic and try to make the scoreboard, standing at 29–3 in France's favour, a little more respectable. Tap-tackled by the first defender, the new cap stumbled a few yards, drew in two defenders and threw an offload to his left as he hit the deck. It found a winger in clear space with an undefended route to the tryline. Sadly, it was Ntamack. The famed three-quarter ran in unopposed to round off a 36–3 win for the visitors.

Thankfully for Welsh fans, rather than let the experience crush him, Williams instead used it to spur him on. He felt that if he could get over the disappointment of making that mistake just minutes into his debut for Wales at Cardiff, he could ride out anything.

Henry kept the faith too and Williams was selected for the next game in Rome. He rewarded his coach with a try in a 46–16 win. By the end of 2001, Williams had won ten caps and bagged ten tries – including four in one match against Japan in Osaka. His fame had spread outside Wales and he gained fans around the world with his footwork, acceleration, eye for a gap and a willingness to take risks. Nonetheless, there were still plenty of doubters who questioned if he had the size and strength to compete at an elite level.

Wasted years and then redemption

After appearing in the Wales v Ireland Six Nations disaster in Cardiff in October 2001 (the game had been delayed due to an outbreak of foot and mouth disease in the UK), Williams fell out of favour with Graham Henry. When the New Zealander himself fell out of favour with the WRU and left the job, his successor, fellow Kiwi Steve Hansen, took over and he simply didn't see a place for such a small winger in his plans for the national side.

Lack of interest from Wales and a run of injuries crushed Williams' confidence. Things got so bad he later confessed he considered giving up the sport as he felt there was no way back to the top. Some of Williams' fitness problems stemmed from him bulking up and attempting to pack on muscle to end criticism of his physical abilities. His small frame simply wasn't built for this kind of body shape though and he eventually realised he had to rein in his training and make sure he didn't lose his explosiveness and agility.

After his appearance for Wales in late 2001, Williams, now representing the newly-formed Neath-Swansea Ospreys team, didn't win another cap for his country until August 2003, when he was selected to play against Romania in Wrexham in a World-Cup warm-up. Even this recall failed to give him much cheer. Williams felt Hansen was trying to silence the press by giving him a run ahead of the World Cup in a game in which Wales were expected to score an avalanche of points. He claimed two tries in a 54–8 demolition job over a weak Romania, but he doubted it would do him much good.

To his surprise though, Williams got asked shortly after by Hansen if he would be prepared to go to the World Cup in Australia as a third-choice scrum-half. He wasn't over the moon with the concept, but wasn't going to say no either. Hansen didn't play Williams for a single minute in the opening three group games, as Wales beat Canada, Tonga and Italy to secure their place in the quarter-finals. Wales's last opponents were a team they had not beaten since 1953 and certainly had no hope of beating in 2003: New Zealand.

The Dragons had lost 11 games on the bounce under Hansen between late 2002 through to the summer of 2003, and their only wins had come against Romania and Scotland in near-irrelevant warm-up games. With this in mind, Hansen essentially put out a second-string team to avoid injuring his starters against New Zealand. After all, there was no chance of a Welsh win. Williams was one of those put up for sacrifice to the All Black gods and pencilled in on the right wing. If that wasn't a daunting enough challenge, he spent four days in bed ahead of the game with a dodgy tummy.

New Zealand showed their contempt for the Welsh challenge from the kick-off, choosing to run from their own 22 and effortlessly getting to their opponent's 22. From the subsequent scrum they scored. It was 5–0 in less than two minutes and the conversion that followed was a good one: 7–0 and the All Blacks hadn't even broken a sweat. It looked like it was going to be a long afternoon for Williams and co and Welsh fans around the world began watching from behind their metaphorical sofas.

Yet what followed was one of the most extraordinary games in World Cup history as both sides produced rugby that wouldn't have looked out of place in a Jonah Lomu video game (see page 239). After half an hour, New Zealand led 28–10. But then the underdogs, with Williams to the fore, bit back and bit hard.

In the 34th minute, Williams took a ball slap bang on the halfway line. Spotting a mismatch – with forwards seemingly twice his size having to mark him – he took two steps left, then let loose with an explosive step off his left foot, followed rapidly by another short step off his right. This sudden double shift caused several defenders to lose their balance and Williams accelerated through the gap they had left. After crossing the 22, he then somehow seemed to both turn full-back Mils Muliaina inside out with a swerve while simultaneously stepping the legendary Richie McCaw before squeezing out a pass to left wing Tom Shanklin who fed centre Sonny Parker for the try.

Just a few minutes later, taking a ball five metres outside his own 22, he set off across the pitch. Williams shaped a pass to a support runner, then instead shot off like a bullet and burst through the small gap between two defenders. Wales advanced to the 22 and the All Blacks killed the move. A penalty came out of it though and Wales kicked to the corner and drove over. It was now 28–17. Four and half minutes into the second half Williams got on the scoresheet himself when he rounded off a try to put the men in red into the lead.

After 54 minutes, Wales, astonishingly, led 37–33. To put that into context, this understrength Welsh team had smashed Wales' previous highest record score against New Zealand of 17 points. The hope that the Welsh hoodoo against New Zealand was finally going to be laid to rest, was short-lived, however. With just under 20 minutes remaining, order was restored and the All Blacks took a lead they would not relinquish on the way to a 53–37 win. But Williams had been spectacularly reborn at international level and had helped provide rugby fans around the world with a series of thrills that rivalled any pieces of individual brilliance they had ever seen at a World Cup.

The performance essentially etched Williams' name onto the Welsh team sheet until he retired from Test rugby in 2011. Hansen rewarded him with selection against eventual tournament winners England in the quarter-final. While Wales lost 27–18, they outscored England three tries to one and Williams once more dazzled. His run from near his own 22 sparked one of the great World Cup tries. Apart from his initial risky run which set the play in motion, Williams magically popped up again in the 22 to take a harsh offload from a falling Gareth Thomas. Juggling the ball at full pace, he somehow recovered it and flicked a superb pass over the head of Ben Cohen to find Stephen Jones, who put Wales into a shock lead. Many considered it the try of the tournament and it all but confirmed Williams as a household name in rugby circles. Furthermore, any arguments that he lacked the physical ability to play at the top level had been comprehensively dismantled. He proved that if a player had the talent, he could make up for supposed shortcomings in stature. Williams became an inspiration for smaller players of all ages as well as the poster boy of the rugby romantics.

International glory
Williams was to be first-choice for Wales until he stepped down in 2011. He played a key part in the 2005 and 2008 Grand Slams as well as in Wales's 2011 World Cup campaign, which saw them agonisingly miss out on a final by losing to France by a single point despite being down to 14 players for most of the match.

His performances in 2008 were off the charts and he was voted World Player of the Year after a 12-month period in which everything he did seemed to turn to gold. Arguably no winger has been more deadly in a calendar year than Williams had been when he deservedly won the award.

Williams won three caps across three Lions tours in 2005, 2009 and 2013. The latter tour call-up was well after his international retirement and came about due to a huge injury crisis suffered by the tourists. By this time Williams was seeing out a nice contract in Japan with Mitsubishi and was in Australia only as a commentator. When the Lions had no time to call up replacements, Williams stepped in for one game against ACT Brumbies.

An Osprey between 2003 and 2012, Williams was part of the region as they won four league titles and an Anglo-Welsh Cup. His most dramatic moment in an Ospreys shirt was his last. In the dying moments of his final match for them in Dublin against Leinster in the league final, he scored. With the Dan Biggar conversion that followed, it gave the Ospreys the title with a score of 31–30.

Williams scored 58 tries for Wales, putting him far ahead of any other Wales international (George North is next nearest on 43 as of 2023). His try tally is so impressive it puts him seventh on Wales's all-time scoring list, despite the fact he never kicked a penalty, drop goal or conversion for Wales.

Having always played for the love of the game, Williams didn't hang up the boots when he finished with professional rugby. He has turned out on several occasions for his local club Amman United, including one cup final appearance at the Principality Stadium. His willingness to swap the fields of international rugby for the humble fields of home was the perfect romantic ending for a romantic rugby story.

GIANT KILLERS
USA
(1991 WOMEN'S WORLD CUP WINNERS)

'The World Cup tour will cost each player about $700 for air fare, $450 for accommodations, and $200 for ground transport; so $1350 at least, not including food or income lost for missing two weeks of work.'
Letter to USA players from the USARFU Women's Committee ahead of the 1991 World Cup

In 2022, Ruahei Demant of the Black Ferns (New Zealand) lifted the ninth Women's Rugby World Cup in a stadium packed with over 42,000 people and with a global television audience watching on. The women's version of the World Cup has become one of the showpiece events in rugby.

In 1991, Mary Sullivan and Barbara Bond of the USA lifted the inaugural World Cup in front of a Cardiff crowd of around just 3,000 (this author was among them as a young boy). Highlights were later shown on television, but there was no live broadcast.

The tournament had been held in spite of the fact World Rugby (then the International Rugby Board) had refused to officially sanction the event. Few of the teams playing had the official backing of the national rugby unions that governed their men's team and a good number of rugby men openly challenged the whole concept of women playing rugby, let alone a World Cup.

The resistance the core rugby unions had shown to the 'smaller' rugby nations when it had come to growing the global game over the past century was being displayed towards the women's game. For many, rugby was a game with great human values, but they only applied to half the world's population. Luckily, the 1991 Women's World Cup was a key moment in the sport's development and a major catalyst for a shift in attitudes to women and rugby.

Bringing the world together

The fact the 1991 tournament even happened at all is testament to the tenacity, courage and vision of four women in particular: organisers Deborah Griffin, Alice Cooper, Sue Dorrington (who also played for England in the tournament) and Mary Forsyth. Rugby historian Ali Donnelly sums up what they went through to make the event take place:

'They had no sponsor and had to beg and borrow equipment. They lost track of how much of their own personal money they put into the competition. They took time off work, worked through maternity leave and had limited to no experience organising major events.'

Griffin had been involved in the formation of the Women's Rugby Football Union (WRFU) in 1983 (it took responsibility for England, Scotland and Wales) and also helped found Finchley WRFC in 1986, which was the first non-university women's side in England.

Originally, the idea had been to run a European tournament in 1991, but the hopeful organisers soon realised, from faxes and letters crawling in from around the world, there was interest from well beyond the borders of mainland Europe. Even then, the initial idea was a World Cup with about half a dozen teams involved.

When the WRFU reached out to the IRB (International Rugby Board) about the concept, they didn't exactly receive an enthusiastic reply. The two organisations had no formal links, but Griffiths hoped their male counterparts may see it as a chance to grow the sport. Instead, the letter hinted at concern the event could undermine the men's tournament which was also taking place in 1991. No support was offered, but the IRB did ask to be kept informed over what was planned. They also had issues with the logo that was being used by organisers and after much pressure, forced them to change it.

Wales, or more precisely Cardiff and the surrounding area, was chosen as the venue for the tournament as it offered a true rugby culture, plenty of grounds and facilities and was cheaper than other potential UK options. There was also the fact that Cardiff Arms Park (the club ground, not the then National Stadium) was available to host the final and would add a sense of occasion to affairs. There was additional support offered from the Welsh Sports Council and South Glamorgan County Council.

After bagfuls of drama, hundreds of letters and faxes around the world, the following 12 teams made up the inaugural World Cup: Canada, England, France, Italy, Japan, Netherlands, New Zealand, Soviet Union, Spain, Sweden, USA and Wales.

All players and teams had to fund themselves, with support from official unions minimal or non-existent.

Women's rugby in the land of the free
In his excellent book on the 1991 Women's World Cup, author Martyn Thomas writes of how, in some ways, rugby's lower profile in the United States helped the early female pioneers of the game there:

'Women who wanted to play rugby in the USA did not, initially, at least, come up against the same systematic discrimination encountered in France. Those keen to pick up an oval ball were able to ride the wave that was the boom in female sporting participation sweeping through the States in the 1970s and 1980s, a largely unintended consequence of educational reform.'

Thomas highlights how a piece of legislation in 1972, known as Title IX changed things forever in the United States when it came to women's sports. Title IX declared that: 'No person in the United States shall, on the basis of sex, be excluded from participation in, be denied the benefits of, or be subject to discrimination under any educational program . . . or activity receiving Federal financial assistance'.

Whilst the change was primarily about levelling opportunities in the classroom, it transformed athletic activities in the US colleges and universities as it meant that funding and opportunities for sporting activities for females now had to be equal to those for males. A 2022 Boston University article highlighted the impact: 'In 1972, women comprised 15 per cent of all student athletes, now it's 44 per cent, women were less than 10 per cent of doctors and lawyers, today it's more than 50 per cent.'

Title IX would help set the US on to women's rugby glory. Rugby did have a historical foothold in several colleges in the USA, especially those on the West Coast. The sport also appealed to universities that had to offer female students the equivalent funds that they pumped into male American football. Rugby was cheaper, lacking the amount of equipment and facilities and staff members American football needed, but provided similar thrills and spills to female students who liked ball and contact sports. As a result, many female students began playing rugby and getting access to healthy funds and resources.

Female students who took an interest in rugby hugely benefited from the fact this code of football held little cultural sway in the United States. Unlike in the game's global heartlands, there were not quite as many grey middle-aged men who got worked up in righteous indignation over the concept of women playing a so-called 'man's game'.

A significant portion of the USA team that would go to Wales for the 1991 World Cup would come through the university system where they not only played rugby, but took part in a wide range of sports and got access to world-class coaching and sport science. The impact of coaching and technical knowledge cannot be underestimated in how it shaped better all-round athletes and helped make the USA team extra special. From weight-lifting and fitness programmes to knowledge around nutrition, recovery and injury treatment, US female athletes had an edge over many of the players they would later face from traditional rugby playing nations.

Tara Flanagan was a key player in the 1991 side and made up the unit that became known as the 'Locks from Hell' with her second-row partner Tam Breckenridge. Flanagan had earned a scholarship to play basketball at university and was even selected in the opening round of the first-ever Women's NBA draft. Breckenridge too was an elite basketball player and, as their nickname suggests, the two formed a formidable partnership.

Speaking for this book in 2023, Flanagan offered insight into what being an athlete in an American college could offer. 'I personally believed that Title IX being enacted was a turning point for the American success in the Rugby World Cup. I had access to the weight room at university and during the season we practised two to three hours a day. We had athletic training room facility access with physios which was so helpful if we had a niggle or injury. We had access to coaching, team psychologists, a team doctor and nutrition advice.'

In an interview for the BBC during the 1991 World Cup, Flanagan praised the physical nature of rugby: 'The best thing for me is that I played basketball in college and you can't foul out of rugby. So that's a good selling point to me.'

A BBC interviewer, who was impressed that some of the Americans trained six times a week, then asked the lock if she liked dishing out punishment. Flanagan wryly replied: 'Oh, absolutely. Yeah. Yeah, we're gonna beat the hell out of somebody and enjoy it. Sure.'

The first official game of women's rugby in the United States was a contest between Colorado State University and the University of Colorado and it took place just a few months after the passing of Title IX. By 1974 there were 29 teams across the country and in 1977 there were enough sides for the Chicago Rugby Club to host the first national championship (won by Portland Maine). Ali Donnelly, in her history of women's rugby *Scrum Queens,* wrote of this tournament: 'The first ever National Championship in Chicago in 1984 was run magnificently. Had they known about it, Europe's leading sides would have been amazed at how professional and organised the competition already was on the other side of the Atlantic . . . it highlighted, although hardly anyone else knew about it at the time, that the US were much further ahead in their development than the rest of the world.'

Donnelly estimates that in 1985, the USA had 'over ten times as many teams and players as Britain or France'. By the end of the decade the US had 210 women's teams and the USA Rugby Football Union (USARFU) had formed a Women's Committee to help administer the women's game.

One obstacle that has always hampered rugby stateside is the vast distances involved in travel to face opponents. The US Women's Rugby Foundation website addresses this issue on its wonderful rugby history pages:

'Given the geographic challenges of the early years, women's rugby relied heavily on tournaments. Players would drive for hours and play up to four matches a day often on different teams. These tournaments, often part of men's tournaments, and always hosted by beer companies, helped elevate the overall quality of play as they exposed women's teams to different levels and styles of play and allowed women opportunities to share ideas during the many raucous social events.'

In 1987, the United States played their first women's international, beating neighbours Canada by 22–3. The squad included American rugby legend Kathy Flores at number eight. She went on to be part of the 1991 World Cup win and would later coach the side too, ultimately earning herself a place in the World Rugby Hall of Fame. Other players from that game that would feature in the first World Cup were centre Candice Orsini, full-back Mary Sulllivan (who would be a co-captain), fly-half Chris Harju, lock Janice Rutowski, prop Colleen Fahey, back row Barbara Bond (who would also be a co-captain), centre Tracy Moens, prop Annie Flavin and lock Tam Breckenridge. The side were coached by Welshman Kevin O'Brien who would be at the helm in 1991 too. The team were not allowed to wear an Eagle logo on their shirts as the USARFU did not permit them to do so for several years.

Orsini, a talented centre who had attended Florida State University, has one of the most colourful biographies in all of rugby. She had won ESPN Female Athlete of the Year in 1985 and earned her living as a stuntwoman. In her death-defying profession, she appeared in films such as *Super Mario Brothers*, *Cocoon* and *Die Hard with a Vengeance*.

That first Test match had been part of a double header with the US men's team. Fred Paoli, the men's American captain that day, grimily etched his name into rugby history by giving a speech later in the evening that included some pretty awful comments about females playing rugby. It was so ignorant that both women's teams left the room in disgust along with several male guests as well. While the initial explosion in women's rugby in the United States had been relatively unfettered by the chauvinistic attitudes that blighted the growth of the game in the 'British Empire' countries, there did nonetheless exist plenty of men in the USARFU who held dinosaur-like views.

Preparations for the assault on history
The funding that helped boost rugby in colleges and universities didn't extend to the national side when it came to money to travel

to Wales for the World Cup in 1991. Not even the USARFU would chip in. The selected players had to pay their own way. A fundraising letter from the Women's Committee outlined the hypocrisy around the lack of union support:

'Since we are representing the United States, you may wonder why the USA Rugby Football Union is not sponsoring our tour. The USARFU sanctions both men's and women's rugby, and collects the same dues from all clubs. However, the men's Rugby World Cup is also scheduled for later this year, and the USARFU executive board is not willing to commit any funds to the women's event. (That's another battle to fight.)'

Flanagan is still angry at the lack of support from the union. Speaking for this book, she says: 'I found it incredibly unjust, but I thought, "forget them". If they are not behind us, we won't let that deter us. And now I think "shame on them". And even now there are people who will trivialise what we did in winning the World Cup. I personally found out about a women's sports foundation grant and applied for it on behalf of the team and we got a $5,000 grant. And that was a lot of money and it made a big difference.'

Going into the tournament, many tipped the Americans as favourites. It was a strange concept to those who only followed the men's game. Surely, they thought, it would be an England or New Zealand team that would be most likely to win? Yet the US had shown their ability, power and flair in their early Test matches. Many of the team had also gone on a tour to the UK and France in 1985 with a representative team called the Wiverns. This team had swept all before them and showed players and administrators in Europe that the Americans were a serious force to be reckoned with and had set the benchmark for those nations wishing to progress.

The tournament

In 1991, when the Eagles squad (they had finally been given permission to use the name) was picked to head to Wales, the national selectors had 162 teams and 3,000 players to choose from. The World Cup would take place over just nine days, starting on 6 April and ending on 14 April. There simply wasn't the money and resources available to have it last any longer. All participating teams would play two pool games, with the group stage consisting of four pools of three teams. The top team from each pool would progress to the semi-finals.

United States 7 Netherlands 0 (Pontypool Park, Pontypool) Pool match. 6 April 1991

USA opened their campaign with a match against the Netherlands. While modern day rugby fans may assume a team from the lowlands would likely be a pushover, the women in orange were a team with history and a core of strong players.

The Netherlands had played in the first ever women's Test match in 1982 when, to celebrate the 50th anniversary of the Netherlands Rugby Board, an invitation was extended to France for a women's international. A surprising number of Dutch universities had women's rugby teams by the early eighties and the country hosted many key early tournaments and would later go on to hold the 1998 edition of the World Cup.

The USA though were favourites and not expected to face too much trouble. Mother Nature, however, decided to level the playing fields. Freezing rain and gale force winds made the game an endurance test. At one point US flanker Cathy Seabaugh, who some said later was hypothermic, set down in a scrum facing the wrong way, so much had the cold gotten to her.

Flanagan was told by the coaches to go on to win her first cap, but Seabaugh simply couldn't comprehend the signals from her teammate to come off and somehow carried on playing in a sort of autopilot and lasted the match.

It wasn't just the cold that hampered the Americans. Just six minutes into the contest their scrum-half, Barbara Fugate, had to be replaced after a serious knee injury that would end her tournament.

The game finished with the USA winning by just seven points. The key moment was a first-half try (four points back then) from influential winger Patty Jervey, who had been set up by Patty Connell, the replacement for Fugate. The final scoring of the contest also came before the break, with lock Andrea Morell slotting a penalty.

After the game, some players took their hot teas into the shower and poured them over themselves instead of drinking them. They were that cold.

United States 46 USSR 0 (Memorial Ground, Cardiff)
Pool match. 10 April 1991

This clash of two political superpowers offered few sparks that may have reignited the Cold War between the states, which was petering out at the time.

The USSR were easily the most bizarre and controversial of the sides that took part in the competition. Years later organisers would say the only hassle caused by any of the teams was created by the Soviets and the trouble started as soon as they arrived. With the team seriously low on funds (understandable in view of the political and economic situation at that time as the state they represented was rapidly collapsing into history), they arrived in the UK with unimaginable amounts of vodka, caviar and champagne which they intended to barter with to pay their way. Custom officials were not amused. Luckily for the cashless tourists, officials were unable to communicate properly with them and eventually let them in anyway. The story made headlines and plenty of help was forthcoming from the rugby community, local people and businesses to ultimately see them through. Some who helped out have claimed that there was little to no gratitude for the assistance and the organisers of the tournament had to deal with several problems including accommodation damage and financial bills that could not be blamed on lack of funds.

The Soviets had struggled to eat properly in the early days of their visit and, combined with the travel and a 28–0 battering by the Netherlands a couple of days earlier, it's hardly surprising they would crash so badly to a USA team that was so well prepared, rested and nutritionally superior. The favourites had made six changes to the starting line-up, producing a XV that would become the core of the side that would contest the knockout stages.

In particular, Kathy Flores took over at both number eight and co-captain in place of Barbara Bond, and Chris Harju and Jen Crawford came in at 10 and 12 respectively. Flores and Bond were both exceptional players and leaders and would rotate in the role of co-captain and number eight depending on the opposition.

Jervey grabbed three tries to add to her effort against the Netherlands and the US crossed the Soviet line nine times in all. The other scores came from Orsini (2), left wing Sandy Meredith, Crawford, captain Sullivan and Flanagan (who when asked about her score for this book had no memory of it). Fly-half Harju slotted five conversions.

The match was the swansong of the Soviet women's rugby team as the state would soon cease to exist.

United States 7 New Zealand 0 (Cardiff Arms Park, Cardiff) Semi-final. 12 April 1991

Most in the know fancied the US to lift the first World Cup, but several believed New Zealand were just as likely to win it. The final score showed just how close the two teams were. In fact, when the two sides had met for the first and previous only time in 1990 in Christchurch, New Zealand had run out 9–3 winners. This was a team that knew they could beat the Americans and had a recent result to prove it.

Coach O'Brien made five changes from the USSR win, again changing his number eight and captain as he restored Bond back to the leadership hot seat and base of the scrum. Annie Flavin came in at prop for her first game of the tournament and Flanagan lined up with Breckenridge to form a second-row partnership that would be nicknamed the 'Locks from Hell'. *Rugby*, a US magazine, explained the origins of their moniker:

'Instead of the large, immobile 2nd rows that seemed to populate the other teams, the Eagles possessed two very athletic, mobile women who also happened to be tall. Flanagan and Breckenridge held their own against larger women in the sets and then played like flankers in the loose. Furthermore, the possession they did secure was clean and crisp, unlike the sloppy ball coming from most opponents.'

The Gal Blacks (their nickname at the time) dispatched Canada 24–8 and hosts Wales 24–6 en route to the semi-final. Like many other competitors, they hadn't received a great deal of support from their union back home and had received zero financial funding to help them compete.

In light of the previous year's loss to New Zealand, the US put a huge emphasis on the scrum. Speaking to author Martyn Thomas for his book *World In Their Hands*, head coach O'Brien spoke of how he put the squad through a gruelling scrummaging session the day before the match: 'I believed in scrummaging and rucking, and basically that's what I was going to do. If they could survive the scrummaging sessions, they could survive the game.'

Flanagan, like all the forwards from that squad, still recalls the brutal session, recalling: 'We now call that session 'scrum for your life'. We all remember it. I think it wasn't just about training, you are already as fit as you are going to be. It was a little bit about fixing technical things, but O'Brien was trying to find the right combinations of people. Remember, how big is America? We didn't have training camps. The first time I had ever lined up behind my front row was at this World Cup. We didn't have chemistry from playing together, so he was trying to see who worked best with each other.'

The game kicked off at 6pm in light rain, after the USA had faced the haka by standing in a huddle in their own half chanting 'Harder. Stronger. Faster'.

The scrummage obsession from the US paid off as the only try of the game was scored by captain and number eight Bond (back in again for Flores) via a pushover try after 65 minutes. That, and a first-half penalty from Harju were the only times the scorers were troubled. The Americans had a fantastic reputation for skilful and fast attacking play, so the fact the win came from a score created by the power of their pack was ominous for England, who would be their opponents in the final.

After the match O'Brien praised the defensive efforts of his entire team: 'The key to it all was the pressure and incredible tackling from every single player.'

No one knew it at the time, but this would be the only time the North Americans would ever beat the New Zealanders. When the sides next met in 1996, the USA would be humiliated 88–8. The record for this fixture now stands at 13 New Zealand wins to a solitary American victory. The Black Ferns, as they are now known, have also gathered up six World Cups.

United States 19 England 6 (Cardiff Arms Park)
Final. 14 April 1991

On the day of the final, the US team only had to stroll a few hundred metres to Cardiff Arms Park from their hotel. It was a short, but memorable trip. Flanagan recalls the journey with great emotion. 'We got dressed in our number ones, got our kit bags and set off as a team. And people were driving by and would stop their cars and roll down their windows and cheer. People would come to the door of their shops and cheer. People in upper story windows would cheer: 'Go on, America! Beat England!' To hear that and feel it was amazing, I'd never felt or experienced anything like it.'

The USA made only one change for the final, bringing Flores back in as co-captain and number eight in place again of Bond. The coaches felt Flores would offer more agility around the park, which would be vital in the game plan they had forged to beat England. Mary Sullivan retained her co-captaincy role at full-back.

An experienced England had beaten France 13–0 in their semi-final, having earlier overcome Spain, who were then a major nation in the sport, 12–0, and Italy 25–9. Again, while the USA were generally seen as favourites by those who followed the women's game, there were more than few willing to back England's chances. Indeed, local bookmakers had the England side as favourites.

In front of around 3,000 spectators, England, utilising the wind the Americans had let them have in the first half, had the honour of being the first side to put points on the USA. The score came after a strong opening period for England's forwards and smart kicking from England outside-half and captain, Karen Almond. The Red Roses knew they had to starve the US backs of the ball and they had begun their task well. After a quarter of an hour, England were rewarded for relentless pressure with a five-metre scrum. Following a good old-fashioned Anglo-Saxon shove, the scrum collapsed and Welsh referee Les Peard awarded a penalty try, which number eight Gill Burns converted.

In response, all the USA could muster before the break was a penalty from Harju, to make it 6–3. The match report from *The Times* said the opening clashes of the game demonstrated that: 'England had kept the Americans penned back in a tight and turgid show of muscle. The "locks from hell" and the "turbo props" could do little to counter a disciplined display from the England forwards. Facing the heavier American line-up, the English pack finally proved that organisation can counter brawn.'

The favourites were not worried. They had given their opponents the wind and expected them to come out all guns blazing, but didn't feel England had the fitness to maintain their ferocity they began with against the elements in the second half.

The Eagles' response came from blindside flanker Claire Godwin, who by this stage was regarded by many as the best athlete in the tournament. Her try came after just two second-half minutes and made up in some way for the fact she had been the player called out by the referee for conceding a penalty try in the first half. Godwin scored from a rolling maul set up by a take from Flanagan.

A few minutes later, the US had a line-out on the English ten-metre line. Seeing several of their opponents weren't concentrating, the Eagles took a quick throw and, just a few seconds and 40 metres later, Godwin had recorded her second try. She would later be named Most Valuable Player of the World Cup by a US rugby magazine.

The score essentially knocked the wind out of the English challenge and, as predicted by the US coaches, they began to tire. England had made limited changes in their four tournament games, while their opponents had cleverly rejigged their line-ups throughout so that fatigue was far less of an issue. All but two of those wearing a red rose on their shirt that day were playing their fourth game in just a week and a half.

Any hope of an England rally was killed off by a third try from scrum-half Connell. Once again, Flanagan and Godwin were involved. The star flanker tapped down to a charging Flanagan who burst through with knees high and soon built up a huge head of steam. Just yards out, Flanagan felt she could beat the final defenders, but heard a call on her shoulder from her scrum-half. 'At the last minute Patty Connell called for the ball,' says Flanagan. 'And if someone called from the ball in an American team, you knew that that person was in a better position. She was on my right hip and went in right in under the post.'

With Harju adding conversions to two of the three second-half tries, it meant the score of this historic occasion finished 19–6 to the USA.

Mary Sullivan and Barbara Bond, the latter of whom had not played but had been co-captain in earlier games, went up the steps to lift the silverware to confirm the USA were world champions. The trophy had cost the organisers £1007.50, an amount that caused a serious argument among the committee in light of how tight budgets were.

On their return home the Eagles were invited to the White House and those that could afford to attend, met Barbara Bush (her husband had been called away on a national emergency).

'It was a little bit bittersweet,' recalls Tara when asked about the reaction in the US. 'America is a non-rugby nation and not a lot of people paid attention and we didn't really get our due. Our union didn't give us money and they barely could acknowledge the success of the women.'

Amazingly (and quite insultingly), the tournament would not be officially publicly recognised by the IRB as an official World Cup until 2009. Thankfully, the 1991 USA team are now rightly and officially regarded as pioneers and game-changers. More than any of the early international sides, they showed the potential of the women's game. The USA would go on to reach the final of the 1994 and 1998 editions of the World Cup, but were never quite able to scale the peak again.

Over the years, their achievements in winning have slowly come to be recognised. Other players who took part in the inaugural tournament have also spoken of how much the Americans taught them about how to train and prepare for elite rugby. They can be proud that their legacy lives on well beyond their own border and the era in which they played.

SQUAD DETAILS*

Front rows: Colleen Fahey, Annie Flavin, Jennifer Hertz, Maryanne Soreson, Val Sullivan, Julie Thompson

Second rows: Tam Breckenridge, Tara Flanagan, Andrea Morrell, Jan Rutowski

Back rows: Barbara Bond (co-captain), Clare Godwin, Cathy Seabaugh, Morgan Whitehead, Kathy Flores (co-captain)

Scrum-halves: Patty Connell, Barbara Fugate

Outside-halves: Mary Dixey, Chris Harju

Three-quarters/full-backs: Jen Crawford, Elise Huffer, Patty Jervey, Krista McFarren, Sandy Meredith, Candi Orsini, Mary Sullivan (co-captain)

Travelling reserves: Ann Barford, Elise Huffer, Joan Morrissey

Coach: Kevin O'Brien

Assistant coach: Chris Leach

Team managers: Anna Holzhauer, Jane Tierney

USA Rugby women's chair: Jami Jordan

MIKE GIBSON

'Rugby is like love, it is a game of touch and of feel and of instinct.'
Mike Gibson

The complete package, Mike Gibson ranks among the greatest players ever to represent Ireland and the British and Irish Lions.

Main teams: Cambridge University, North of Ireland F.C., Ulster, Barbarians, Ireland, British & Irish Lions
Position: Centre, outside-half
International caps: 69 (1964–79)
International points: 112 (9 tries, 7 conversions, 16 penalties, 6 drop goals)
Lions caps: 12 (5 tours between 1966–1977)
Lions points: 0

Before the arrival of Brian O'Driscoll in the emerald green shirt of Ireland in 1999, there was very little debate about who had been the greatest player to represent Ireland since the team first entered the international arena in 1875. Almost all of those who knew anything about the game's history ranked Cameron Michael Henderson Gibson as the finest talent to play for Ireland.

Indeed, plenty of 'old timers' can set out a robust case for this son of Belfast to remain atop the pile. But no matter which player you throw your support behind, Gibson's greatness is undisputed.

Born in Belfast in 1942 and educated in the city's Campbell College, Gibson was a keen footballer in his youth. However, at Campbell College rugby was the only option, so he simply went with the flow. In later years he claimed that he didn't begin his rugby career with any ambition, but played simply for the love of the game. Gibson would go on to attend Cambridge University where he played with distinction in the famous blue and white shirt. After finishing his studies he went on to work as a lawyer.

A complete player

Gibson possessed a superior skill set to most of his peers, in part due to pushing himself at a young age. He would often set himself a challenge when playing, such as only kicking with his left foot in one game and only with his right in another. This forced him to learn to use both feet under pressure in actual match situations and become someone who could be trusted to kick off either foot as and when needed. He possessed an elite rugby brain too and was a great anticipator of what was about to happen on the field, enabling him to combine his grey matter and athletic ability to devastating effect.

Thanks in part to the influence of his coach at Campbell College, as well as his father, Gibson learned the importance of analysing his choices in a game. Both mentors would pose him questions after a match, asking him to explain why he did the things he did in certain situations. This encouraged Gibson to focus on the mental side of the sport. He learned not just how to make correct decisions on the field, but to also anticipate the flow of a game so he could put himself in the right place at the right time for his team. Indeed, the great Gerald Davies of Wales once said that Gibson played 'rugby of an intellectual kind'. This awareness of what could be gained by considering the mental side of rugby was an unusually professional approach to what was then an amateur sport and was another reason he excelled and had such a long and glittering career.

Before matches, when passionate teammates could be making dramatic speeches, or banging parts of their bodies against floors and walls, Gibson would close his eyes and visualise the things he would do in different situations during the forthcoming match. He was, quite frankly, light years ahead in the mental aspect of sport.

Yet he was far from a cold-blooded machine. Gibson was often emotional, even teary-eyed, when playing. He would be overcome with the passion of the crowd, the melody of an anthem or the presence of his parents in the stands. His skill was in knowing how to channel it to make him excel.

A glorious start to Test rugby

Gibson won his first cap for Ireland in the 1964 Five Nations, being selected at fly-half to face England away at a sprightly 21 years of age. The youngster had impressed Irish selectors in the 1963 Varsity Match, which saw Cambridge triumph 19–11 over Oxford. He had also done well against the touring All Blacks for both his university and Ulster.

The task ahead of Gibson on his Test debut was a big one. Ireland had not emerged victorious from London for 16 years. In total, Ireland had won just four times in 20 visits to Twickenham. This was the 76th meeting of the old rivals and *The Times* previewed the game by pointing out that England had won 46 of the previous matches to the visitors' 23 (there had been six draws).

The Times also wrote that while Gibson had 'shown every quality that his position demands . . . it may have been tempting to hold him up as a bombshell for next season, when new laws should give him even further scope'. History, though, shows that the Irish selectors were right to unleash Gibson when they did.

The new cap was praised for his performance in the impressive 18–5 win (a proper beating by the scoring averages of the era) and labelled as a diamond that was already 'cut and polished'.

The men in green grabbed five tries and the debutant fly-half was the key player in crafting three of them. For Ireland's first try, Gibson showed both his impeccable timing and his strength. He burst on to a reverse pass from his scrum-half, James Kelly, at devastating speed and at a cutting angle. The pace and suddenness of this action took him past two of the England back row that were breaking from a scrum. Gibson's power then knocked England's scrum-half Simon Clarke off his feet, before the Irish ten then stumbled into England full-back and captain John Wilcox and opposite number Tom Brophy. Gibson had enough power to tie them both up and enough composure to pop a gorgeous little ball to his supporting flanker Noel Murphy who crashed over the tryline.

In the Monday paper *The Times* wrote: 'Gibson does not waste energy needlessly. He has the easy anonymity of a superbly cut Savile Row suit, but if there is a gap he is through it, fast and unfussily, before opponents or even spectators even realised that he is there . . . he has a calm unflappability . . . [and] was an inconspicuous menace whenever the ball was in his hand.'

A year later, *Rothmans Rugby Yearbook* would reflect that 'Gibson had made his reputation with one of the most brilliant international debuts at fly-half in the history of the game'.

Despite the wonderful start to Ireland's season, they failed to win another match. No one, however, thought that was Gibson's fault. Ireland were an inconsistent side during his years playing Test rugby and won just 29 of his 69 games. But there is little doubt that if he hadn't been on the scene, that record would have been even worse.

For all his longevity in the Ireland team, Gibson would only be part of one championship-winning side. In 1974 a win over England at Twickenham (in which Gibson scored two tries and two conversions), a victory over Scotland at home and a draw in Dublin with Wales was enough to give Ireland an outright title, despite an opening loss in Paris.

After winning his first 23 caps in the number ten shirt, Gibson was moved to centre to accommodate the talents of Barry McGann. He would only win three more caps at outside-half. Remarkably though, Gibson would earn three caps as a winger in the 1978 Five Nations at the grand old sporting age of 35 and another one in 1979 against Scotland. Proof, if any more was needed, he was a complete footballer.

A key reason that Gibson was able to play as an international winger during the twilight of his career was his dedication to fitness and conditioning. In an era when even top players often had a far from ideal approach to their physical conditioning, Gibson worked with a sprint coach to maximise his speed and carefully watched what he drank and ate (he also avoided the party lifestyle many of his teammates embraced). Few players in world rugby at the time would have had such dedication to their body's wellbeing.

To get himself in peak physical condition, Gibson would train with athletes, pushing himself further than he would ever be forced to in rugby training. That way, he knew he was ready for anything on matchday.

Gibson's last spell in an Irish jersey was during the 1979 tour of Australia. At 36 years old, he ignored the influence of Father Time to help steer his nation to an historic 2–0 series win. It was a fitting end to a Test career in which he had been captain of Ireland on five occasions.

A proud and persistent Lion

Gibson was selected for five tours with the British and Irish Lions. These were Australia/New Zealand (1966), South Africa (1968), New Zealand (1971), South Africa (1974) and New Zealand (1977). His extraordinary tour tally has only been equalled by fellow Irish star Willie John McBride.

Gibson won 12 caps during those expeditions and cemented his place in the pantheon of rugby greats with his performances as part of the legendary 1971 side. Not only was he a core component of the only Lions team to conquer the All Blacks, Gibson won over the knowledgeable rugby folk of New Zealand too. Kiwi legend Colin Meads – not a man to dish out praise lightly – said: 'Gibson's presence in the Lions backline was the most frustrating influence of all'. He estimated that '80 per cent of All Black back movements came unstuck through Gibson's quickness, skill and courage'.

Rugby historian Huw Richards points out that Gibson's extraordinary memory helped Lions coach Carwyn James coach his team to victory: 'In an age before coaches were offered huge amounts of film analysis, Gibson's pitch-perfect ability to recall every incident in a match was of immense value to coach Carwyn James.'

On the 1968 tour of South Africa, Gibson also became the first ever replacement in international rugby, when he came off the bench for an injured Barry John against the Springboks. The laws of rugby union had only just been changed to allow replacements and, prior to this, players either had to play on injured or leave their team with a numerical disadvantage. Amazingly, replacements could not get changed into their playing kit until a doctor had confirmed an injury. So, when Gibson got the call to come on, he was wearing a tie and blazer!

Legacy

Gibson made an astonishing 56 appearances in the Five Nations between 1964 and 1979. Upon his retirement, no other Ireland player had played so often in the Championship. His record was finally broken in 2012 by Munster's Ronan O'Gara. O'Gara, of course, was playing in the Six Nations era, meaning he had the opportunity to play in one extra game a season, as well as win caps as a tactical replacement (something not possible during Gibson's career).

Gibson retired with 81 caps in total (69 for Ireland and 12 for the Lions). At the time this was a world record. Famous rugby commentator Bill McLaren said he was the 'most complete footballer I ever saw'. Gibson's tally of 112 Test points – aided by an ability to place kick and dropkick – may not seem a formidable amount to modern fans, but at the time of his international retirement it put him in the top 20 international scorers of all time.

Even after stepping away from the Test arena, Gibson played on well into his 40s at club level. He was awarded an MBE for his services to the game and was among the first batch of players inducted into the International Rugby Hall of Fame in 1997. After his induction, he said: 'There were so many elements within rugby that are of use in dealing with life . . . the satisfaction comes from being a member of a successful side, but more from the fact that you were in a team that fought together and those memories will just not leave me.' Gibson was also accepted into the IRB Hall of Fame (now the World Rugby Hall of Fame).

Unlike a great many of his contemporaries, Gibson has never written an autobiography and seldom gives interviews. He told journalist Paul Kimmage in 2016 that he had no interest in writing a book and that his views on modern rugby were 'not worth much' as he does not believe he is 'au fait with the current demands of the game'.

His silence only adds to the aura of one of rugby's true global greats.

JILLION POTTER

'Rugby has saved my life in a lot of ways.'
Jillion Potter

Few players in the history of rugby have overcome such serious illness and injury as USA's Jillion Potter. Despite the horror of a broken neck and cancer, Potter fulfilled her dream of playing sevens in the Olympic games and became a cult inspirational figure in rugby.

Main teams: University of New Mexico, Denver Raptons, Minneapolis Valkyries, USA, USA Sevens
Position: Flanker, prop
International caps: 22 (2007-15)
World Sevens Series: 60 games (2012-16) (16 tries)
Honours: 2016 Olympian, 2013 Rugby World Cup 7s (Bronze), Collegiate All-American (three times), 2022 US Brewers Cup Competitor (as a barista!)

Jillion Potter didn't know anything about rugby growing up. But one thing was clear: bumps, bruises and bangs were not an issue for her when it came to sport. As a youngster she enjoyed skateboarding and her attitude to the dangers and often painful consequences of the pastime tell you everything you need to know about her sporting character. Speaking for this book, Potter explains: 'I was competitive at it and loved jumping off stairs, sliding down rails and falling on cement. I cut myself, got scratched, bruised and even chipped my teeth. But none of those things are things you can call injuries.'

Born in Austin, Texas, in 1986, Potter was one of three children. Alongside skateboarding, she played basketball growing up and represented her high school in the sport. Rugby was simply not on her radar. Yet not long after turning up at the University of New Mexico in 2005, she was approached by a few of the college's women players to try out for rugby. Her initial response was to refuse. After all, she didn't even really know what rugby was. But a few days later another group of players looking for fresh talent saw her and also asked her to try out. Thinking it was possibly a sign she should at least give it a chance, she agreed to attend a training session. Just a few minutes in, Potter was given a tackle pad to hold.

'I remember it so vividly,' says Potter looking back in 2023. 'This girl named Joslyn runs up and just smashes me to the ground. And I lay there thinking: "Oh, this is how it's going?" And I stood up and went "Ok". That helped me understand the level of intensity and contact people were bringing. Joslyn was a flanker and when she saw red, she saw red. She was fierce and intimidating and everything you expect when you show up in rugby. So, when she knocked me down I was like "Oh, ok. Alright." Then I held my ground and when it was my turn to hit her . . . oh boy, did I.'

A steep learning curve, but glory follows

Potter was hooked, but she still knew nothing about the sport she had fallen so hard for. Luckily for the fresh convert, she got her eager hands on a copy of the book *Rugby for Dummies* from her mother who had purchased it off Ebay. Potter had a personality that made her not just desperate to learn, but utterly unafraid when it came to asking questions that others may have found embarrassing. This came in handy when her athletic ability, natural skill and outright willingness to do the rough stuff, saw her fast tracked into a US national team camp while aged just 19. She openly admits she still barely understood the laws and terminology of the game. During her first camp she had to ask the coach what he meant when she was told to run to the 22 line.

'It's funny when I think about that now, how little I knew about the game,' says Potter. 'But I am not afraid to ask questions or to raise my hands. I would make mistakes and I had so many penalties given against me in the early days. I wasn't really a student of sport until I made the under-23 squad. In the under-19 team I simply focused on having fun and raising my hand when I had questions and just did the best I could.'

Potter rapidly became a hot prospect in US rugby and was put into the High Performance Development Pathway and by 2007 was making her Test debut (after having played at both under-19 and under-23 level). Extremely strong and a lover of the physical stuff that rugby encourages, Potter flitted between flanker and prop. So impressive was her early impact in US rugby, she was one of the first eight women to be contracted by USA Rugby. No one in women's rugby in the country had ever played with her gung-ho physical approach. She was both admired and openly feared by others in American rugby. Players in the US game spoke of her with genuine awe and nobody relished coming into contact with her, even in training. By the time the 2010 World Cup was on the horizon, Potter had become an established and key figure in the USA team.

Speaking to *Bleacher Report* in 2016, Sevens Olympian Kelly Griffin said: 'I first heard about Jill when I was in college at UCLA and she was at New Mexico. She was known as a crazy-ass flanker. I mean, totally crazy, 100 per cent beast. She'd just lay people out like it was nothing. I'd never seen anything like it.'

A slight pain in the neck

During a Test away to Canada, Potter felt terrible pain in her neck following an attempt to poach a ball after a tackle. She fell to the ground and, for a terrifying moment, couldn't feel her limbs properly. Despite this, she managed to walk off the pitch with the help of her teammates.

'As soon as I stood up I was in the most pain I've ever been in,' says Potter. 'It was tremendous agony and I almost collapsed. But my teammates were holding me and helped me off. I was crying the whole time for the rest of the game on the sideline. The game was in Canada and the hospital gave me what turned out to be a misdiagnosis and told me to wear a neck brace, go back to the States, have an MRI scan and see a specialist to find out what to do next.'

Potter returned home and booked an appointment in three weeks' time. In the meantime, with a World Cup looming, she decided a neck brace wasn't going to stop her training: 'I thought I may as well keep working out while waiting to get the results from my scan. So I worked out and kept my neck brace on. Well, most of the time I kept it on. I lifted weights and, well, I was so dumb.'

Three weeks later, she got a voicemail from the specialist saying: 'Jillion, whatever you do, don't take off your neck brace you need to come in immediately, your neck is highly unstable. Be careful walking on stairs and don't drive and get other people to drive you anywhere.'

Potter picked the message up while returning home from the gym. It turned out her neck was displaced and the C5 was cracked. 'It didn't even look like my neck was connected,' recalls Potter, who looks back now in horror at how bad things could have been and how close she came to paralysis. Of course, some said she would never play again, but one physician, who had worked with NFL players who had suffered and recovered from similar injuries, gave her hope. Potter reflected that 'as soon as one person said you can play, that was all I needed to grab onto.'

While Potter was unable to recover in time for the 2010 World Cup, she did get back on the field and was soon back in national colours. Having cruelly missed out on her first chance at a World Cup, Potter got to represent her nation at the 2014 edition in France and fulfil one of her rugby dreams.

Not only had she become a well-respected figure in the fifteen-a-side code, Potter was also making an impact in the seven-a-side format too, overcoming the concerns of those who felt she had the wrong physique and playing style to thrive in the sport.

Sevens, sarcoma and Rio

Before Potter made it to the 2014 15-a-side World Cup though, she got to play in the sevens World Cup – a mark of her versatility and athleticism. Fully recovered from her neck injury, in 2013, she was selected to be part of the World Rugby Sevens World Cup in Moscow. The USA took bronze in the tournament, only narrowly losing to eventual winners New Zealand in the semi-final. She considers it one of the highlights of her career.

With her relentless energy and excellent stamina, Potter was a natural for sevens (she was also a co-captain of the team) and set her sights on the unbelievable opportunity of being part of the 2016 Olympics. Rugby had not been part of the Olympic games since 1924 and then, of course, was for men only. For the games in Rio, Brazil, in 2016, rugby was to return in spectacular style. This time, the game would be the shortened seven-a-side code and both men and women would compete.

Rugby being in the Olympics was huge for the women's game in terms of both profile and the extra funding that being an Olympic sport brought for the nations and athletes involved. For the Americans it was particularly exciting as it significantly raised awareness of the sport in a country where it has a relatively low profile.

Then, in 2014, something happened to Potter that was even more devastating than her broken neck. Not long before her appearance in the 2014 15-a-side World Cup, she began to suffer painful swelling in her jaw and discovered an unusual lump. At first she dismissed it as some kind of infection and tried to treat it herself. That didn't work. Neither did a course of antibiotics. The lump turned out to be a tumour.

Despite the obvious concerns, doctors gave Potter the go-ahead to play in the World Cup in France, believing the tumour was benign. So, like the warrior she is, she played. It wasn't easy, but she played. In an interview in 2018 Potter described how she got through the tournament and the horrific aftermath that followed: 'I went to Europe to compete, and every week [the tumour] got bigger and bigger and bigger. You couldn't tell if you looked at me because the tumour was pressing up into my mouth instead of out. I just remember that I was so exhausted. Luckily for me, I had been training all year to be super-fit and able to combat fatigue. You are trained as an athlete to just push through.

'I had surgery in San Diego two days after the World Cup. We found out that it was a sarcoma, which is a soft tissue cancer classification. Because of the tumour size I started treatment very fast. There was no digestion period. It was like: you need to start chemo right away, and this is going to be the regimen. It was a four-day, inpatient hospital stay, so I had chemo for four days back to back. That was the worst part about it, in my opinion – the hospital stay. Of course, the nausea and how you feel afterward is a bummer too.'

Unbelievably, Potter would continue to push herself to her physical limit during the chemotherapy treatment. She would work as hard as possible in between the rounds of treatment (every three weeks) and then, when at the hospital, force herself to walk around the campus with the support of her partner, Carol Fabrizio (Potter had met Carol through rugby). The cancer Potter had was a rare one, with typically less than 1,000 cases seen annually in the whole of the United States.

In a 2018 interview with *lennyletter.com*, Potter expanded on how she combated the terrible toll cancer treatment took on her:

'It would take about two days at home after the chemo before I exercised again. Generally I would just walk to my community acupuncture place down the street, maybe a five-to-ten-minute walk. By day ten or twelve, I usually felt pretty good. The nausea would subside, my appetite would be back, so I would lift and run and basically do everything I could. Sometimes I was so tired I wouldn't be able to do as much as I wanted to. But some days I would be feeling so good that I would completely just go crazy in the gym.

'I also went to physical therapy twice a week to work on chronic athlete things like thoracic mobility. I wanted to try to get better as much as I could so that by the time I could actually start "really" training again, I would have a better foundation. Coming back from chemo and rebuilding my cardio was definitely harder than any conditioning session I've ever had in my life. The chemo affects your red blood cells . . . all of it, it kills everything, basically . . . I remember that when I ran I was definitely scraping the bottom of the barrel. It is hard to dig yourself out of that.

'Then I moved to Houston for radiation. It is completely the opposite of chemo because when you have chemo, it's like you are smacked in the face, and you are exhausted from day one. With radiation, it kind of creeps up on you. I remember on my first day of radiation I thought, "Well, this seems like it will probably be pretty easy." But it's cumulative, so by the end of radiation you might have skin burns and burns in your mouth, and you might feel more fatigued.

'I had radiation every day at 11. I would have a good breakfast, drive down there, and go straight to the gym after, every day. I kept to a pretty solid schedule and amped up my lifting and cardio. Initially, it was all about getting my size back. I had lost some weight during treatments, and it was about getting my muscle back and my strength back before I could add anything else. I am really fortunate for the strength and conditioning coaches that got me back to where I needed to be, and the doctors and the radiation department.'

Even in these awful times, Potter's human spirit shone through and one teammate remarked that even on a day when the toll of the treatment meant she was only awake three hours the whole day, she would visit the hospital's children's ward bearing gifts or colouring books and games.

In total, Potter underwent 18 weeks of chemotherapy and two months of radiation. Yet just two months after finishing her treatment, Potter ran a half marathon with her now wife Carol. And, staggeringly, Potter was able to return in time to be selected for the Olympic Games in 2016. Not just as a player either, she was named co-captain along with Kelly Griffin.

Further testament to Potter's athletic ability and mind can be made by the fact that she had to adjust how she played the game in light of her illness. Speaking for this book in 2023, she explained what she had to do to adapt to a new physical reality:

'Before that illness I was way more physical. I think I had a lot more speed and in my mind, the way I showed up on the field was different. After the treatment I was a lot slower, and I couldn't regain the weight that I had before or regain the same level of strength. It was hard to watch videos of myself and see what I could do before and realise I wouldn't be the same. Before I would have these dominant hits and now my body couldn't take that. So I had to figure out how to change. How, for example. would I bring people down and get a turnover now? Before I was hunting for the big hits, but not anymore. I had to think about how I moved across the field. I knew my aerobic fitness needed to be higher as I was the slowest person in the squad, so my weakness was my speed. How did I then build my stamina?

What were my strengths now? I had to redefine and discover my new strengths. I was a better player before the illness, but I became a better leader after.'

While Potter may have changed how she played, she could never quite tame the aggressive spirit that drove her. Her coach at Rio still described her as the team's 'enforcer' and claimed there was no other player like her in the women's game.

The USA secured fifth place at the Olympics, beating Fiji and France in the play-offs. While the Americans may not have got a medal, Potter was singled out for praise for her performances and considers watching the subsequent medal ceremony as one of the most powerful moments of her career, even getting emotional recalling it all over six years later:

'I was so proud of those women. It was super emotional. You see their struggles, you see them giving everything they've got and they know they had similar feelings getting picked for the Olympics. So in Rio, it didn't matter if we had gold or not. Well, of course I wanted to win gold, but the women worked so hard to be there, that's what really mattered. I would relive watching that moment again above all others in sport if I had the chance.'

New challenges

Despite overcoming the impact of cancer treatment to make her Rio dreams come true, the illness again reared its ugly head. It returned shortly after the Olympics, with USA Rugby announcing the news in early January of 2017. The diagnosis was unexpected and came after a routine check-up.

The sporting world quickly rallied around Potter, generously helping with fundraising to donate some of the hefty fees that come with expert medical care in the USA. Once again, Potter overcame initial scares to seemingly beat the disease, undergoing an operation in 2018 after the cancer had spread to her lungs.

In 2023, by now a proud mother, Potter again was diagnosed with cancer. In speaking for this book, she remained as defiant and determined as ever to again overcome the disease.

As always, Potter never stands still. After retiring from rugby, she dived into a totally new professional challenge: running a coffee roaster with her wife. Helm Coffee, based in Indianapolis, is run with Carol and donates parts of its proceeds to local good causes and offers up its space for fundraisers for reproductive healthcare.

Just as she threw herself into rugby without knowing anything about the sport, so Potter dived into the coffee world with almost zero knowledge. She had taken an interest in coffee after getting a taste for it in San Diego while prepping for the Olympics. Not long after getting the bug, she was competing in brewing competitions, despite admitting she had so much to learn at the time.

Of course, Potter has quickly upped her game and now has some serious coffee skills. Asked if there was something in her that liked taking risks when it came to trying new things, she answered: 'I'm the type of person that likes to take chances and I am not afraid to walk through doors and not be good at something. And two weeks from now I'm competing in a coffee competition and I'm not that good at it. I do ok, I am maybe now perhaps one of the best in my state. But I'm not afraid to ask questions of other competitors to see if they share ideas and knowledge with me. That's my mindset.'

The Olympian believes the lessons she learnt in her rugby career have helped her immensely in life. She said: 'The values rugby mostly instils in you are discipline, community, connection, openness and everything that defines you as a human. In my experience, rugby can help create great humans, not just great rugby players. I can go anywhere in the world, and this is true even if I had never made the Olympics, and say 'I need a job and can you help me?' Every rugby club in the world would help you. That's not true in other sports in my experience.'

Just as rugby has given her so much, so Potter has given countless people in and outside of rugby huge inspiration. Her zest for life, her enthusiasm on the pitch, her incredible charisma (I've never enjoyed interviewing anyone as much as I did interviewing her for this book) and her refusal to ever give up make her a genuine role model that people from all walks of life can look up to and learn from. Which is why this book features Potter as the 'captain' of our fantasy team on the front cover.

Asked about her impact on others and how it makes her feel, she answered: 'I think it's worth all the suffering and hardship if one person's life is changed from hearing about my story.'

That statement simply sums Potter up. If her suffering has helped others, then she thinks her suffering was worth it.

What a player and what a person.

GIANT KILLERS
FRANCE (1911)

'The result was greeted with wild enthusiasm by the spectators, who, in spite of unfavourable weather, numbered about 10,000. The match is said to have been the finest ever held in France.'
The Times

In 1911, France won their first ever match over a major international side. It was a significant victory for a nation that would later go on to become one of the sport's dominant forces.

France 16 Scotland 15 (Stade Colombes, Paris)
2 January, 1911 – Five Nations
To the modern rugby follower, France winning against Six Nations rivals Scotland may not seem like the stuff of epic legends. After all, in the 100 meetings between the sides between 1910 and the 2023 Championship, France have won 58 of the contests. Yet, when France arrived on the international scene in 1906, Scotland had been playing Test rugby for almost 35 years.

Unsurprisingly, the French were whipping boys for the more established nations in the early years. Rugby's complexity and its requirement for strong domestic roots which produce a large enough quantity of Test players well-versed in the subtleties and technicalities of the game's set pieces, mean it can take decades for new nations to get up to speed.

The sport was brought to France by students and merchants (as it has been in so many nations) in the early 1870s. A national XV represented France in the bizarre rugby tournament that was part of the 1900 Olympic Games, competing with a team from Frankfurt (representing Germany) and Moseley Wanderers (representing Great Britain). The French side beat Germany 27–17 and Great Britain, who had arrived in Paris that very morning, 27–8. No match was played between Germany and Great Britain. As a result, France took gold and the other nations shared silver! However, these are not recognised as official Test matches for France. Their first full international was against the All Blacks on New Year's Day 1906. They fell 38–8. It was nothing to be ashamed of as the debutants were facing one of the greatest sides of all time (see page 299).

Scotland were the last of the Home Unions to face France. The conservative Scottish Rugby Union (SRU) have a pretty poor track record in establishing ties with developing nations or those new to the scene. In 1905 they churlishly refused to award caps against the great New Zealand team in a dispute over gate money and treated the visitors poorly. Ahead of what was then a risky and epic tour, the New Zealand Rugby Football Union (NZRFU) had to ensure the tour would be financially viable. They wrote to all unions, counties and teams to form arrangements for how ticket income would be split. In most cases, the home side offered up a guaranteed sum for the tourists. Not expecting much of a crowd for the game against a colonial side, the SRU refused to agree to these terms. They had previously hosted a Canadian team and given them guarantees and then been left out of pocket when few came to watch. Instead, the SRU said the New Zealanders could have the match income, minus whatever expenses were incurred in hosting the game. Sadly for the home union, the All Blacks swept across Europe and the Scottish game was a packed sell-out of 21,000. The SRU were mocked in many quarters when it came to light what they had done and, in a pathetic tantrum caused by how much cash they had lost out on, they refused to award caps for the clash. Edinburgh was also the only place on the whole tour that the All Blacks did not receive a 'warm official welcome' when they arrived in town. That's not even the worst of it. When the All Blacks next visited Europe in 1924, a full 19 years later, the SRU refused to arrange a fixture as they were again upset with pre-tour arrangements!

Furthermore, in 1908, when Australia first came to British shores, Scotland and Ireland declined to play them due to disagreements about how the RFU had arranged the tour. With this context, then, it's perhaps not too surprising that France had played New Zealand (once), England (four times), Ireland (once) and Wales (three times) before the SRU deemed them worthy opponents.

The big shock

The first meeting between Scotland and France occurred in January 1910 in Inverleith and the home side trotted comfortably to a 27–0 win. France were beaten in every match of that season, losing to Wales (49–14), England (11–3) and Ireland (8–3). When they came to face Scotland in the first game of the 1911 Five Nations, France had lost all 12 of their international matches since their debut in 1905. For most of these matches they had been battered from pillar to post and had played with a loose, ragged, some would even have said a 'devil-may-care' approach.

In contrast to the French, Scotland, along with Wales, had been the dominant team in the Home Championship at the start of the 20th century. They had won the title in 1901, 1903, 1904, and 1907. The team was entering a decline by 1911, but no one seriously expected them to struggle when they travelled to Paris to play at Stade Colombes on 2 January, 1911. The Scottish selectors named six new caps in a side led by fly-half Patrick Munro of London Scottish. In later life he would serve as president of the SRU and as a Conservative Member of Parliament for Llandaff and Barry.

Any excuses about fielding an inexperienced side that may have been put forward for the defeat that was to come could be countered with the fact the home side were fielding seven new caps. The French were led by lock Marcel Communeau of Stade Francais (pictured at the start of this chapter).

Scotland entered the field of play accompanied by a piper in Highland dress. France joined them a few minutes later, but with one player missing. *The Times* writes of a home player arriving late and not making the start of the match, but fails to report who exactly was missing in early action.

The early stages of the contest went according to script, with France having more work in defence than they did in attack. Early on, Scottish forward John MacCallum bagged a try which went unconverted, putting the visitors 3–0 up. The French didn't cave in as they may have been expected too by those who had seen them crumble in the previous fixture between the sides. Not only that, their three-quarter play was sharp and exciting and they were causing the favourites plenty of problems. Soon an intelligent attack ended in a try for French scrum-half Guillaume Laterrade which was converted by forward Paul Decamps. 5–3 to France.

This was no blip either. France kept coming at the shocked visitors with wave after wave of attack; all excellently marshalled by Laterrade and debutant fly-half Georges Peyroutou. The pressure again told and debutant winger Pierre Failliot scored his side's second try, although this went unconverted. Failliot, at 1.82m (6ft) and 88.9kg (14st) was a huge man for the period. He also possessed serious pace and had been French champion over 100m, 200m and 400m distances. Rounding off a remarkable half for France, Latterrade bagged a try of his own before the interval. Again, Decamps missed the extras.

Scotland rallied before the break, getting a try through captain Munro and adding the extras through the boot of forward Freddie Turner (both sides employed a forward as place kicker).

It meant Scotland were 11–8 down at the halfway stage. The Scottish piper who had led the side out returned to entertain the crowd as the players took a breather. Perhaps inspired by the sounds of home, Scotland started the second half strongly and it took some firm and smart defending by France to keep them out. Full-back Julien Combe and winger Gaston Lane were singled out for praise, in particular, for their efforts in keeping the French line intact. Unable to cross for a score, Scotland had to settle for a drop goal from winger Jimmy Pearson. Drop goals were worth four points back then and a try just three, so this was no bad return. It also meant Munro's men were in the lead again (12–11).

The French almost immediately struck back as the magnificent athlete that was Failliot got his second score and this time Decamps added the crucial extra points. Now it was 16–12 to the home side. Desperate to avoid a humiliating defeat, Scotland attacked with all they could muster and the latter part of the game was described as 'very fast, though perhaps less brilliant than the earlier stages'.

Then, Scotland almost did it. A try came from forward Cecil Abercrombie and a victory would have been possible if the conversion had been added by Turner. It wasn't. The French held on to claim a famous victory as they brought down one of the founding teams of the international game.

The Times reacted to the match as follows: 'The result was greeted with wild enthusiasm by the spectators, who, in spite of unfavourable weather, numbered about 10,000. The match is said to have been the finest ever seen in France.'

In his wonderful *Phoenix Book of International Rugby Records*, rugby historian John Griffiths wrote: 'The French backs were the architects of a fine win . . . Many observers noted that for [the] first time France played with a collective purpose, abandoning the happy-go-lucky approach which had characterised their early international performances.'

The loss signalled the start of a tough period for Scotland, who lost the remainder of their games that season. They had some revenge the following year when they dismantled France 31–3 in Inverleith.

France may have tasted glory, but it was to be the last time for a while. It was to be nine years and 19 games before they won again, beating Ireland in Dublin 15–7. They would not win the Five Nations outright until 1959 (although they were exiled for the period 1932-1939).

The results of their grim early years often make for surprising reading to modern fans and among the multiple stories of defeat sits a valuable lesson in how long it can take a 'second-tier' international team to adjust to a new level of competition. Who, now, can imagine the game of rugby without the magnificent French?

MATCH DETAILS
France: Julien Combe (Stade Francais); Pierre Failliot* (Racing Club), Marcel Burgun (Racing Club), Andre Franquenelle* (Vaugirard), Gaston Lane (Racing Club); Georges Peyroutou* (Club Athletique Perigueux), Guillaume Laterrade (Tarbes); Paul Mauriat (FC Lyon), Joseph Bavozet* (FC Lyon), Pierre Guillemin (Racing Club), Fernand Forgues* (Bayonne), Marcel Communeau (captain) (Stade Francais), Paul Decamps* (Racing Club), Pierre Mouniq* (Toulouse), Marcel Legrain (Stade Francais).
Tries: Failliot (2), Latterrade, Peyroutou
Conversions: Decamps (2)

Scotland: Borth Tod* (Gala); Walter Sutherland (Hawick), Fletcher Buchanan (Kelvinside Academicals), Thomas Young* (Durham), Jimmy Pearson (Watsonians); Patrick Munro (captain) (London Scottish), Frank Osler* (Edinburgh University); Robert Stevenson (St. Andrew's University), Freddie Turner* (Oxford University), Rowland Fraser* (Cambridge University), Cecil Abercrombie (United Services Portsmouth), Alexander Stevenson* (Glasgow University), John Scott (Edinburgh Academical FC), Alexander Moodie (St. Andrew's University), John MacCallum (Watsonians).

*Denotes first cap.

Tries: Abercrombie, MacCallum, Munro
Conversion: Turner
Drop goal: Pearson

ERROL TOBIAS

*'I [needed] to play to show white people that not only am
I good enough, but that other people of colour are good
enough and maybe even better than you are at this game if
you give them a proper chance. I wanted to prove to the
world that South Africa had talented coloured players.'*
Errol Tobias

**Errol Tobias made history as the first non-white player to
represent the Springboks. An immense talent, he refused
to allow the system and people that worked against him to
break him.**

Main teams: Boland, Caledonians RFC, Proteas (South African
Rugby Football Federation), South African Barbarians, South
Africa
Position: Fly-half, centre
International caps: 6 (1981-84)
Points: 22 (1 try, 4 penalties, 3 conversions)

Errol George Tobias was born in 1950 in Caledon, South Africa.
He grew up under apartheid, a system of racial segregation that
operated in the country at the time. As a black rugby player he
seemed doomed, like countless thousands of people of colour
before him, to be denied the opportunity to play at the highest

level of the game in his native land. Yet, in spite of the seemingly insurmountable hurdles he faced, he overcame incredible odds and prejudice to succeed and earn a special place in rugby and sporting history.

The All Whites

Apartheid, which means 'apartness' in Afrikaans the 'white language' of South Africa, took root in the late 1940s. It divided the people of the nation into four distinct racial groups: white, black, coloured (people of mixed descent) and Asian. The group a person was in determined where they could live, what work they could do and what schools they could attend.

The white government actively discriminated against non-white groups and created conditions which helped whites prosper and live well, while all the other groups faced severe restrictions, limited opportunity and enjoyed fewer basic rights. Black people were forced to live in designated areas of the country called 'homelands' and they were not allowed to travel in 'white' areas without special paperwork and identification. Black people weren't even allowed to vote. Non-whites could face punishment or even jail for using the wrong public bathroom or trying to eat in a white-only restaurant.

As a result of apartheid, many countries, including the United States and Great Britain, limited their interaction and trade with South Africa in an attempt to persuade the South African government to change its racial policies. Eventually, over many decades, several other countries joined this boycott either through trade sanctions, or by limiting interaction and engagement through sport and culture. The impact on international sport was significant, with South Africa not being part of the Olympics between 1964 and 1988.

For all the talk of 'rugby values' by those who love the sport, rugby was rarely on the right side of history during apartheid. Teams from around the rugby world regularly toured South

Africa during the apartheid era, often leaving their own non-white players at home to keep their hosts happy. Similarly, the Springboks frequently travelled overseas. Many of these tours saw huge protests and violent incidents as citizens (and sometimes even those in the rugby community) tried to prevent the Boks playing or tried to raise awareness of the racial injustices in South Africa. As far back as 1906, while touring Europe, South Africa appear to have pressured England into not selecting Jimmy Peters, England's first black player (see his profile on page 85).

Before the 1990s, rugby was seen by outsiders as a white man's sport in South Africa. Political institutions and the sport's main governing body, the South African Rugby Union, had no desire to allow non-whites to play for the national team. Yet, inside South Africa it wasn't just a white man's game, even if the main power brokers and national side were exclusively white. White and non-white players traditionally played rugby, but did so in different competitions. In a 2022 article, *The Economist* explained: 'that rugby had already [been] played for generations in black and mixed-race communities. In fact, rugby was not a white sport belatedly embraced by non-whites, but a sport enjoyed by all races – only separately.

'[Non-white players] wanted to show that they were as good, if not better, than Afrikaners; at the same time, for political reasons, they supported South Africa's sporting opponents.'

It was into this complex and often cruel world that Errol Tobias was born and it was the world he would have to continually rally against.

Good enough, but not the right colour

Tobias followed in his father's footsteps by picking up an oval ball. The sport was all around Tobias growing up and he was a natural. At the time, whites, blacks and coloureds played under three different organising bodies. There was the South African Rugby Board (SARB) for whites, the South African Rugby

Federation (SARF) for coloureds and the South African Rugby Association (SARA) for blacks.

Tobias's father would take the youngster to Newlands in Cape Town to see the likes of the British Lions and the All Blacks when they came to visit and he idolised players like winger Jannie Englebrecht (South Africa), Cliff Morgan (Wales) and Mike Gibson (Ireland) (see page 121).

As a 12-year-old, Tobias, who was already a skilful player known for exceptional handling skills, walked past a rugby session with young white boys practising. He overheard the coach admonish one player for dropping the ball, saying: 'You will never become a Springbok if you cannot catch the ball properly.'

As he almost never dropped the ball himself, Tobias thought this meant he could become a Springbok, until his mother told him the colour of his skin would stop him achieving his dream. Nonetheless, he became fanatical about being able to handle and catch a ball well and blossomed into an exciting fly-half who blended speed with power, and could also control a game intelligently and create space both for himself and his outside backs.

Global experience

That Tobias was of international class was of little doubt to those who knew their rugby and had seen him play. In 1971, Tobias was selected to play for the Proteas team, a side representing SARF. They were the first coloured rugby side from South Africa to tour internationally, playing six fixtures in England against mainly county teams. He continued to represent the team in the coming years. Highlights included facing a touring England in 1972, in which Tobias scored all the Proteas points as they lost narrowly by 11–6, and playing against the 1974 British Lions. His side lost 37–6, but he again bagged all his team's points.

Tobias would later represent the multi-racial South African Barbarians both abroad and in the UK and played with them against the 1980 British Lions.

His appearances in these international tours and fixtures helped earn him an international reputation as a fine, creative player. It also led to many putting forward the case that he was good enough to represent South Africa. Around this time Danie Craven, a former international and key figure in the administration of rugby in South Africa, said that if a player of colour was good enough to represent the Springboks, he would be selected. Many doubted the truth of this statement and others saw it as cynical tokenism, designed to placate those who demanded full integration or the continued isolation of South African sport.

However, some believed that despite what Craven proclaimed in public, he uttered different things in private. Former England international Derek Wyatt has stated he was told by Craven in 1980 that: 'Black players should stick to soccer; that's their game. We don't want black players in our game.'

By the early 1980s, Tobias was getting offers to play in Europe from clubs in Wales and France. It must have been incredibly tempting to go and live abroad where he would have been able to live a life on equal terms to his fellow teammates. But Tobias wanted to stay and fight. Not just for himself, but for others like him. He knew he was good enough to wear the green and gold of his country and, having stayed for so long and battled so hard, he didn't want to give up as his playing career drew to a close.

A nation finally calls
In 1980 South Africa, whose options for touring were severely limited, decided to head to South America to play six matches in Paraguay, Uruguay and Chile. They would have preferred to play in Argentina, but the Argentine government had refused to sanction such a visit due to their opposition to apartheid. Instead, the Springboks arranged a six-match tour which included two games against the South American Jaguars, which was effectively Argentina in disguise.

By now 30 years old, Tobias's call-up made international news and, combined with the unusual circumstances of the tour, seemed a somewhat surreal event. One UK newspaper wrote: 'The tour has been arranged quietly in a bid to avoid possible protests abroad against South Africa's apartheid policies. The dates and venues of the matches have not been officially announced . . . Tobias, a fast-running player, had been on the verge of full Springbok honours after excellent performances during the British Lions tour of South Africa earlier this year. His selection was widely predicted and was seen as an effort by rugby authorities to show that South Africa's national game was moving towards full racial integration at all levels.'

Tobias played in three non-cap games on the tour, facing Paraguay, British Schools Old Boys and Chile. He scored a try against the British Schools and kicked ten conversions against Chile (a game often not listed in tour records). All three matches were won and Tobias had defied the odds and racist opposition to wear the Springbok shirt. However, the fact he didn't feature in the Test matches (the Boks preferred the dull, but steady play of Naas Botha at fly-half), led to suspicions that his selection, while no doubt worthy in terms of sheer rugby ability, may have been a PR effort to show South African rugby was changing. When Tobias was not selected for the subsequent match against France in Pretoria, it seemed to indicate his 'chance' of winning a cap was gone.

The cap fits

In 1981, Ireland undertook a controversial tour of South Africa. There was plenty of opposition to the tour with several protests taking place in Dublin to try and stop it going ahead. A newspaper poll in the *Irish Times* found just 32 per cent of Irish people were in favour of the trip and even the Irish taoiseach (prime minister) asked the Irish Rugby Football Union (IRFU) to cancel the trip on ethical grounds. Shortly after the IRFU confirmed the tour would go ahead, a school match in Pretoria was called off because a visiting touring side had two black players in their line-up. It didn't change the IRFU's attitude.

Ahead of the tour, the South African Council on Sport said: 'You cannot have normal sport in a racial society. Because of poor education, nutritional standards, abysmal coaching and training facilities, it was much more difficult for blacks to excel at sport than whites. Even when blacks do reach a level where they can play alongside white sportsmen, the scope for off-field contact was severely limited by a maze of race laws . . .'

Despite the political tension, Ireland travelled to face the Boks in a two-match series. And it was here the historic call-up finally came for Tobias. He was picked at centre, instead of in his usual fly-half position. The ten shirt was, of course, occupied by the seemingly immovable Botha.

The decision was, unsurprisingly, controversial. Some praised it as a sign of progress in race relations, others as a cynical attempt by the Springboks to show they had modernised so that the sporting world would again open up to them.

Tobias was 31 years old when he finally got to wear the Springbok shirt in a Test. Making things even more challenging was the fact the concept of him pulling on the green and gold didn't just anger white racists, it also upset many people of colour who thought he should refuse to play for the team. However, he felt that if he didn't grab the opportunity he had been offered, the Springboks would remain a white-only team for a long time. He later told the *Irish Times* that: 'I [needed] to play to show white people that not only am I good enough, but that other people of colour are good enough and maybe even better than you are at this game if you give them a proper chance. I wanted to prove to the world that South Africa had talented coloured players.'

It's hard to imagine what must have been going through Tobias's head on 30 May, 1981, when he sat in the dressing room in Cape Town's Newlands Stadium. All players making their debut for their country have to deal with the pressure of entering the Test arena for the first time. And all players, even experienced ones, have to cope with the self-doubt and nerves that come before running out in front of thousands of fans and millions of television viewers to engage in a physical, brutal and unforgiving sport. But on top of all these things, Tobias shouldered the burden of effectively representing millions of people of colour. He was doing something countless non-white people before him had not been allowed to do. He couldn't help but feel the weight of their hopes and dreams on his shoulders. Even worse, there would have been millions of his own countrymen willing him to fail – perhaps even members of his own team and national union.

Tobias has since revealed that his teammates may not have been rude to him, but could often be stand-offish when they were not on the field. It meant his debut preparations would be even lonelier than for any other player.

As his team were at home to the green shirts of Ireland that day, he had to wear the alternate Springbok shirt for the match. It was, ironically, white. He later remembered that a friend said: 'The white jersey is perfect, Errol, you will stick out, and you will show the Afrikaners just how good you are.'

Tobias seized his chance with an excellent display that ended any doubt his selection wasn't fully justified on playing terms. One notable highlight was his contribution to a try from back row forward Rob Louw. Taking the ball from fellow centre Danie Gerber in the middle of the field just one metre inside the Irish half, Tobias unsettled and unbalanced Irish centre Ollie Campbell with an inside and outside swerve, followed by a hand off. Three Irish defenders collided in bringing Tobias down, but not before he was able to offload a sweet ball to winger Edrich Krantz. Smart combination play followed between Krantz and flanker Theuns Stofberg and the move ended with Louw crashing over. It was a crucial score in a 23–15 win.

'Errol, Errol. Errol!'

If Tobias playing for the Springboks at the time wasn't extraordinary enough, what happened after the match was another example of the potential for change in the country.

When the debutant got back to the changing rooms he was welcomed by the jubilant sound of his Afrikaner teammates chanting: 'Errol, Errol, Errol!'. His performance on the pitch had proven to all he was good enough to wear national colours. Tobias didn't know it at the time, but his excellent performance for South Africa even inspired a man who would go on to change South African history. Political prisoner and future president Nelson Mandela was overjoyed at Tobias's exploits, feeling it would help show that by working together the nation could become a better place.

Tobias retained his place for the second Test against Ireland a week later in Durban, which South Africa won 12–10.

Garden training

Tobias was a committed trainer who wasn't averse to inventing some unusual methods to improve his game. When he was selected to tour with the Boks to New Zealand in 1981, he decided he needed to get fit for the wet, swampy fields of the Land of the Long White Cloud. First, he ripped up the flowers and plants in his garden, leaving only turf. Then he watered the grass heavily every single day to turn it into a quagmire. By running around his soaking and sticky garden, Tobias felt he was giving himself the stamina needed to succeed on tour.

As an amateur player, his training had to be fitted in around a full-time job. During his time with the Boks he worked as a brick layer and his working day would often start at 5am and last at least 12 hours. He trained for three hours each day too, making it incredibly tough to spend time with his wife and daughter. His brother, who had been a prop, even gave up playing to run more aspects of the family business so that Tobias had more time to focus on his game. To top off the family support, the Springbok got diet advice from his sister who worked as a nurse. Drinking and smoking were not part of his fitness regime. He told *The Times* in 1981 that: 'From my childhood all I have done is play rugby. To become a Springbok you must train because only the fittest survive.'

The ability of Tobias as a rugby player created strange situations. After he had proved himself good enough to wear national colours, he would find himself being accepted by white people who were still openly racist against other non-whites. Tobias was once served in a restaurant by an owner who recognised him as a Springbok. As he was waiting to eat, Tobias saw, to his horror, the same owner refusing another man service because he was black. Rightly upset, Tobias paid his bill and left without eating. The owner would later call up Tobias to offer him a complimentary meal as an apology and also said that from that point on he would serve people whatever their skin colour.

A lasting legacy
In total, Tobias won six caps and made nine non-Test appearances for the Boks. The caps came in pairs against Ireland, England and South America. Tobias played in his favoured position of fly-half against England and South America in 1984 and racked up 22 points in these games through a try, four penalties and three conversions. The 35–9 second Test win over England at a packed Ellis Park was, at the time, the worst defeat England had ever suffered.

He dedicated his international try against England to three black boys he had seen on the way to the stadium. On the team bus before the match, Tobias had witnessed the boys going through rubbish bins trying to find a bite to eat. It was a stark reminder of the division of wealth and opportunity in South Africa. The Springbok side that faced off against England in 1984 also featured winger Avril Williams, the second black player to win Test honours for South Africa. Williams's nephew, Chester Williams, would win fame as the only non-white player in the 1995 World Cup-winning side.

After his masterful performances against South America, one Afrikaner fan even said he would allow Tobias to marry his daughter. Hugo Porta, the great Argentine fly-half who lined up for South America in that Test series, said that he thought Tobias was the best outside-half in the world and did not grasp why Naas Botha was usually selected ahead of him.

Despite his success on the rugby field, until apartheid was brought crashing down, Tobias would still have to live under the oppressive restrictions faced by his fellow blacks.

In 1990 apartheid finally ended in South Africa and Nelson Mandela became the nation's first black president. The changes in society allowed South Africa to come back into the sporting fold. In 1995 they even hosted the Rugby World Cup and won it at the first attempt, with Mandela famously joining in the celebrations in a Springbok jersey.

Tobias would later work as a rugby commentator and pundit and also became the first black mayor of Caledon, his home town.

After his retirement from the sport, Tobias said: 'It was everything to me to represent my country, despite tremendous political pressure from certain circles. I knew I was opening doors for others.'

He admitted to shedding tears when in 2019 Siya Kolisi, South Africa's first black captain (see page 207) lifted the World Cup: 'I never thought I would live to see it. The tears flowed from my eyes, the same as the day when I was selected for the Springboks.'

GIANT KILLERS
ROMANIA (1980S)

'It is a country in the shadow of Russia, seeking to improve its lot under a system that we may not favour, but as Welshmen seeking to play all countries, we judge the players only as they behave on and off the field. In this they have been immaculate and whatever happens today, one would like them to come again to Wales.'
J.B.G Thomas, 6 October, 1979

Frozen out by the rugby community for decades, Romania were once a fearsome force in the game and arguably should have been invited to join the Five Nations in the 1980s.

Anyone whose memory of international rugby stretches fewer than 30 years will likely consider the Romanian national team as bit-part players on the Test scene. A side that will likely make few ripples worthy of notice in the pool stages of any World Cup. Unless, perhaps, you consider conceding record scores in pool matches something worthy of note.

Yet for several decades it seemed very possible that Romania would be capable of joining the rugby elite. Perhaps, if the rugby community had shown a few more of the open and welcoming values it likes to always speak of, it could have had a period when the bright yellow and blue of the Romanian shirts dined and dined well at the top table.

A short history of rugby's unwanted cousin
Rugby came to the country via Romanian students discovering
the game in France and bringing it back to their homeland. The
first match on Romanian soil took place in 1913 and every single
player involved was a native. This was unusual as more often than
not, rugby was introduced to fresh lands with a hefty portion of
oversea 'missionaries' involved both on and off the field.

By 1914 a national championship was taking place and just
five years later Romania made their entrance onto the Test stage
with a match against the USA. The Oaks, as they would come to
be known (their emblem is an oak leaf and symbolises force and
endurance), lost their debut 21–0.

Romania took part in the bizarre rugby tournament that
occurred during the 1924 Olympics in which the only other
teams were France and eventual winners USA. The East
Europeans lost both games, but can perhaps be forgiven for that
after travelling by train for four days to Paris in a third-class
compartment.

As is so often the case when it comes to rugby's gospel being
spread, the French can take more credit for going forth and
preaching the game than the Home Unions and the three major
Southern Hemisphere powers. When France were accused
of breaching amateur principles by the Home Unions in the
1930s and were expelled from the Five Nations, they forged
stronger links with countries like Romania, Germany and Italy.
In 1934, France joined Belgium, Catalonia, Czechoslovakia,
Germany, Italy, Romania, Netherlands, and Sweden to form
the Fédération Internationale de Rugby Amateur (FIRA). To
help rugby in Romania grow, France even sent coaches to assist
in developing their domestic game. These ties still bear fruit for
French rugby today.

In 1953, the Romanian Rugby Federation asked the
International Rugby Board (today's World Rugby) about
membership. They were refused. Historian Huw Richards notes

the IRB had a 'go-slow' policy when it came to its member unions organising 'foreign fixtures'. The IRB held strong suspicions that amateur principles were not always being followed behind the Iron Curtain, where the now Communist Romania dwelled as a Soviet satellite state after having been occupied by the Soviet Union between 1944 and 1956.

Nonetheless, British teams like Swansea and Harlequins visited during the 1940s. The Romanians earned a reputation as brutally strong up front and fanatical adherents of the ten-man, forward-oriented style of play. The tactics didn't win many plaudits, but were enough for them to claim their first win over France in 1960 with an 11–5 triumph in Bucharest. Romania would win one and draw two of the next three fixtures as well. As of 2023, the sides have met 42 times with the Oaks winning eight of the clashes and drawing two. In 1966, Australia were refused permission by the IRB to accept an invitation to tour Romania.

Despite the sporting and political isolation, by the late 1970s Romania – now under the rule of the cruel dictator Nicolae Ceaușescu – were a serious force to be reckoned with on the rare occasions they were permitted to play the big boys of the IRB. They drew their national squads mainly from military and police sides, where the players essentially worked as full-time athletes in violation of the amateur code of the time.

In 1979 the Romanians travelled to Cardiff Arms Park to meet the great Wales team at the tail end of its golden era. No caps were awarded by Wales, with the WRU following IRB policy on the matter. Romania took their illustrious hosts right to the wire, going down just 13–12 to a Wales team with names like Ray Gravell, Steve Fenwick, Terry Holmes, Robert Norster, Graham Price and Derek Quinnell. It took a late drop goal from Gareth Davies to save Welsh blushes.

The *Rothmans Rugby Yearbook* wrote: 'The Romanians achieved what they had set out to do – to prove that they are now capable of challenging any of the four home countries, just as they do France . . . the team was extremely fit, as well as physically well-equipped; but there was a lack of imagination and flair behind the scrum.'

In 1980, Romania crushed France 15–0 in Bucharest. The visitors' line-up contained the great full-back Serge Blanco and the French were good enough to recover by winning their third ever Grand Slam in the subsequent Five Nations. Also in 1980, Romania held an Irish XV to a 13–13 draw in Dublin (the IRFU and IRB would still not award caps).

Even the mighty New Zealand were rattled by the Romanians. In October 1981, the All Blacks grafted to a 14–6 win in Bucharest, with Romania being unlucky to have a key try disallowed that could have made things very scary for the famous tourists. The following year, France again fell in Bucharest, going down 13–9. Romania had clearly arrived as a major power in the world of rugby union. In the coming years they would defeat or scare several of the old guard.

1983 – Romania 24 Wales 6 (23 August Stadium/Dinamo Stadion, Bucharest)

In 1981, the IRB had granted official permission for major nations to award caps against Romania. Wales became the first of the Home Unions to bestow the 'honour' on the so-called minnows from behind the Iron Curtain as they travelled to Bucharest. Romania were coming off a six-game winning streak, but the most recent of those victories had been an unimpressive 31–0 over East European rivals Poland. The Oaks failed to score in the final quarter of the match and the selectors held a trial match to settle on their line-up and get players in condition. The visit of Wales was considered the biggest moment in their nation's rugby history.

Wales, captained by the late broadcasting legend Eddie Butler, arrived with a risky selection that included six new caps. Among them were Bleddyn Bowen, future Triple Crown captain and Mark Brown, the first black player to be capped by Wales. Critics expressed concern that Wales lacked a middle-line-out jumper or a specialist blindside and Wales coach John Bevan found himself facing plenty of negative media sentiment ahead of the clash. The press made much of the fact the home pack would have two players at 6ft 5in and one at 6ft 7in, huge for the time. Adding to the concerns, Wales had won just one away clash in four years, a 1983 victory over Scotland at Murrayfield.

The critics were right to be worried. The Romanians featured six of the pack that had taken a star-studded Wales XV to the wire in Cardiff in 1979 and they gave Wales a torrid afternoon this time around too. The giant local forwards took Wales apart. Steve Bale, writing in the *Western Mail*, lambasted the visiting team: 'Wales were made to pay a penalty as severe as anything they could possibly have imagined for their desperate lack of forward strength in Saturday's shattering defeat . . . Wales simply did not have men on the field . . . equipped to cope with the physical presence and superb athleticism of the Romanian forwards.'

Romania banked tries from winger Marian Aldea, lock Gheorghie Caragea, centre Adrian Lungu and flanker Florica Murariu, with fly-half Dumituru Alexandru kicking a conversion and two penalties.

Years later, Eddie Butler, speaking to me about this game, said: '[I] always felt that if we could win some ball and go as wide as the pitch allowed we'd be ok. But it never happened. They were diabolically good up front.' He added that the Welsh dressing room afterwards was 'as black as Bucharest could be at that time. That's black.'

1984 – Romania 28 Scotland 22 (Stadionul National 2, Bucharest)

Scotland arrived in Bucharest fresh off a Grand Slam in the Five Nations. They had also held New Zealand to a 25–25 draw the previous season, which to date is equal to their best-ever result against the All Blacks (they drew in 1964 too).

Romania had 11 survivors from the Welsh win of just six months previous. Scotland held no fear for the Oaks, who had pushed them hard in a 12–6 loss at Murrayfield in 1981. The Celts travelled with key players Iain Milne, Iain Paxton, Colin Deans, Jim Calder and Roger Baird unavailable, but still put out a more than capable XV.

On a hot day in front of 20,000 home supporters, the Five Nations champions led 16–9 at the halfway stage thanks to tries from flanker David Leslie and full-back Peter Dods. Romania answered with a try of their own from Gheorghie Dumitru.

The second 40 minutes was a different story though. *The Times* reported how: 'In the second half the bigger Romanian pack took over as the Scots wilted in the heat.' The Oak pack starved the visitors of the ball and slowly, but surely, ground down the Grand Slam champions. The key moment came nine minutes from time, when a high kick caused chaos in the visitors' defence. Some reports indicate that Dods may have been taken out ahead of playing the ball. Whatever happened, number eight Alexandru Radulescu gained possession and 'beat off clawing tackles to barge over for Romania's third try'. A final penalty kick in injury time from fly-half Dumitru Alexandru sealed Scotland's coffin firmly shut. Another scalp had been taken.

1985 – England 22 Romania 15 (Twickenham, London)

England great Rob Andrew celebrated his first cap by racking up 18 points from four penalties and two drop goals (the first kicked after a mere 45 seconds) as Romania took England close in their first Test clash. *The Times* wrote that England 'encountered opposition intent only on defence and spoiling'. Romania failed to cross the English line, having to settle for five Alexandru penalties.

1988 – Wales 9 Romania 15 (Cardiff Arms Park, Cardiff)

Of all Romania's glorious wins, this is the most celebrated, coming as it did on foreign soil and on the hallowed turf of what is still considered perhaps rugby's greatest cathedral: Cardiff Arms Park. While Wales were in a slump after a brutally embarrassing tour of New Zealand that summer, they were still joint Five Nations champions with France after winning the Triple Crown the previous season. They had also finished third in the 1987 World Cup.

It's a sad indictment of the nation's rugby supporters that just over 19,000 attended the match. Despite cheap tickets and the fact Wales played as few as three or four home games a season at this time, traditionalists scoffed at it being a minor nation and fans failed to turn up in decent numbers. Yet, as this chapter has shown, Romania had taken plenty of serious scalps and had a fantastic record against Wales. Even the match programme for the game discounted the caps that Romanian players had won against non-IRB teams, making them an inaccurate source of information for anyone keen to learn more of the rugby world.

Romania's hooker for the 1988 clash was Gheorghe Ion of Dinamo Bucharest. Speaking for this book in 2022, Ion gave some fascinating insights into just how well-prepared the Oaks were and why, in retrospect, the win isn't perhaps the shock it has always been portrayed as. 'I knew a lot about Wales and did a lot of research,' says Ion. 'Our management gave us a report on the strong and weak points of the team and details on our opposite numbers.'

Packing down directly opposite Ion that day was Ian Watkins, then of Ebbw Vale. He recalls that the Welsh players had a totally different preparation to the Oaks. 'We weren't given anything at all on the Romanian team," he admitted. "I can't remember even seeing footage of them playing.'

If Romania's preparation for the game seems incredibly professional for the amateur era, that's because it was. A significant portion of Romania's top players were in the military or police and essentially state-supported athletes. Ion explains how Dinamo Bucharest were the 'police team' and he and his fellow players were full-time when it came to rugby, only working if they were injured. 'It wasn't until I retired at 36 that I started to actually work on the streets as a police officer.'

This meant that they had serious time to work on their fitness. It's fair to say their training programmes involved far more weight training, for instance, than what would have been the norm for players in the Home Unions at the time.

'I was crazy about weights,' recalls Ion. 'I wanted to feel strong. It was like a tradition that I would have a sauna and weight session before the game. I would spend time with the team in the morning, but also find time to be on my own and do weights and have a sauna.'

Ion's personal regime also included extra time after training every day, throwing around 500 balls through a target to ensure his line-out throwing was as accurate as possible.

In contrast, Watkins explains how the Wales team and WRU approached the game: 'The WRU had a dyed-in-the wool amateur ethos. We had to work and train in our free time. I was a dedicated trainer and would follow fitness programmes and would even do weights on a Sunday after playing for Ebbw Vale the day before. But at this point we were only just starting to introduce more formal training programmes with the national team.'

The match

On a grey December day in Cardiff, Romania were led into the history books by experienced flanker Florica Murariu. And, as in 1983, the Welsh pack could not get into any kind of rhythm and Wales's backs, including the legendary Jonathan Davies, were starved of any decent ball to work with. The Dragons couldn't even argue they didn't get the rub of the green, with Wales being awarded 18 penalties to just six for Romania.

'What struck me was their efficiency.' recalled Watkins. 'That can only come from continual training and preparation. They were fit and technically very good, like a rugby machine.'

The Oaks did not come to play with flair. Fly-half Gelu Ignat kicked so often, so long and so well it still gives Welsh fans of a certain age nightmares. Romania's solitary try was set up by a monster kick from the number ten that started 15 metres in from the left touchline near the Romanian ten-metre line and ended up in touch 15 metres from the Welsh touchline on the right wing. From the subsequent line-out, Romania stole possession with a tap down from the throw in. As the ball bounced, scrum-half Daniel Neaga gathered at pace, drew Welsh flanker David Bryant, before slipping an inside ball to his openside flanker, a charging Alexandru Radulescu. The Romanian pack arrived in numbers to drive him to within metres of the line. Captain Murariu dug it out of the ruck, spun to his left and was only stopped inches from the line. Ion, in a wonderful show of athleticism, body position, timing and handling, somehow collected the ball at his toes and drove through the final defenders to score arguably his country's most important try.

Wales went in trailing by 9–3, with replacement wing Paul Thorburn kicking a penalty for Wales and Ignat slotting a conversion and penalty.

The only Welsh try came from centre Jonathan Devereux in the second-half and it briefly brought Wales level. But Ignat was having the day of his life with the boot and he seized the limited opportunities he had to shoot at goal by putting over two penalties to place the game beyond Wales.

Romania celebrated long into the night, despite the presence of secret police monitoring their activities and ensuring there were no defections. Try hero Ion even got caught by one of the Romanian security men afterwards as he was 'entertaining' a Welsh lady in a small room.

The result meant Romania led by two wins to zero in matches between the nations. In the traumatic fallout, Wales captain Jonathan Davies, stung by the post-match criticism, signed to play rugby league and one of the darkest periods of Welsh rugby history had truly begun. Ray Williams, Wales's chairman of selectors, heaped further embarrassment on the WRU and Welsh rugby by churlishly blasting the style of the visitor's ten-man approach and claiming that his side had played all the rugby.

'They deserved their win,' said Watkins when he looked back decades later.

Romania returned home as heroes. 'We were invited everywhere,' reflects Ion. 'It is still talked about today. But now it is impossible for us to beat Wales.'

More enlightened folks in the rugby community saw potential in inviting the Romanians into the Five Nations. Their claim was certainly valid. It was ignored.

The revolution brings down communism . . . and rugby

Just over a year after the famous win, revolution swept across the Eastern Bloc and the cruel reign of Ceaușescu came to a bloody end with the dictator and his wife executed. Among the many that died (estimates vary between 689 to 1,290 people), was the captain of that famous win in Cardiff: Florica Murariu. Five other Test players lost their lives too.

Without the state support it had previously enjoyed, rugby went into freefall. Economic conditions and the drastic political and social change that followed the end of communist rule upended the country and rugby was far from a priority. There was simply no longer the funds or infrastructure to support it. There was one final high, though. One final swansong of Romanian rugby as a serious international force: Romania's eighth win against France. It came in 1990 and was the first on French soil, a 12–6 victory in Auch. Once again, Ignat's boot was key, with the deadly marksman kicking three penalties and a drop goal.

Ion was hooker again that day. 'The French were very tough, but dirty. I played them eight times and almost lost an eye once against them. When you play against France they think they are the best and they are very arrogant. I was very happy to beat them and to do so in France was very special. I finished the game with a cut on both eyebrows and a broken nose.'

Outside of a win over Fiji in the 1991 World Cup, the only results most rugby fans will know the modern Romanian team for are record defeats. England's 134–0 win over the Oaks at Twickenham is the darkest of the many grim hours that have passed on rugby fields the world over since. By 2003 playing numbers had dropped from 12,000 to a paltry 4,000. The best players these days tend to ply their trade in France, rather than in the low-quality domestic scene.

In 2003, former Oaks captain Alin Petreache summed up the state of rugby in Romania: 'When the rest of the rugby world was amateur, we were professional, now rugby is professional we are completely amateur.'

The Romanian team that won at Cardiff Arms Park, 12 December, 1988

Marcel Toader (Dinamo Bucharest); Nicolae Racean (University Timisoara), Nicolae Fulina (Baia Mare), Adrian Lungu (Dinamo Bucharest), Daniel Boldor (Steaua Bucharest); Gelu Ignat (Steaua Bucharest), Daniel Neaga (Dinamo Bucharest); Gheorghe Leonte (Steaua Bucharest), Gheorghe Ion (Dinamo Bucharest), George Dumitrescu (Steaua Bucharest), Sandu Ciorascu (Steaua Bucharest), Haralambie Dumitras (Contactoare Buzau), Florica Murariu (captain) (Steaua Bucharest), Ioan Doja (Dinamo Bucharest), Alexandru Radulescu (Steaua Bucharest).
Replacements used: Traian Oroian (Steaua Bucharest).

SQUIDGE RUGBY

*'A desperate attempt to understand a sport
where not even the ball makes sense.'*
Squidge Rugby, YouTube channel description

**Robbie Owen and Will Owen of Squidge Rugby have helped
transform the way rugby is analysed and their insightful and
irreverent videos have even forced major broadcasters to up
their own game.**

'Teams': Squidge Rugby (YouTube), Long Eaton RFC,
Nottingham Corsairs RFC
YouTube debut: December, 2017
YouTube subscribers: 216,000*
Views: 34,234,040
*As of June 2023

Of all the 'major' global team sports, rugby has perhaps been the
slowest to adapt to change when it comes to evolving the format
of how it presents itself to its audience.

American football, baseball, cricket, football and basketball,
for instance, all handled the transition to the social media age far
quicker and more effectively than rugby union did. At the same
time that basketball's NBA league was encouraging fans to share
game content on social media – believing it keeps the game in the
spotlight and helps build interest, engagement and community

– rugby's main bodies were enthusiastically geo blocking content and restricting sharing of game footage by fans. Even posting a few seconds of action on a Twitter post can see users get reported by the likes of the Six Nations and World Rugby and accused users banned or suspended from the platform. Just as rugby resisted recognition of the game's growth among 'smaller' Test nations for as long as it could, so it seems to want to resist the new digital landscape that is reshaping the sport.

Rugby broadcasters and print media have also been largely complicit in gatekeeping the old ways of doing things. With few exceptions, television producers and print editors have lazily served up lowest-common denominator-type analysis. The mantra has effectively been: 'Keep things very simple. Cling to cliche. Treat the audience like they are incapable of understanding the finer details of the game. Repeat.'

Traditionally, qualification for being a pundit, especially on UK commercial channels like ITV, has been about no more than name recognition and nationality. Which is why Jonny Wilkinson and Clive Woodward can openly admit, while being paid a good wage, they don't know much about the players they are watching in the Six Nations as they don't follow domestic rugby. This would and could not happen in other sports. Analysis and punditry have moved on elsewhere.

Things are changing though. And like many sporting revolutions, the impetus comes from outsiders. Among those leading that charge at rugby's crumbling old media walls are Robbie Owen and Will Owen of Squidge Rugby.

Producing insightful, detailed, and suitably irreverent analysis on YouTube, the pair have helped push rugby forward and, in doing so, proved there is an audience for sophisticated, long-form strategic and tactical rugby content and that it's ok to do it with a bit of humour too.

Learning to love the game

Robbie and Will grew up in Nottingham, with a rugby mad Welsh father. Robbie, the senior of the siblings by 18 months, remembers how rugby was always on in the background and has an early memory of hearing some player in an interview describe himself as a 'lean, mean, rugby machine'. Despite the constant stream of rugby action into the living room and the sound of Radio Wales almost permanently on in the family car, neither brother took to the sport immediately.

In 2004, the pair had their first experience of international rugby when their parents took them out of school (citing a 'family emergency') so they could drive down to Cardiff to watch Wales play Japan on a Friday night. Here they saw a green and white clad Wales dismantle Japan 98–0, with Gavin Henson slotting 14 out of 14 conversions. In the following years the trip would be repeated, usually, Robbie says, for the 'cheap' game of the autumn. However, these trips didn't immediately make converts of them either.

The conversion was ultimately to be fuelled by the famous 2008 Wales win at Twickenham. Robbie explained his 'road to Damascus' moment in an interview for this book, saying: 'My mum wanted Will and I in the room for the England game because of how aggressive my dad had gotten during the Fiji game a few months before when Wales got knocked out of the World Cup. She thought if we were there he wouldn't react as badly.'

The pair witnessed Wales win at the home of England rugby for the first time in 20 years. 'It made me think that Wales were one of the best teams in the world,' says Will, who was 11 at the time.

'I remember then quietly asking him when the next game was,' added Robbie. 'But I also didn't want him to know I was getting into it. We ended up watching all the Wales games that Six Nations as Warren Gatland helped Wales win the Grand

Slam. My mum, Will and I even watched the French game alone as my dad was watching elsewhere, which is not something we would ever have ever done before.'

Soon the brothers were obsessively following both Wales and the Ospreys. As Welsh children in English schools, the annual clash between Wales and England always had a special edge. Not long after the Grand Slam, the brothers began playing the game too. Robbie played for three seasons and admits he wasn't the best player but still loved playing it.

'I was one of three kids on the team I joined that hadn't gone to a private school,' says Robbie. 'Lots of the other players had started when they were five and I was starting at age 13. So I was always somewhat of an outsider. I had never been around posh people either and had very different cultural references and experiences. I had certainly never been a rugby lad.

'So I had this weird outsider relationship with rugby and I did get a lot better and had a real burst of form. The team wasn't great and I had my best ever game towards the end of a season in which we had lost every game. It was the only game we won all year and I came off the bench and onto the wing and things just clicked. I had a try disallowed for a double movement, which to this day I swear was a try, but it filled me with confidence. I made some good tackles, which was rare, and then threw a perfect offload in one attack and also got a key interception to save the game at the death.'

Cruelly, Robbie's performance and development were not rewarded. In the last game of the season against the best team in the league, Robbie was not selected, despite all three regular back three players being unavailable.

'The coach picked a flanker on the wing instead of me. I was so upset and I felt that despite doing everything I could, I wasn't able to get into the worst U13 team in the midlands for a game we were never going to win anyway. I played a couple more seasons but never really got over it and then stopped.'

Will also had a rocky start to playing, initially finding it hard to get game time at his first club Nottingham Corsairs RFC. When the side he was in folded, he moved on to Long Eaton RFC, where he plays and coaches to this day.

'I love the place,' says Will. 'I usually play scrum-half with the seconds or, if we have a thirds team, I will captain them. I also coach under-15s and under-16s and have learnt so much about rugby from the coaches there, many of whom are former professionals.'

Stand-up, cinemas, and Sam Warburton

Squidge Rugby was the brainchild of a creatively frustrated Robbie. Rugby had really taken a hold on him and he clearly thought about it in a far deeper way than most young fans did.

'Something in rugby clicked in me when I was a kid in a way no other sport had,' he says. 'I think part of what I love about the game is that you can approach it in so many ways. There are simply thousands of ways to win a game and you can deploy such a wide range of tactics and ideas in doing so.

'Something that I feel is almost unique to rugby is the way in which everything that happens impacts the next play and connects to the next one. One of the big secrets about why rugby works is how hard it is to exit. There is always this continued pressure and sense of narrative where one thing impacts the next. Whereas in football, if a team misses a shot and it goes off the pitch, the goalkeeper just hits it upfield and you effectively reset the game, in rugby if you end up with a scrum five or are camped on the line, the defenders might only succeed in clearing the ball 15 metres. You have to find a way to get the pressure off.

'And a big part of me taking it seriously, is the level of emotional investment you can put into it. You know, for 80 minutes this is all I am going to care about. I've had issues with depression and issues with mental health and I can invest in the sport and focus and think, "It's Wednesday and the Ospreys play Saturday," and that can help give me focus.'

For a long time, Robbie worked with a small group doing comedy and podcasts, trying his hand at sketches and stand-up. Unfortunately, the group dissolved when several people moved away and Robbie found himself lacking a creative outlet. Even worse, he ended up 'accidentally' getting a job he absolutely hated.

'I reluctantly turned up for an interview with UBS,' laughs Robbie. 'It turned out no one else bothered to turn up for the interview and I got the job. I didn't want it, but through sheer British politeness I took it and did it for months.'

Trying to keep his mind active during what he found dull work, Robbie began asking himself why rugby lacked the kind of online content other sports enjoyed. 'I was wondering why there was so little deep analysis in rugby and wondered in particular why no one was doing stuff on YouTube,' recalls Robbie. 'It was a platform where so many content creators were popping up, but there was very little rugby stuff. It felt like most rugby content and coverage was aimed at people who drive Land Rovers and there was nothing for anyone like me.'

Inspired by James Hook having a somewhat ropey performance for the Ospreys against Edinburgh, Robbie took the plunge and channelled the inspiration from a nagging muse and made his first rugby video: 'So what went wrong with the Ospreys?'. He uploaded it to a channel called 'Squidge Rugby'. The name was inspired by his own childhood nickname and the famous quirky logo by the blue headgear of Justin Tipuric.

The opening line of this 16-minute video was unlike any rugby analysis anyone had ever heard before. And it was fantastic. After a black and white clip showing an utterly toothless Ospreys side going sideways and backwards in attack, Robbie announced himself to the wider rugby world with these words:

'You may be wondering why I chose to start what is nominally a rugby video with a clip of a piece of performance art exploring the relationship between befuddlement, pointlessness and abject misery. But what I actually showed you was, and you may struggle to believe this, was a clip of a professional rugby team trying to play rugby. More specifically this rugby team was the Ospreys.'

It wasn't just the words and well-timed delivery either. The video was an explosion of quick-fire game clips, on-screen jokes and subliminal-like messages you needed to pause the video to read. It would cut between rucks and line-outs to things like clips of Spiderman and Gruffalo toys. It was relentless. And, crucially, the analysis was excellent. It was clear that Robbie knew his onions. And could cook with them too. The creator, though, was nervous.

'I had just quit my job,' recalls Robbie. 'I figured out I had about a month's rent in the bank and gave myself two weeks to make the video.'

After posting it online, and sharing it with the likes of cult podcast *Blood and Mud* and writer Paul Williams, Robbie went to the cinema to take his mind off worrying about the reaction to his video. When he emerged, he found that he had about 50 comments and that most of them were positive. It was enough to spur him on to make a second and a third video.

The video was published in January 2018 and Robbie had set himself a goal of getting 5,000 subscribers to his YouTube channel by the 2019 World Cup. He hit that number with his second video: a look at Ireland scrum-half Conor Murray.

The big breakthrough though, was a video he made on Wales and Lions captain Sam Warburton who had retired in July 2018. Fed up with having to defend the flanker on the internet against accusations he was overrated, Robbie made an 11-minute video showing exactly how good Warburton was and why so much of what he did went unnoticed to the casual viewer.

Once again, after posting the video, Robbie headed to the cinema. This time, he emerged to a couple of hundred Twitter notifications and a message from Will saying that Warburton himself had shared and liked the video, posting a message stating: 'I'm glad you appreciated the dark arts of the back row!'.

Amusingly, and quite rightly, that Warburton video also had some well-aimed digs at establishment figures like Stuart Barnes who, as a paid pundit, had offered opinions on Warburton's legacy that, quite frankly, revealed he hadn't really watched Warburton play with any great attention.

The reaction to the Warburton video was a major moment for the channel and helped convince Robbie there was a potential living to be made from what he was doing. Subscriptions shot through the roof and by the 2019 Six Nations Robbie, now without a full-time job, directed his whole energy into making his videos. Soon after, Will came on board with him.

Robbie has stated that for every minute of a video released, he and Will have put around an hour and a half into producing it. Fans support Squidge Rugby through financial backing via platforms like Patreon and the pair also receive income from advertising and sponsorship.

In a nod to his popularity, and a demonstration that the big broadcasters weren't completely blind to progress and what the market really wants (not just what they think it wants), Robbie has now worked for major broadcasters such as the BBC on flagship shows like *Scrum V*.

Digging deep

So how do the pair do it? Will offered some great insight into what goes into their videos when speaking for this book, saying: 'Generally, especially with Wales and the Ospreys, we'll watch the game live purely as fans. Then we will watch the game again that same weekend, having already gotten a general feel for the game, but now paying a bit more attention to who did what, what the teams were trying to do tactically and who played well. This means we've now built a good feel for the narrative and structure of the game before we start the deeper dive which begins either late in the weekend or first thing Monday morning.

'I will make notes and pass these on to Robbie, who will have his own notes and will also start writing and recording a script for the voiceover. I'll edit the audio and then we take forever editing the videos.'

The pair tend to put in 12-hour shifts for several days before getting a video out after three or four days of hard graft.

As well as both being fanatical students of the sport, constantly studying the modern game, Will also draws on the coaching he gets and sees from former professionals at his own club. 'I have the approach that I want to learn something new about the game every time I play, watch or coach,' he says. 'Even if it is something minor. It's such a complicated game, you can't learn everything. It has really helped being coached by people who have played the game at the professional level. What's impressive is that some of the stuff I've learnt from coaching, such as formations in rugby attacks, Robbie had already picked up himself just from watching and following rugby.'

One of Will's proudest analytical moments was spotting that Scotland had taken advantage of their physio being a former full-back to create a try against England in the 2022 Calcutta Cup match. After kicking a restart long, Scotland made sure England were forced to clear from their own 22 into touch. Will noticed that Scotland had kept hooker George Turner back deep, by the touchline. Just a few yards away, physio Stuart Paterson, was standing just outside the field of play with a towel in hand. Usually, Paterson would keep up with play, running up and down the sideline, but on this occasion, he was back where the kick was heading. Will and Robbie did not feel this was pure chance. Paterson quickly dried the ball and handed it to Turner. By touching the ball, the law had to be followed that a line-out had to be formed and the England backs needed to retreat ten metres. Thanks to the fact Turner was instantly set to go, a quick line-out was thrown to the front (utterly uncontested by a surprised England) and the ball was whipped out quickly so the canny Scots could attack an unprepared and over-cluttered midfield. A few excellent phases later and Scotland had exploited the befuddled England defence to score.

It was another example of the nuggets of treasure almost every Squidge Rugby video contains and encapsulates why the channel has been such a success. The channel has even been praised by giants of coaching such as World Cup-winning coach Rassie Erasumus of South Africa.

Pleasingly, Squidge Rugby isn't a lone digital voice in the field of analysis these days either. Social media is increasingly helping other fresh viewpoints get aired from smart thinkers such as Sam Larner (@SamLStandsUp), Graeme Forbes (@thedeadballarea), Geraint Davies (@daviesGDD), EK Rugby Analysis (@ek_rugby), The Loose Head (@TheLooseH) and Tom Savage (@threeredkings).

Together, this new wave of analysts is forcing broadcasters, magazines and newspapers to up their game and, in some cases, realise that even the casual fan is happy to dive deeper if the content is presented the right way.

Preaching the glory of the game
Unlike most mainstream rugby commentators and outlets, Robbie and Will are committed to covering as much of the rich rugby world landscape as possible. From women's rugby to Tier Two clashes between supposed 'minnows', they give it all equal love. For them, rugby is rugby. It's a focus that has, remarkably, cost them subscribers.

'We once lost about 100 subscribers after posting an analysis of a women's game,' says Will. 'Fine. We'd rather help the game grow.'

Their channel dives as deeply into the women's Six Nations and World Cup as probably any rugby site or magazine in the world. Similarly, World Cup qualifiers between sides like Chile and the USA are given as much care and love as a New Zealand v South Africa clash.

'I've always loved that there is a whole world out there,' says Robbie. 'You've got 30-odd teams competing, and it is not as big a world as football and you can kind of learn almost all about it. The rugby world is small enough to be interconnected, and you can engage with it all.'

Will and Robbie both express frustration that unlike in sports such as football, fans who make the effort to learn the names of supposedly 'minor' teams are seen as nerdy or odd. Will speaks of how one former international mocked a fellow pundit for making the effort to learn the names of Uruguayan players. Robbie tells the story of a time he spoke in glowing terms of the try scored by Argentina wing Lucas Gonzalez Amorosino in the 2011 World Cup clash with Scotland. One of his friends, bemused, asked why Robbie had bothered to learn the player's name. He could only answer in despair that he knew the name because he was one of the best players in his position in the world. The incident is another example of how so many in the rugby community still see 'real rugby' as being the eight major traditional nations, and feel anything outside that doesn't quite deserve to be fully recognised.

'Italy are a great team,' says Will. 'People should learn their names.'

The pair are also not afraid to speak their minds on social and political issues within the game, much to the ire of the more reactionary members of the rugby community. The Squidge Rugby video on Israel Folau's homophobia was so powerful and got such a response in the rugby world that it even made Australian breakfast news.

'As the channel has grown in terms of numbers, there is also a level of responsibility that comes with that,' says Robbie. 'We can use our platform to start a conversation where there isn't one being held and we think there should be. Or we can help keep an issue in the spotlight that other media outlets have decided to leave alone.'

'I wouldn't say we've lost subscribers over social issues,' argues Will. 'We probably never had them subscribing in the first place.'

The gatekeepers slam the gate shut . . . briefly

While today Robbie and Will are able to make a living from their videos, it all almost came crashing down just ahead of the 2019 World Cup in Japan. Having not long given up his day job to devote himself full time to his channel and preparing to extensively cover the forthcoming World Cup, Squidge suddenly found himself hit with multiple copyright claims by Six Nations Rugby. As YouTube operates a three-strike system, his channel was removed.

With his content all gone in a single day, Robbie understandably had trouble sleeping that night: 'When I got in touch with someone at the Six Nations, they were quite firm that I should stop.'

What makes the situation laughable, was that in reality, the short clips Robbie was using for his channel were creating massive engagement among fans and helping to keep the Six Nations trending on social media platforms. Common sense tells anyone with half a brain that there was no rugby fan deciding to not watch live games or view official broadcasters or channels because they watched a deep dive tactical video on Squidge Rugby. It was the opposite, if anything.

But as Six Nations Rugby will geo block a short clip of the Five Nations from the 1970s on Twitter in countries like the Czech Republic, it's perhaps not remotely surprising they took such a dim view of Squidge Rugby content.

Despite their initial curt dismissal of Robbie's appeals, they soon had to change their tune. Thousands of fans led an unofficial protest on social media each time Six Nations Rugby posted content. Instead of engaging on the topic or theme Six Nations Rugby hoped fans would, Squidge Rugby fans would reply in bulk criticising the nonsensical decision.

'The response was overwhelming,' says Robbie. 'Each time the Six Nations posted anything, they got about 60 replies talking about them blocking my videos.'

Realising the issue wasn't going away, Six Nations Rugby relented and did a spectacular u-turn. Sadly, they still haven't learnt their lesson and continue to block content left, right and centre. Leagues like the NBA see the benefit of letting people share content. Rugby administrators prefer to block.

As of the summer of 2023, Six Nations Rugby still regularly take down and force the cancellation of plenty of users on channels. Indeed, *The East Terrace* was briefly suspended from Twitter in 2023 for sharing a cropped video about five seconds long of an England player celebrating the awarding of a scrum in his side's favour. Previously, *The East Terrace* had its YouTube channel permanently removed for sharing a 30-second video of an early 1980s' England game that was unavailable anywhere else online and may well never be again.

Outsiders to mainstream

As Welsh boys growing up in Nottingham following a sport no one else in their school really cared about, Robbie and Will have always been outsiders. Their commitment to following what they love and celebrating it passionately is to be applauded. They may be too modest to admit it, but they have changed rugby fandom for the better and paved the way for others to follow. They've also taught a lot of old dogs (or older fans) a lot of new tricks with their insights and observations.

Robbie has spoken of how the aim of his channel was to 'celebrate' rugby. He's done that so well, many in rugby now, quite rightly, celebrate Squidge Rugby.

NORIKO KISHIDA

*'I envied that men could play rugby
and wanted to try to play it too.'*
Noriko Kishida

Noriko Kishida discovered rugby 'late' in life and in a nation where rugby was a minority sport and not considered fit for women. Her desire to play was so strong she helped found a new team and was key in getting Japan to the first ever Women's World Cup.

Main teams: Liberty Fields RFC, Japan
Position: Prop
International caps: 3 (1991)
Honours/positions: Manager of Japan Women's team at the 1994 and 2002 World Cups; founder of Liberty Fields RFC; founder of Japan Women's Rugby Football Union; winner of the ARFU Women's Rugby Development Award (2012)

Noriko Kishida's story is one of the most remarkable in the whole of rugby history. The founders of the sport in early 19th century England could never have imagined in their wildest dreams not just how much their game would spread geographically, but the barriers it would cross socially and economically. And, of course, they would never have dreamed that women would take up the game, let alone women on the other side of the world.

By the 1980s rugby was already long established in Japan (see page 24). But there were also ripples of revolution running through the Japanese game: women were taking an interest in playing. In a country of over 120 million the numbers were miniscule, just a few hundred. But it was a seed. What it needed was some watering.

One of the people who played the biggest role in nurturing those delicate roots was Noriko Kishida. She was 37 years old when she first encountered rugby and was utterly fascinated. Her sport at university had been tennis – indeed she worked as a tennis instructor as well as a teacher. But rugby held an instant appeal to her.

'The first I ever saw of rugby was the university men's team playing,' says Kishida, speaking to me for this book. 'I was surprised when I saw it and it was so interesting to me. I envied that men could play rugby and wanted to try to play it too.'

At the time, not only were the options for a woman playing rugby extremely limited, it was frowned upon for females to play. It was incredibly tough for women in Japan if they didn't live up to the social stereotypes imposed upon them. In 1980s' Japan, women were expected to be feminine, pretty and submissive. Traditional gender roles put many restrictions on what women could or should be seen to do, and getting bruised, bloody and muddy playing a contact sport like rugby was not something that was looked kindly upon by large swathes of society.

Thankfully, Kishida was not a person to be held back by such attitudes. She firmly believed that she had as much right as anyone to play a sport she had fallen for and so she set about trying to find out how to get involved. The trouble was finding a place to play and enough people to play with.

The official match programme of the 1991 Women's World Cup (which Kishida would play a key role in), said the following on the history of the women's game in Japan: 'Rugby started about 10 years ago in Japan with a number of mothers taking up the sport having seen the fun their sons were having. By 1983, other women had taken up the sport and teams were formed in Tokyo, Nagoya and other major cities.'

Kishida would be central to the formation of another side in Tokyo; a club that would play a key role in Japan's adventure in the inaugural women's World Cup.

Liberty Fields RFC

Not long after falling for rugby, Kishida read in a rugby magazine that there were only a small number of women players in the country. This gave her hope, rather than discouragement. She signed up for a short course at the Setagaya rugby school in Tokyo. This helped her establish the foundations of how to play and coach a sport that was completely new to her.

But that wasn't enough. She began recruiting new players – encouraging those who had been tempted to play but not yet found the courage, and convincing those that had never even considered such a thing to give it a try. Soon Kishida, with the help of a few friends, had pulled together over 30 players, enough to form a team: Liberty Fields RFC.

By the late 1980s Liberty Fields, named after the area in which they trained and played, would become the most powerful of the few women's teams that now existed in the nation. They didn't have it easy. The fields were often a quagmire, they had no team doctor and, in the early days, no coach either. What they did have though was an overwhelming love for the game itself and the camaraderie that came with it.

Sadly, the players took a lot of personal abuse from others for even playing the game. Kishida has spoken of how many in Japan considered it 'vulgar' that women should play a male contact sport. Injuries to women from rugby were also seen as proof the sport was too rough for women. This was despite the fact, of course, that men got just as many injuries when they competed.

'It was even difficult to source the right kit and equipment for women at the time,' recalls Kishida, who had settled into the position of prop. 'Proper rugby boots for women were hard to get at the time, so many girls had to use soccer boots.'

Despite Liberty Fields helping to demonstrate there was potential for rugby to grow among women and girls in Japan, the Japan Rugby Football Union (JRFU) was not interested in supporting, or indeed even recognising the women's game.

'We wanted to help the women's game progress,' says Kishida. 'So we set about forming our own union. It was lots of hard work and organisation, but there were advantages too. It allowed us to start contacting other women's unions, such as Wales and New Zealand, to try and begin international tours and fixtures. We may well have not been able to do that as part of the JRFU as it is unlikely they would have helped us.'

Japan rises in the land of dragons

The formation of Japan Women's Rugby Football Federation in 1988 set in motion a journey that would see a national side formed to visit Wales as part of the first ever women's world cup (see page 103) in 1991. Kishida worked closely with the organising committee that helped put in place the plans and funds to get a team over to the other side of the world. In addition to being a player, she was effectively team manager too. An incredible 15 players from Liberty Fields were named in the squad that would be part of this historic tournament.

If all this wasn't impressive enough, Kishida was 45 years old when she lined up for Japan in the World Cup. Interestingly, in the squad profiles for the Japan team in the tournament's official match programme, Kishida is the only Japanese player without her age listed in the player biographies.

There were to be no fairy tale victories on the playing field for Japan, they fell 62–0 to France and 20–0 to Sweden. The scores were unsurprising. Japan had never even played a Test match before they arrived in Wales. The victory for them had simply been in forming a team and getting it to Wales. There was one final game against Spain in the plate tournament, a match that ended in a 30–0 defeat.

'We knew that our level of rugby was not so high,' admits Kishida. 'But still, I was surprised when I watched the final game between England and the USA and realised that women could play at such a high level. It was amazing. It inspired us to focus on raising the level of our game. So in that way, the World Cup was a huge success.

'We set our sights on the second World Cup. And us even being there in the first one had inspired others to play, as well as given those that had played great inspiration to improve further.'

Legacy

As Kishida had hoped, the first World Cup helped push the game forward in her native land. By 1992, the women's union she had helped create was representing approximately 25 teams and 500 players. Even august publications like the *New York Times* were running features on women's rugby in Japan and interviewing Kishida.

The second World Cup took place in Scotland in 1994 and Japan, now managed by Kishida, tasted their first tournament success with a win over Sweden by 10–5. While they suffered heavy defeats in their other matches, the victory meant everything to the Japanese and Kishida has fond memories of the achievement.

For the 2002 World Cup, Kishida was the manager of Japan and a member of the Women's Advisory Committee of the IRB. After qualifying for the tournament via a 62–0 rout of Hong Kong, the Japanese fell by the same scoreline to Spain (a serious power in the women's game at the time) in their opening match of the competition. Another defeat followed to Italy in the next contest, before Kishida's side triumphed 37–3 over the

Netherlands. Unfortunately, they lost to Ireland in the 13th/14th place playoff. While Kishida didn't particularly enjoy coaching and the pressures around fundraising and administration that came with it, she was thrilled to be involved in the hard-earned victories. In the same year, the JRFU finally recognised the women's game in the country and became the union for women's rugby too. Again, the former Test prop had been at the heart of driving great change in Japanese rugby.

For many years after her managing and playing career was over, Kishida was heavily involved in growing rugby in Asia and Japan. She is immensely proud of how far women's rugby in her native land has come and is hugely respected in the game for what she did to promote the sport.

So inspiring was the story of Liberty Fields, Guinness made a short film in 2019 about the club and the sacrifices Kishida and her teammates made so they could play the sport they loved. The powerful film gained global attention and Kishida was quoted widely in newspaper and website features written around the world.

Upon the film's release, Kishida remarked: 'It is a sport that not only makes me feel a sense of belonging in society, but also helps bring me and my friends together from all around the world – from different countries – to play a sport that we all have passion for. For the world to work to its fullest potential, it's crucial for men and women to co-exist together, to have equal opportunities, and to have the same chance for success.

'Even in moments of doubt, I always remind myself of the importance of believing in yourself and what you stand for. It is important to combat prejudices and support the ongoing fight for equality, which all men and women are entitled to.

'As a team of strong women, we were driven and motivated by the philosophies and beliefs behind Liberty Fields, helping us rise above the challenges that we faced. Being aware that our actions were (and still are) having a significant impact on society, fuelled our desire for change in the world of sport and how women were perceived in rugby.'

In early 2023, Japan were ranked 12th in the women's official rankings and had won the Asia Rugby Women's Championship on three occasions. Today, there are 5,000 female players in Japan and 75 teams.

'We made the impossible, possible,' said Kishida upon the film's release. Few would disagree.

GIANT KILLERS
URUGUAY (2019)

*'Can I tell you a little secret? Yesterday I missed
pretty much all my kicks so I had trouble sleeping.'*
Felipe Berchesi

**Uruguay are known the world over for their football prowess.
But in 2019 they showed the sporting world they were pretty
hand with a rugby ball as well.**

**Fiji 27 Uruguay 30 (Kamaishi Recovery Memorial Stadium,
Kamaishi)**
25 September, 2019 – Pool D, Rugby World Cup
Fiji are one of the most loved rugby nations. Their contribution
to the sport, in both its full 15-a-side format and its shortened
seven-a-side sibling, is incalculable. They are, physically and
metaphorically, giants of the global game. 'Arriving' with an
impact in the 1950s (see page 285), they've been a consistent
character on the international stage since the sport's first World
Cup in 1987.

The 2019 World Cup was the eighth time Fiji had taken
part in rugby's biggest tournament. Only the 1995 version of
the competition lacked their unique presence, when the beloved
South Sea Islanders failed to qualify during a grim time for the
national side.

Heading to the jamboree in Japan in 2019, Fiji had won ten of their 28 games in the tournament. Wins had come over Argentina (1987), Namibia (1999, 2011), Canada (1999, 2007), USA (2003), Japan (2003, 2007), Uruguay (2015) and, in one of the most celebrated games in modern Test rugby, against Wales (2007).

The 38–34 pool win over the Dragons in France, knocked the Welshmen out of the event and took Fiji to their first quarter-final since 1987. The game is regarded as one of the most open, thrilling and dramatic matches in tournament history.

Even though Fiji may not have won a huge number of games in the World Cup, they'd given plenty of teams a giant scare, most notably France in 1999 and Scotland in 2003. The men in white have always been firm favourites of fans who have grown up watching their world-conquering feats in the seven-a-side version of the sport. As detailed elsewhere in this book, Fiji have also taken the scalp of major nations such as Australia. They may be technically classed as a 'Tier Two' nation, but they are a colossus of the game in more ways than one and their players are key figures in all the sport's major leagues globally.

In contrast, one of their pool opponents at the 2019 World Cup were genuine minnows. Japan 2019 was Uruguay's fourth time dining at the top table of rugby union, but, judging by their history, they were expected to nibble on no more than a few scraps during their games.

The South Americans had first taken part in a World Cup in 1999, where they beat fellow minnows Spain (27–15), but fell to Scotland and South Africa in their other group outings and failed to score a single try in their defeats. In 2003 they were dismantled 72–6 by South Africa, 60–13 by Samoa and 111–13 by eventual winners England. Despite the hidings, they did at least rack up another win – scoring three tries in a 24–12 triumph over Georgia – a side that had not yet reached the maturity they are now famed for.

As it turned out, Uruguay didn't qualify for another World Cup until England in 2015. It was a somewhat grim adventure as they managed just two tries and were comprehensively beaten by Wales (54–9), Australia (65–3), England (60–3) and Fiji (47–15).

So when the South Americans were drawn to meet the South Seas Islanders again in 2019, few could see past a repeat of the 2015 result. Making the odds of an upset even longer, Fiji had brushed Uruguay aside 68–7 in an autumn meeting in England a year out from the World Cup.

A round ball nation only?

In sporting terms, Uruguay is famous for its football. Los Charrúas, as the national team are known, were winners of the 1930 and 1950 FIFA World Cups and have enjoyed 15 titles in the Copa América (formerly the South American Football Championship).

Surprisingly though, rugby has a proud and long history in Uruguay, even if no one is exactly sure at what point union arrived in the country. Some believe a game was played there as early as 1865, with British immigrants, as is so often the case, being the group that first kicked an oval ball on local soil. What isn't in any doubt is that the national team played their first official Test in 1948 against Chile. The Uruguayan Rugby Union was founded three years later but was not granted affiliation status with World Rugby (then the International Rugby Board) until 1989. The long wait for such recognition shows the attitude to the expansion of world rugby that prevailed among the blazers of the traditional Test-playing nations.

In 1951, the South American Rugby Championship was created, with Uruguay facing off with Argentina, Brazil and Chile. Argentina comfortably dispatched all-comers, but Los Teros (the nickname of the Uruguayan side and taken from the national emblem which is a bird known as the south lapwing), defeated Chile (8–3) and Brazil (17–10) to claim the runner-up spot. The tournament has evolved over the years with different formats and teams, but the Uruguayans have celebrated titles in 1981, 2014, 2015, 2017 and 2021.

Despite regional success, the nation had done little to etch itself in the consciousness of global rugby fans. Which is why, when they rocked up to Japan for their fourth World Cup adventure, few casual fans took much interest. After all, Uruguay was a football nation that hadn't come close to troubling a nation in the top ten of Test rugby. What's more, their squad contained just 22 professional players. Only the curious and the hardcore fans tuned in and most of them did so in expectation of Fijian magic. Few knew, however, just how much work had been done behind the scenes back in Uruguay to transform the fortunes of the national team. Excellent strategic planning and coaching from Esteban Meneses, their Argentina coach, and smart investment from the union had helped to bring the game on in leaps and bounds since their previous appearance on the world stage. Meneses brought in some excellent support staff and helped create the conditions to allow more players to play professionally (the 2015 squad had contained just four full-timers).

Fiji, captained by blindside flanker Dominiko Waqaniburotu, would be playing their second game of the tournament, having already lost to Australia 39–21. While the ultimate scoreline was unkind in that opening match, the Islanders had the Wallabies on the ropes for the first 60 minutes before running out of steam. They now knew that they likely needed big wins against Uruguay and Georgia to keep their hopes of progressing to the knockout stages alive. Fijian coach John McKee made 12 changes to his starting lineup for this match. The Uruguayans, in contrast, were fresh, but would likely be more rusty.

The match

This Pool D clash took place at the Kamaishi Recovery

Memorial Stadium in the Iwate Prefecture of Kamaishi City. The construction of the 16,000-capacity venue began in 2017. Kamaishi had been devastated by an earthquake and tsunami in 2011. Over 1,000 people lost their lives or went missing and the city itself suffered terrible damage. The World Cup marked a significant cultural and historical moment in the rebuilding of the city.

On 25 September, 2019, 14,000 fans came to the venue to see Fiji and Uruguay do battle. Many of the fans were local school children who had all been encouraged to adopt one of the teams to support. After the South Americans had blasted out their national anthem, 'Orientales, la Patria o la Tumba' (and a few tears were certainly shed as they did so), they accepted the challenge of the Fijians' famous war dance, the Cibi.

Los Teros, captained by flanker Juan Manuel Gaminara, kicked things off. They immediately showed their state of mind and just how much the game meant to them when loosehead Mateo Sanguinetti and number eight Manuel Diana smash-tackled Fiji's giant number eight Leone Nakarawa within 15 seconds, driving him back and causing him to lose the ball.

Fiji had a strong breeze behind them in the first half and Uruguay knew to have any hope of victory, they needed to stay in the hunt in the first half and limit the Fijians' ability to utilise the wind.

The favourites showed their confidence early on, happily running the ball from set pieces in their own half and mixing up their attacks with a potent blend of speed, width, kicks, steps and crash balls. But the underdogs were not fazed and put their own cards on the table in the fifth minute when they took a quick throw-in and set off a wide attack from just outside their own 22. While the attack ultimately came to nothing, it demonstrated that if they were going to lose, it wasn't going to be because they focused on playing it safe. If something was on, no matter where they were on the field, they would go for it.

The opening exchanges were free-flowing and full of dare and pluck from both sides, which only reinforced the feeling that Uruguay would be outgunned ultimately as rugby is a crueller sport than most when giants and minnows meet. Eventually, size, weight, experience and money usually triumph.

Sure enough, Fiji bagged their first try after just seven minutes. Gaining a five-metre line-out after a wonderful deep attack, a simple throw to the front of the line-out followed by a quick loop around and pass, saw hooker Mesu Dolokoto stroll over. So far, so good for Fiji. The script was being played out.

From the kick-off Fiji ran out at Uruguay again and stormed to halfway with ease. It really did look like a long afternoon was in store for the men in blue. But then, in the 14th minute, the unexpected happened. Flinging the ball about in their own half, the Fijians made their first big mistake. Nakarawa tried a second fancy offload in less than 20 seconds, but this time the ball went loose. Uruguay hooker Germán Kessler, winning his 50th cap, pounced on the loose ball and then popped it up to scrum-half Santiago Arata who hit it at impressive speed. Taking the ball on the Fijian ten-metre line, he showed some nimble footwork and a sturdy handoff to beat multiple tacklers and go over from 40 metres out, despite one tackler briefly grabbing his shirt and another almost tap-tackling him at the end. With the conversion from his half-back partner Felipe Berchesi, the minnows held a shock 7–5 lead.

In the 19th minute, the lead swung back to Fiji after a controversial try that didn't even get referred to the TMO (Television Match Official). Prop Eroni Mawi was bizarrely allowed three goes at trying to burrow over while being held by a tackler. The conversion made it 12–7 to Fiji.

Then another shot was fired after Uruguay charged down Fiji's exit attempt after the restart. Los Teros drove over for a second score and put them back in the lead. It had come about after they bravely turned down a shot at goal from a penalty they had been awarded and opted for a line-out. The reward was powerful number eight Manuel Diana adding his name to the scoresheet. Berchesi added the extras and it was 14–12 after 24 minutes.

The game refused to settle down. Rattled, Fiji began to make unforced errors. Confusion in covering a simple kick just inside their own half, saw the Islanders surrender a bouncing ball to Diana. Uruguay immediately put width on it, and, after an initial fumble near halfway, full-back Gastón Mieres fed centre Juan Manuel Cat who gave the ball instantly to left-wing Rodrigo Silva. The flyer took possession with about 45 metres to go – gassed his opposite number, who had been put off balance by Cat thanks to the timing of the pass – and he was off. He was brought down as he reached the 22 thanks to an excellent cover tackle, but he flipped a lovely inside ball back to Cat who had run a wonderful support line. There was no one near the centre and he burst over to extend his side's lead (see image on page 194). The conversion made it 21–12 after 28 minutes. There was no doubt now, David was starting to rain down some serious blows on Goliath. The question was: could David maintain the effort?

Seven minutes before half time, after just about holding out a dangerous Fijian attack, Uruguay again pounced on a loose ball and, 60 metres later, almost got another try after a frantic hack and chase from inside centre Andrés Vilaseca. Replays denied the score, but it further heightened the sense Fiji were in trouble.

If anyone expected Uruguay to go into their shells and try to defend their lead, they were soon proven wrong. Los Teros kept up the pace, width and pressure and relentlessly attacked. After stealing a line-out on halfway, the Uruguayans marched 30 metres through multiple phases and were rewarded with a penalty. Berchesi nailed the kick and took his side into the dressing rooms at the interval with a 24–12 lead.

The second half

During the break, rugby commentators, live-match blogs and

fans around the world on social media shared their disbelief at what was happening. Everyone agreed the match was a thriller and debated whether it would have a fairy tale ending or if the natural order of the rugby union world would restore itself and see the flying Fijians popping the dreams of their plucky opponents.

Less than two minutes after the restart, Fiji blew a certain score, with the final pass carelessly being thrown to a blue shirt instead of a white one. There was plenty of time left. But it was another one of those signs, things weren't clicking for the favourites.

Fiji had come out firing though and relentless pressure helped them earn a very kickable penalty for fly-half Josh Matavesi a few minutes later.

He missed.

But the Fijians, who just seemed to become bigger and faster the more the game went on, kept coming at the upstarts and in the 48th minute, second row Api Ratuniyarawa powered over. Matavesi again missed the extras with a terrible hooked kick. The score stood 24–17 to Uruguay.

Los Teros seemed to redouble their efforts. Their line speed and aggression in defence was incredible and time and time again they frustrated their opponents just as it seemed they would break through. And when they had the ball in hand, they continued to attack, simply refusing to play the percentages as underdogs are far too often wont to do.

To their credit, Fiji remained steadfast in their commitment to an attacking 15-man approach too, frequently running set-piece ball from deep in their own half, often making huge gains in territory before a last-ditch effort from Uruguay threw a spanner in the works.

The match continued to be an end-to-end thriller, only now more and more players were suffering from bangs, bruises and burning lungs. Fresh legs continually entered the fray to try and change the game for Fiji and save it for Uruguay.

In the 60th minute, Uruguay earned a shot at goal after a 15-phase sequence in attack which started in their own half had ended ten metres from the tryline. Berchesi coolly made it 27–17 as the contest entered its final quarter.

Fiji rallied once more and Uruguay began to look tired. With 14 minutes left on the clock, Fijian replacement Nikola Matawalu finished off a 16-phase attack by bursting over the line from a yard out. Again the conversion, eminently kickable, failed as replacement Ben Volavola hooked his kick. It now stood 27–22 to Uruguay.

From the restart, Fiji once more refused to put boot to ball, opting to run their way to victory. It was foolhardy, but it all made for mesmerising sporting theatre.

Ten minutes remained.

By this stage, almost every phase of play seemed to feature a South American player being treated for an injury, leaving his team a man short. On several occasions, Uruguay had two men down. Still they clung on. In fact, a crucial penalty was won by Uruguay while two players were out of action. Taking advantage of Fiji's failure to roll away, Berchesi showed the men in white how to slot pressure kicks as he nailed his sixth kick from seven attempts.

30–22. Five minutes left. History was in touching distance.

Fiji continued to launch attacks from deep and almost scored a spectacular try with just over three minutes left, only for the last pass to once again miss its target.

At this point, the television broadcasters flashed some match stats on the screen and revealed that Uruguay had missed an astonishing 44 tackles to Fiji's 16. Los Teros had also had to make 136 energy-sapping tackles to Fiji's 103. Both stats reveal the pressure the men in blue had been under. But still, it was Uruguay that retained a vital eight-point cushion. Fiji needed a miracle.

It never arrived.

In the final play, Matawalu grabbed his second try from a five-metre scrum, but all it did was give Fiji a losing bonus point. The game was lost. Fittingly, perhaps, the conversion again failed.

On the referee's final whistle the Uruguayans erupted in joy. The players on the field embraced and were instantly joined by the rest of the delirious squad and management. There were the inevitable tears of joys and the wonderful victory hugs of which sporting dreams are made. They had done it: their first World Cup win in 16 years and their first ever against a top-ten nation.

Moments later, the triumphant captain Gaminara, drenched in sweat and draped in a national flag conducted his post-match interview. Through tears, he said: 'I'm really proud of my country. We are not the biggest or the tallest. We came here to win and we've been preparing for four years . . . since we qualified we have been thinking about this game. And you saw the passion.'

Fly-half Berchesi added: 'It's unreal. We lost by 60 points to them in November. It's outstanding. It's a really good day for Uruguayan rugby today. I hope everybody could see that, and everybody joins to play rugby in Uruguay. We need more players.'

To rub salt in the wound of devastated Fiji fans, the man who had made six of his seven shots at goal added: 'Can I tell you a little secret? Yesterday I missed pretty much all my kicks so I had trouble sleeping.'

The aftermath

Fiji managed a win against Georgia in their next match, but went out of the tournament after losing to Wales. Uruguay failed to follow up their heroics against Georgia, not helped by having to play them on a hot day just four days after this momentous victory. They fell 33–7. Once again, a minor nation in the World Cup was handicapped by a ridiculous playing schedule. Further defeats followed against Australia and Wales. But the 45–10 and 35–13 scorelines in those two matches were a far cry from previous tournaments when they truly were whipping boys. Their performances in the 2019 tournament proved to the rugby world they had stepped up to another level. They went home with their heads held high and their place in tournament folklore well and truly secured.

MATCH DETAILS

Uruguay: Gastón Mieres; Nicolás Freitas, Juan Manuel Cat, Andrés Vilaseca, Rodrigo Silva; Felipe Berchesi, Santiago Arata; Mateo Sanguinetti, Germán Kessler, Diego Arbelo, Ignacio Dotti, Manuel Leindekar, Juan Manuel Gaminara (captain), Manuel Diana, Santiago Civetta.

Replacements: Guillermo Pujadas, Facundo Gattas, Juan Rombys, Franco Lamanna, Juan Diego Ormaechea, Agustín Ormaechea, Felipe Echeverry, Tomás Inciarte.

Tries: Arata, Diana, Cat.

Conversions: Berchesi (3)

Penalties: Berchesi (3)

Fiji: Alivereti Veitokani; Filipo Nakosi, Semi Radradra, Jale Vatubua, Vereniki Goneva; Josh Matavesi, Henry Seniloli; Eroni Mawi, Mesu Dolokoto, Manasa Saulo, Tevita Ratuva, Api Ratuniyarawa, Dominiko Waqaniburotu (captain), Leone Nakarawa, Mosese Voka.

Replacements: Ratu Veremalua Vugakoto, Campese Ma'afu, Lee Roy Atalifo, Tevita Cavubati, Sam Matavesi, Nikola Matawalu, Ben Volavola, Levani Botia.

Tries: Dolokoto, Mawi, Ratuniyarawa, Matawalu (2)

Conversion: Matavesi

SIYA KOLISI

'I'm not only trying to inspire black kids but people from all races. When I'm on the field and I look into the crowd, I see people of all races and social classes. We as players represent the whole country. I tell my team-mates that you should never play just to represent one group. You can't play to be the best black player or to be the best white player to appeal to a community; you have to play to be the best for every South African. We represent something much bigger than we can imagine.'
Siya Kolisi

Siya Kolisi rose from utter poverty to become a world-class rugby player, the first ever black captain of South Africa and a World Cup winner.

Main teams: Western Province, Stormers, Sharks, South Africa
Position: Flanker
International caps: 75 (2013–)
Points: 45 (nine tries)

When Siyamthanda Kolisi lifted the Webb Ellis Cup above his head in 2019 he had reached the top of the rugby world. Captaining their nation to World Cup glory is an incredible achievement for any rugby player. But for those who know the history of South African rugby, the fact Kolisi had reached the pinnacle of the sport was truly astonishing. His tale is one that just a few decades before, would have been unthinkable.

Hungry and painful early years

Kolisi was born in 1991. As a boy growing up in Zwide, a township near Port Elizabeth, he knew real hunger. Sometimes, when his family were really struggling for money, he would wake up at night and scream with the pain of hunger pangs. His grandmother would try to ease his suffering with sugar water as there was simply not enough food at times to go around. Often she gave up her own food and went hungry to make sure he had something to eat.

The family house was barely fit for human habitation and rainwater would rise up through the floor or pour its way in through the leaky roof. That wasn't even the worst of it. Kolisi didn't have a bed to sleep on and would lie instead on cushions piled up on the floor. Occasionally he would feel rats run over him as he tried to get to sleep.

Kolisi regularly had to endure the horrors of seeing his mother and aunty suffering physical abuse in a world where domestic and public violence was all too common. He himself couldn't avoid the dangers on the streets around him – he once got stabbed in the neck with a glass bottle and on another occasion almost lost his ear in a fight. When he was 12, he saw a man get stoned to death on the streets.

With Kolisi's father rarely around, he was raised by his mother, grandmother, aunt and uncle. Kolisi has praised his grandmother, Nolulamile, for how she brought him up, calling her a 'positive, loving, supportive and protective' influence and admitting that without her he, quite literally, would not have made it to adulthood. She died in his arms when he was still a boy and Kolisi's mother passed away when he was just 15. With such a difficult home life and upbringing, it would have been little surprise if Kolisi had got caught up in a cycle of violence or remained trapped in poverty.

Despite the difficulties he had at home, Kolisi excelled at sport whenever given the opportunity. He loved playing football on the dusty hard streets by his home. A handy and fearless goalkeeper, he thought nothing of flinging himself around the hard ground to stop a shot getting past him and between the bricks they used as goalposts. Kolisi and his friends played games against children from other streets for money. If they won they would usually share five rands (about 30 pence) among themselves and buy food to celebrate.

With no money to buy proper sporting equipment, Kolisi and his friends had to improvise. Sometimes they would play rugby with a brick and he has stated that growing up, his brick was his favourite toy.

No matter the lack of real balls and goalposts, his clear talent for sport shone through and at age 12 he won a scholarship to play rugby at Grey Boy's High School, which ran one of the most prestigious rugby programmes in South Africa. While it was an amazing opportunity and would ultimately change his life, it wasn't easy at first. Still a young boy, the scholarship meant he would be away from his family for long periods of time. His first language was Xhosa, which meant he also had to rapidly learn to speak English so that he could engage at school.

It may have been a baptism of fire, but Kolisi instantly excelled on the playing fields and quickly established himself in the back row of the first XV. By 2007, he was part of the youth set-up for Eastern Province Kings and played at both under-16 and under-18 level in the two years he was there. Next, he spent two years at the Western Province youth set-up and won national honours with the South African schools team and later South Africa Under-20s. By 2011 he was making appearances for the senior team at Western Province. After 34 games for them, he moved to the Stormers, where he would remain for eight years and 118 games.

Kolisi succeeded so quickly at senior level due to his exceptional athleticism. Brutally powerful in contact, he also possessed speed in the open and the ability to beat – and sometimes even embarrass – defenders with footwork as well as force. His attacking skills have seen him frequently employed by coaches in wide attacking positions where he can be a lethal finisher. In defence he is highly valued by coaches as he is capable of making open-field tackles on nimble backs as well as hitting brutally in close quarters.

Becoming a Springbok and leader

In 2013, with just two years of senior rugby under his belt and aged just 21, Kolisi was called up for the full Springbok team. And, boy, did the loose forward announce his arrival in style.

He had been named on the bench for a clash with Scotland at the Mbombela Stadium in Nelspruit. The match was part of a four-team tournament with Italy and Samoa. Kolisi had to wait just five minutes to earn his first cap as he replaced an injured Arno Botha. He had a dream debut with and without the ball and was named man of the match in a storming display that saw the Boks overcome an early scare to win 30–17. He turned 22 the next day.

Kolisi quickly established himself as a squad player, winning most of his first dozen caps as a substitute and earned himself a spot at the 2015 World Cup in England. Pretty soon he was nailing down a starting place and looking every inch a world-class flanker. He was also gaining attention for his professionalism and leadership skills and in 2017 was named as captain of the Stormers.

Making history

After such a challenging start to his life, that Kolisi played for the Springboks at all was a remarkable achievement. But that was only the start of things. In 2018 he was named as national captain by Rassie Erasmus, South Africa's director of rugby.

This made Kolisi the first black man to captain the Springboks in their 127–year history. Due to the history of racism and apartheid in South Africa, no non-white player had even played for the Boks until Errol Tobias in 1981 (see page 149 for more details on Tobias and the history of race and the Springboks). His appointment was a major moment not just in the history of South African rugby, but in South African society and world rugby.

In his autobiography, Kolisi wrote: 'For so long, the Springbok emblem of a leaping antelope represented only a small part of the country and reflected how that part felt about themselves: that rugby was a sport for real men, white Afrikaners.'

Now here he was, representing real change and standing as a beacon of hope for the generations to follow. His first game as captain was against England at Ellis Park, the opener of a three-match summer Test series. Ahead of the encounter, Kolisi told the *Guardian*:

'I don't shy away from where I have come from and I'm aware that my story is a typical South African story in some ways. It's my motivation. Yes, being a professional sportsman can be tough and occasionally you question if it's all worth it. But then I just think about where I've come from and about the people that look up to me. For me to be able to help people inspired by me, I have to play every week. That is my duty.

'I'm not only trying to inspire black kids but people from all races. When I'm on the field and I look into the crowd, I see people of all races and social classes. We as players represent the whole country. I tell my teammates that you should never play just to represent one group. You can't play to be the best black player or to be the best white player to appeal to a community; you have to play to be the best for every South African. We represent something much bigger than we can imagine.'

It was a hugely emotional moment when Kolisi led the team onto the field among a cacophony of noise and an explosion of flames and fireworks. Kaunda Ntunja, who gave the Xhosa commentary on this historic occasion, said with pride and excitement: 'Siya is our grandson, our son, our nephew, our younger brother . . . A cement truck with no reverse gear!'

Yet the visitors paid no heed to the drama of the occasion and England stormed into a three-try lead after just 17 minutes. At 24–3, it looked like it would be a disastrous result for the 61st Springbok captain.

In the end, it turned out the early deficit just made the whole day even more dramatic as Kolisi's men stormed back with five tries of their own in an epic encounter. The Boks hung on and emerged 42–39 winners. They would go on to win the series two games to one. It was a fantastic start to mark a new chapter in the nation's rugby story.

Kolisi would go on to skipper South Africa to the 2019 World Cup. Leading from the front, he took his men to the ultimate glory and followed in the footsteps of Francois Pienaar and John Smit and lifted the Webb Ellis Cup. The win made South Africa the most successful side in World Cup history. While both the Springboks and New Zealand have won three titles each, South Africa missed the first two World Cups due to apartheid and sporting isolation, so have claimed their wins in two fewer tournaments.

It's fair to say that anyone who lived during the apartheid era would never have imagined even in their wildest dreams a black player from the townships taking a Springbok team to a world title. Errol Tobias has spoken of how he broke down in tears when Kolisi raised the trophy. It will remain one of the most iconic moments in rugby and sport.

A true role model
Kolisi, who has since joined Western Province and captained his country to a series win over the British and Irish Lions, has inspired countless young boys and girls across South Africa and symbolises the progress the South African team have made when it comes to truly representing the whole nation.

To use his position and profile for good, Kolisi, and his wife Rachel, created the Kolisi Foundation. The charity works to support people who live in deprived areas in South Africa and helps with food security, education, sports and also to prevent domestic violence. 'We want kids to be able to dream the same wherever they live,' said Kolisi in 2022. 'That means they need fair, equal societies and freedom. The vision I have for my country, South Africa, keeps me going,'

Perhaps Kolisi's approach to life is best summed up in his own words: 'If someone told me I can't do it, I would keep on going until I make it.'

RONALD POULTON

'Rugby is too good a game to be confined to a particular class.'
Ronald Poulton

Few biographies in English rugby history are so fascinating as that of Ronald William Poulton. And few, sadly, end so tragically. He was an exceptional player, an extraordinary leader and, most importantly of all, a thoroughly decent human being.

Main teams: Oxford University, Harlequins, Liverpool, England
Positions: Centre, wing
International caps: 17 (1909–14)
Points: 28 (8 tries, 1 drop goal)

Ronald William Poulton came into the world on 12 September 1889. His father was Sir Edward Bagnall Poulton, Hope Professor of Zoology at Oxford University – a pioneer in his field and a prominent believer in the teachings of Charles Darwin (still a hugely controversial theory at the time).

Affectionately known as 'Ronnie', Poulton grew up in a wealthy family with four siblings who were all attended by six servants. The family's impressive stately home, Wykeham House in Oxford, is now a Grade II listed building.

From a young age Poulton revealed a sporting talent. In junior school he is said to have scored 15 tries in a single game and his headmaster claimed he was the best athlete to have attended the school. Fittingly for a boy who would become a rugby icon, Poulton went on to attend Rugby School and was joint-captain during his fourth and final year in the school team. He excelled not just with the oval ball, but in cricket and athletics too and won the school's 'Athletic Cup' for pupils for three consecutive years.

At Oxford University Poulton played both centre and wing, while also appearing for the Harlequins. He had been recruited to the Quins by England legend and strategic genius Adrian Stoop (after whom the club's home ground is named). The quality of the Oxford University team was such that Poulton failed to get selected in the 1908 Varsity Match, the famed annual game against rival Cambridge University, but he did get selected for England two months later. From 1912 he would also represent Liverpool, having moved to the city to study engineering.

A star is born

Poulton's Test debut, at centre and aged just 19, came against France in 1909 at Leicester. England won at a canter 22–0. As France were young whippersnappers in international terms and the match was not part of the Championship (they would join in 1910), the French match did not attract the same level of public or press attention as clashes against the other Home Unions of Ireland, Scotland and Wales. However, Poulton had an assured debut and retained his place in the subsequent matches of the season against Ireland (an 11–5 win in Dublin) and Scotland (an 18–8 loss in Richmond). Before the outbreak of war in 1914, Poulton established himself as one of England's most exciting and talented players.

After the disappointment of missing out on the Varsity Match in 1908, Poulton was selected for the 1909 edition.

Once more, the quality of the Oxford University side was so great that even then, after consolidating his place in the England backline, his selection was a close-run thing. He celebrated his selection with five tries. Poulton is one of only three players to have bagged a hat-trick in the history of the Varsity Match and stands alone with his record of five in a single game. By 1911 Poulton was captain of Oxford and it is claimed his presence on the field boosted the gates significantly at the Varsity Match.

His consistency and dazzling displays for Oxford, Harlequins and England soon established him as an 'idol of English rugby'. The rugby historian Barry Bowker, writing in the 1970s, wrote that Poulton ran 'with his head well back and the ball in both hands at arms' length; he had an instinct for seeing a gap and, thanks to a peculiar trick of crossing his feet without stumbling, the ability to swerve either way without losing speed. He was a Rugby genius and one of the best players to don an England jersey.'

Glory with the red rose
Poulton played in two Grand Slam-winning England sides (although the term itself was not coined until 1957). His first was in 1913, when his performance in Cardiff against Wales went down in English rugby folklore. England, captained by Norman Wodehouse, travelled in hope of winning in Cardiff for the first time since 1895. By this point, Poulton was so acclaimed in rugby circles that in Wales posters advertising the clash were put up which proclaimed: 'Come and see R.B. Poulton'.

He lived up to the hype. Poulton was so brilliant that day the contest, which England won convincingly 12–0, was dubbed 'Poulton's Match'. He scored a drop goal, with one reporter stating Poulton had discovered 'a small green patch in a sea of mud' from which to kick. The centre was also instrumental in

England's first try. Afterwards, one of the dejected Welsh players said: 'How can one stop him when his head goes one way, his arms another and his legs keep straight on?'

In 1914 England did the clean sweep again, this time with Poulton leading his nation to the Grand Slam as captain. His approach to captaincy revealed a lot about his attitude to life and leadership. In those days, international teams would have their photo taken ahead of each match and captains would always sit in the centre of the photo holding a ball. Poulton would not pose with the ball as he did not wish to stand out from his teammates. His final game for England secured the Grand Slam in a 39–13 win in Paris before the Great War halted international rugby for six painful years. Poulton signed off in style, claiming four tries. It was a national record no England player equalled until 2011.

A rugby radical

For all the interest his on-field history generates, to the student of rugby Poulton's off-the-field life was even more fascinating. Born into wealth, he was, as rugby historian Huw Richards wrote, 'by rugby standards a radical'. He was not afraid of openly criticising the RFU, something that was a far, far riskier thing to do in the amateur age than it is in today's professional game.

Rugby union was a fanatically amateur sport at the time of Poulton's career. In 1895 the game had reached a momentous tipping point and the 'Great Split' occurred over the issue of 'broken-time payments'. Many individuals and clubs, particularly in the north of England, believed players should be able to receive compensation for taking time off to play rugby. In the late 19th century, workers usually endured six-day weeks, only having Sunday free or, as new 'factory laws' came in, a limited amount of time off on a Saturday. As Sunday was a religious day, sport was usually forbidden. That meant that many working men had to take time off work to play, putting them out of pocket and potentially taking away their ability to financially support themselves or their family. And, of course, a bad injury from playing could see someone with no job or income as employers had no legal duty to pay workers in these circumstances.

Most of those in rugby's corridors of power, however, were firmly against broken-time payments, believing they violated the amateur ethos of the sport. Furthermore, it's clear many within rugby's middle-classes feared losing control of what they saw as their sport. After all, association football had, since going professional, been dominated by the working classes.

Against this background, 22 clubs in the north of England broke away from the RFU in 1895 to form the Northern Union and what would ultimately become the sport of rugby league. Any player who pulled on their boots for a Northern Union club was banned for life from rugby union. Similarly, any player in union found to accept any kind of payment or reward connected to playing union would also be banned for life. Talking about the issue of professionalism as a rugby union player was a risky move in an era when teams were selected by a conservative and reactionary committee, rather than a head coach. Airing unorthodox opinions about professionalism was gambling with your playing career. Vengeful selectors would have had little hesitation in ending a career over a perceived failure to toe the party line.

This didn't faze Poulton. When the RFU banned ten West Country players and officials who had broken rules on amateurism, he spoke out. Poulton believed that such a decision risked making rugby a game for one class only. Despite the fact the furore of 1895 was still reverberating around the sport, he went as far as to publicly call for broken-time payments for players who could not afford to take time off work to play. And he wasn't just muttering complaints in the clubhouse over a beer or gin, he put it in writing.

Letter to *The Sportsman*, December 1912

THE RUGBY UNION AND PROFESSIONALISM.

It is with much apprehension that I read this morning the finding of the General Committee of the Rugby Union concerning the charges brought against certain players in Devonshire clubs of having received money for 'broken time'.

If it is the desire of the Rugby Union Committee practically to limit the game to players who learn it at the Public Schools, and in the Services and Universities, such a finding is reasonable. But I cannot believe such is their desire.

Was not this, then, the opportunity to put the game on an immovable basis among all classes of the community by making an alteration in the laws of the game relating to professionalism, so as to legislate for a carefully arranged payment for 'broken time' for men who are paid weekly or monthly for the hours they work?

And it is difficult to see how such an offence can be construed as professionalism. A man does not, or under careful regulation would not, receive any addition to this normal weekly wage, but would be paid merely for the hours of work missed through football. Such hours of work would, of course, not include 'overtime'.

He would then be exactly in the position of many business men who, in the enjoyment of a settled income, leave their work an hour or so earlier to catch the necessary train to the match. The most optimistic must feel that such an action as the R.U. Committee have taken will do much

to prevent the expansion of the Rugby game, and so reduce
the value to England of the most democratic of sports.

I only venture to write this to find out if there are any
other present or past players of the game who think as I do.

Yours truly,
RONALD W. POULTON.
16 Portland Place, Reading

In today's full-blown world of professional sport where even the blades of grass on the playing field feature digital or painted advertisements, it's hard to appreciate how fiercely people opposed broken-time payments.

Poulton had form in reaching out across the class divide in England. At university he was an advocate of the Balliol Boys' Club, a society which helped the homeless and hungry. He would often react angrily at Oxford University to the Eton elites who belittled the efforts of groups like the Balliol Boys' Club. Poulton frequently gave up his free time to volunteer for lads' clubs in Manchester and Reading.

After university, Poulton began working with his uncle, George Palmer, for the Huntley and Palmer biscuit company. Even then he concerned himself with others. He tried to encourage factory workers to play rugby and took an interest in their welfare and working conditions. When his uncle died in 1913, he became heir to a biscuit fortune. As part of the inheritance arrangement he had to change his surname to Palmer and is now often referred to as Poulton-Palmer.

A tragic and early end

Like so many tens of thousands of young men, Poulton volunteered to serve his country in the First World War, requesting overseas service. He was angered by the concept of civilised nations going to war, but also felt that Germany had to be defeated. In letters home he set out his frustration that more hadn't been done to secure peace and in one letter he wrote: 'international socialism could stop the war, and that alone'.

In Belgium, in May 1915, aged just 25, Poulton was shot by a sniper while he was repairing a trench. A story has become commonplace in the rugby history books that the young man's last words aired his regret that he would never again play at Twickenham. More likely, and a view put forward by his commanding officer, death was instantaneous. He was one of eleven players from the 1914 France v England match to die in the war. In total, 27 England internationals lost their lives in the barbaric conflict.

While Poulton never got to grace the playing field of Twickenham again, his spirit in some way did return. In 2018 soil from Twickenham was taken to Poulton's grave in Belgium and earth from his grave was taken back to Twickenham and buried pitchside.

Poulton left a bequest in his will to the Workers Education Association. At a memorial service for Poulton in Oxford in 1915, the Reverend William Temple said:

'Many of us believed that with his ready sympathy, his utter freedom from selfishness, and his courage to follow what he saw to be right, he would grasp the causes of our labour unrest and class friction, and by removing them from the great industry in whose control a large part was to be his, set an example which would prove a great force in our social regeneration . . . What he hated most in our usual manner of life was the artificial barriers that hold people apart, and the suspiciousness of one class towards another . . . There are many of us who, if asked to point to a life without blemish, would have pointed to Ronald Poulton.'

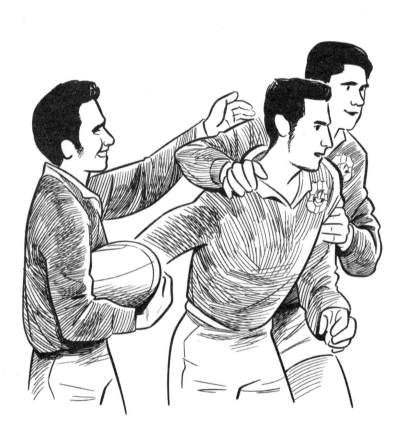

GIANT KILLERS
TONGA (1973)

'The tour of the happy Rugby warriors from the Friendly Isles to Australia had almost a fairytale quality about it.'
Phil Tresidder, *Sydney Daily Telegraph*

Tonga and Australia have only met four times on the international field. Two of those clashes came in 1973 and the second of them would turn out to be one of the great upsets in rugby.

Australia 11 Tonga 16 (Ballymore Stadium, Brisbane) 30 June , 1973

A win by a Tier Two nation over a Tier One nation is still rare enough to send shockwaves through the game. Tonga's 1973 win over the Wallabies is even more remarkable as matches between the countries are so rare. Despite the relative proximity of the two nations and the heavy social ties between them both (the 2011 Australian census lists over 10,000 Australians born in Tonga and over 25,000 claiming Tongan ancestry), the sides have only met four times on the rugby field in capped internationals: twice in 1973, with others games in 1993 and 1998. All of the games have been on Australian soil. It is a sad reflection on the 'brotherhood' of rugby that the Wallabies have made so little effort to meet the Tongans at the elite level, but it does mean the shock Tongan win in 1973 leaves the Polynesian side with a 25 per cent win rate in the series.

While the contact between Tonga and Australia at Test level has been unfortunately limited, to their credit, the Australian Rugby Union (ARU) decided to award full caps for the two-match series in 1973. Bestowing that status on Tonga was not something the Home Unions and most other major nations would have considered at the time. Indeed, many founding members of the International Board (today's World Rugby) still resisted such declarations of support for 'minnows' well into the 1980s.

The tour had been dreamed up to mark the golden jubilee of Tongan rugby. Rugby union had been brought to the 'Friendly Islands' in the early years of the 20th century, with sailors and missionaries responsible for introducing the oval ball. By 1923, the Tonga Rugby Football Union had been formed and the following year the national team played its first Test against Fiji, winning 9–6. For most of the early years of Test rugby in Tonga, they played Fiji and in 1954 first met Western Samoa (now Samoa).

Tonga's player resources when they ventured to Australia to play their ten-match tour of 1973 were limited. A report from 1974 (a year after the tour) claimed the pool of players Tonga could draw upon was just 550, coming from 20 'senior clubs' and 16 'others'.

In 1973, the Tongans were led by number eight and national rugby legend Sione Mafi (grandfather to Tonga and London Irish player Steve Mafi). The novelty of the tourists to the Australian public is clear to see in the contemporary newspapers and rugby annuals. The prose around the Tongans drips with a somewhat twee romanticism and, at other times, even allowing for the attitudes of the era, crosses into what is to modern eyes outright racism. Phil Tresidder of the *Sydney Daily Telegraph* wrote after the tour:

'The tour of the happy Rugby warriors from the Friendly Isles to Australia had almost a fairytale quality about it. The muscular Tonga giants had to be outfitted on arrival with studded boots, the largest ranging from size 13–15. Rugby innocents abroad they were captivated by the sight of themselves on television – rookies on the international scene.

'The Tongans arrived in a blaze of colour – crimson blazers, shell necklaces, and cream sarongs, with *ta'ovala* belts showing their rank in Tongan society. Of the party, 10 were police constables. They took the field brandishing menacing wooden spears and rattling chains of paanga seeds around their ankles. They were warming their bodies, they explained, for the 'big war', making the emblem of the dove of peace on their jerseys a little incongruous!'

Tresidder's language in describing some of the star players is jarring to the modern reader: 'They produced several personalities, notably the little golliwog half-back, Ha'unga Fonua, and the captain, Sione Mafi, who proved a stirring runner with the ball. Australia crowds should have been ready for the unexpected from a touring team that boasted eight apostrophes among the players' names!'

The first Test

Coming into the first Test, the Tongans had beaten South Australia and Sydney, but lost to Victoria, New South Wales and Australian Capital Territory. After the latter defeat, just days before the first Test, the Tongan management implemented a drinking ban on the squad. There were rumours of homesickness plaguing the touring squad, but this is something Tongan flanker Fakahau Valu denies. Speaking for this book in 2022, he said: 'The only obstacle that was new was going to a developed country and being exposed to a new environment, but the team was not homesick.' Either way, it is clear that in the eyes of home media, Tonga were not fancied to trouble their hosts in their historic first international meeting in Sydney. Indeed, the *Canberra Times* wrote:

'Australia's prestige as a rugby union nation will be at stake. The pressure will be on, although it will probably not come from the Tongans. The real acid will come from the stands, where supporters, selectors, and the critics will be ready to damn the team if it does not win soundly.'

The article continued to explain that the Wallabies would 'go out to crush Tonga'. And, sure enough, they did. With a star performance from debutant winger (and former All Black) Owen Stephens, who grabbed a brace of tries, the Wallabies were 10–0 up after just as many minutes and 14–0 after just a quarter of the match had been played. With Wallaby captain and flanker Peter Sullivan in fine fettle, the game was, to all intents and purposes, over not long after it had begun. It finished 30–12. The match was also notable for the fact Australia's Farrick Fay became the only specialist second row to ever score a drop goal in Test rugby.

The Tongans followed up the disappointing loss by falling 22–11 to New South Wales. The result meant they had lost five of their seven games on the tour. Despite this, Australian coach Bob Templeton naturally talked up his side's opponents ahead of the second Test. He said: 'We have definite tactics for certain contingencies. But these fellows are so unpredictable I cannot say which ones we will use. That will be left to the captain, Peter Sullivan . . . We were not an 18-point better side and the presence of their star centre Tali Kavapalu has me concerned. I hear he is a beauty and I prefer the devil I know to the one I don't.'

Kavapalu was absent from the first Test, but was incorrectly listed as playing in some contemporary match reports. He was a central figure for the Tongans and his return for the second match would have given some hope to his side.

The Canberra Times previewed the second meeting (penned the day before the Test) by writing: 'The Tongans passed up a training session today, preferring to rest after a solid morning of social engagements. They had planned a late afternoon training session. It is difficult to assess their chances although it is generally agreed that they are much better than they were in the first Test.

'At their best they were irresistible. They are strong, fast and rely almost entirely on long passing, incredible handling and the demoralising up-and-under . . . The Tongans are appreciating the warmer Brisbane weather and they are expected to respond with better play.

'They have a brilliant half-back in Fonua and a clever fly-half in 'Alatini and a forward pack which, though still ignorant of rucking and mauling techniques, is a greyhound to the loose ball.'

Heading into the eighth match of the tour, the Tongans were perhaps unsurprisingly carrying injuries and feeling the fatigue. Valu, who played in eight of the ten tour games, recalls how the side lacked the resources of modern touring teams: 'We had no physio or doctor. However, the rugby team also played the roles of a physio when required. However, if they were sick they were taken to the hospital.'

Valu also states that Tonga were far from discouraged by the result of the first international: 'After the Test we strategised on how we could do better for the second Test. We learned from our mistakes. As Tongans, we had the heart for winning.'

The match
On 30 June 1973, in warm weather and with a slightly blustering cross-field wind, Tonga full-back Valita Ma'ake kicked off from an oddly painted halfway line that was marked at its centre point with a double circle – making it look like the kicker was positioned in a giant target for an aerial assault. The referee was Bob Burnett of Brisbane. There were no neutral officials in these distant touring days.

The opening play lasted about 40 seconds and saw both teams drop and kick the ball multiple times. Nerves and adrenaline were clearly thick in the air. Eventually, after a fumble from Australia, a scrum was awarded about 12 metres inside the Australian half and slightly to the right of the middle of the pitch. In a sign of how much the game has changed, the time it took from the ref blowing his whistle for the scrum to the ball emerging for scrum-half Ha'unga Fonua was just 22 seconds. As it rapidly arrived at his feet, the number nine picked up and burst off to his right. There was a decent amount of daylight as his pack – as allowed under the scrum laws of the day – had wheeled the home back row and defending scrum-half away from him. Fonua accelerated past the covering flanker and inside left wing Owen Stephens to reach the edge of the 22. Seeing full-back Arthur McGill covering over, the scrum-half expertly drew his man and threw a lovely inch-perfect inside pass to captain Sione Mafi. The number eight, who had run an excellent support line, hit the ball at full speed, and sprinted in from 20 metres. Mafi, who was probably too stunned by how perfectly the game had opened for him, failed to go nearer the posts and dived over as soon as he crossed the line, leaving a conversion to come from about 13 metres inside the right touchline.

In another example of how much the sport has changed, Mafi jogged back from the score with no celebration and all alone as all his teammates, other than kicker Ma'ake, had already retreated for the restart. The full-back just missed the unnecessarily difficult conversion, leaving the score at 4–0 after just two minutes.

Five minutes later, Australia's McGill missed a kickable penalty with the wind, which was coming and going in spurts, doing nothing to aid his effort. The attempt was part of a long period in which all the territory and possession was in Australia's favour. Twelve minutes into the match and Australia grabbed an equalising try. Tonga lost control of their own ball at a scrum on their own line and Wallaby scrum-half Eric Tindall, on his debut, poached a four-pointer after stealing the ball from Fonua.

The try was not converted, but just three minutes later McGill converted a penalty for an offside at the scrum by Fonua. The score stood at 6–4 to Australia and the visitors had not had a sniff since their remarkable opening score. Order, it seemed, had been restored.

Yet Tonga kept pulling things out of the hat. Twenty minutes in and with a scrum ten metres from their own line, they attacked on the blindside through full-back Ma'ake and winger 'Isikeli Vave. The latter took the ball deep in his own 22 and sprinted to halfway, but in trying to kick over the last defender he saw his kick deflected into touch. It was thrilling stuff and an excellent example of just how quickly Tonga could turn the game on its head in the blink of an eye. Time and time again, Australia dominated possession and then the tourists pulled out some elaborate move or made a spectacular break to give their hosts a serious fright.

Half an hour in and Tonga gained a kickable penalty in the Australian 22. The place kicking of this Tongan side had been erratic all tour and this was to be one of eight kicks at goal squandered by Tonga, including one almost comical miss late in the first half that barely left the floor.

But the miss worked out well. In the sequences of play that followed, Australia were unable to get out of their half and eventually, Tonga earned a line-out on the left touchline on the Australian 22. The long throw-in from winger Vave (teams back then had the winger from the relevant wing throw in, usually overarm) found flanker Siaosi Selupe who leapt up and used his outside arm to tap a ball to Mafi who had been inside him at the line-out. The Tongan captain released almost instantly to Fonua who outfoxed a rushing defender with a dummy, then accelerated into the space he had created and drew the next man and passed to 'Alatini who had burst up on his right shoulder. Inside centre Sione Foliaki ran an excellent dummy line and the ball was then transferred to Kavapalu, who had so worried the

Australian head coach earlier in the week. The outside centre took only half a dozen steps, drew a tackler and then passed to winger Sami Latu who sped over from 20 metres, just making the corner before the despairing cover defence. It was, again, a rapid moment of magic that Australia had no answer for. Mafi missed the difficult conversion.

When the half-time bell rang (yes, a literal bell), the Tongans led 8–7.

The second half

Early in the second period Wallaby captain Peter Sullivan threw a punch out of the blue at the back of the line-out as the ball sailed over his and his opponent's head. This was one of several punches thrown in the game and the referee immediately awarded a penalty. Sullivan claimed an act of shirt pulling led him to retaliate. Either way, such acts rarely led to much of a fuss back in 1973, especially when a referee was officiating his own countrymen.

Not long after though, Australia stole a line-out in the tourists' 22 and quickly moved it infield from the right-hand touchline. After a few passes, number eight Mark Loane made inroads in the middle of the pitch. With quick ruck ball and under severe pressure, Tindall switched the attack back to the left of the field. His diving pass found the wonderfully named centre David L'Estrange, who fed McGill who then provided a scoring pass to right wing Jon Cole who had to run only a few yards to score.

The conversion failed and the score sat at 11–8 to Australia ten minutes into the second half. McGill missed another penalty a few minutes later, continuing the day's trend for inaccurate goal kicking.

With just over 25 minutes remaining, Australian fly-half Geoff Richardson rolled his ankle and was struggling to play on it. His replacement, Russell Fairfax had to change out of his civilian clothes to get dressed in case he needed to come on! In the end, he wasn't called upon.

Tonga missed another penalty with 11 minutes to go. It was clear that to win this match, Tonga were going to need to score tries. Once again, the missed kick was a blessing. From the subsequent 22 drop out, Tonga gathered a bobbling ball and launched an attack. Mafi took the ball to the right of the breakdown and then, suddenly, switched back and ran left and offloaded to support runner and second row Fa'aleo Tupi. The lock took it into the 22 and then lobbed off a ball in the tackle that may well have been forward or knocked on, the grainy match footage is unclear. The pass went to ground, but bounced kindly for Valu who charged up to within five metres of the line. He was brought down and temporarily injured in a collision with two defenders. Fly-half 'Alatini zoomed in to pick up and fired the ball quickly to Kavapalu who ran just a few yards but, crucially, tied up the final covering Wallaby, and then gave a simple pass to Vave who sprinted about four metres and squeezed over in the corner. 12–11 to Tonga. The conversion, inevitably, failed (Vave tried this time and almost put it straight across the 22 line it was struck so poorly). But with the stadium clock showing just nine minutes of normal time remaining, people started to sense that history may well be on the cards.

Australia stepped up the pressure. Tonga, however, would not yield. Not long after the Tongans' third try, Wallaby winger Stephens received a brutal, but legal, hit when seemingly in space. The tackle was from Ma'ake and, when compared to the 'passive' tackling style of the day, it looks like something from another sport. The Tonga full-back hits him like an express train around the waist and the crowd, surprisingly supportive of the visitors at this point, roared their appreciation. The hit led to a Tongan penalty too and they wasted a precious minute by having a more than optimistic pop at goal. Amazingly, Mafi hits the worst kick of the day – which is quite something. The captain scuffed the top of the ball and it bounced like a lovely grubber kick into the welcome arms of Wallaby hooker Chris Carberry just ten metres away.

With five minutes to go, Australia made huge yardage from a clean line-out and quick ball to right winger Cole. Despite the game being in its dying moments, the Tongans were corner flagging and covering the field with incredible commitment. They ran with a sense of history in their heads and hearts. While speedster Vave ultimately made the textbook cover tackle and drove Cole into touch, several of the Tongan pack hustled their way over with burning lungs to give him support. The effort was all the more remarkable as for some of these players it was their third game in a week.

Three minutes remained.

Tonga, through running and kicking, were able to relieve the pressure and get a line-out near halfway.

Two minutes remained.

Australia put it wide from a scrum only for full-back McGill to have his turn getting cut in half by Ma'ake, who crunched the open ribs of the Wallaby like a demolition ball crashing into a moving car.

One minute on the clock.

Australia were now forced to go all out. After recovering a kick inside the Tongan half, they again put width on the ball to try and find a way through a backline that had been, to this point, an iron blanket. Stephens and Cole attempted a switch to avoid the right touchline and bring play back infield. But it was fumbled. Kavapalu, missed so much in the first Test by the tourists, gathered off the floor and sprinted 50 metres to the corner to seal one of rugby union's greatest wins. For the first time all game a Tongan try received the congratulations of teammates. Just two of them. Quite calmly. But by the standards of the day it was a riot and shows what the score meant to the men in red.

Mafi, of course, failed with the conversion. It was the eighth and final missed Tongan kick of the day. It didn't matter. The score was 16–11 to the islanders and the match was over. Rugby immortality had been achieved. The match commentator spoke of the Tongans' jubilation on the final bell, but the cameras managed to miss it all, lingering on the conquered players and then panning all too slowly to the victors. A small crowd of local youths ran onto the pitch to show their appreciation, but there were no laps of honour or dramatic celebrations, the players simply came together and shook hands and swapped shirts.

The aftermath

The win was a national humiliation for Australia. The back page of the *Canberra Times* wrote:

'In an incident without precedent at Ballymore Park, the 10,000 strong Queensland crowd barracked against its own side as the Tongans gave the football lesson of the year. They scored four tries to Australia's two and on the effort should have swamped Australia, but all of its eight attempts at goal missed . . . The Tongans' play was unorthodox, and confused and bewildered Australia.'

Another article in the same paper blasted the whole set-up of Australian rugby and the culture it believed had allowed such a result to happen: '[Tonga] missed every kick at goal and, it is not widely known, went into the Test a team of tired, despondent and homesick young men. They should have been the greatest pushover in the history of international rugby and there are not many teams going round today which could have managed Saturday's loss.'

The Tongan coach, Lupeti Finau summed things up nicely: 'We couldn't go back home to our king without winning.'

Valu, who had played such a key part in the match's third try, today remembers the physical toll of the game and the pride of his side. 'I recall seeing after that most of our players had injuries,' he says. 'However, we had the spirit of representing our Island Kingdom, injured or not. I also recall the Tongan people being overjoyed with the win. We prayed and thanked our Heavenly Father for his blessings, his love, guidance and protection. We gave the glory back to him and then we continued with a feast – Tongan style.'

Meanwhile, the Lord Mayor of Brisbane, Alderman Clem Jones, said the result had 'whipped up such enthusiasm and interest in the capital that a tie-breaker was essential'. He even went as far to offer $1,000 dollars to have another match played. Sadly, it would be 20 years before the sides met again. And except for the 1998 encounter, as of 2022 the sides have not met since.

Tonga won one (Darling Downs) and lost one (Queensland) of their remaining two games after the dramatic Test win, to finish the tour with a record of four wins, six loses and 125 points for and 158 against. They went to the Palace to greet their King when they returned home as conquering heroes.

The following year they toured the UK and faced a Scottish XV and Welsh XV, losing 44–8 and 26–7. Despite the Tongans having beaten Australia away from home just one year before, both the SRU and WRU declined to award caps for the fixtures.

While Tonga are now well-established on the international scene, the only wins they've achieved against Tier One nations since 1973 are France (1999 and 2011), Italy (1999 and 2016) and Scotland (2012).

The win of 1973 still stands supreme in the annals of Tongan rugby history.

MATCH DETAILS

Australia: Arthur McGill; John Cole, David L'Estrange, Trevor Stegman, Owen Stephens; Geoff Richardson, Eric Tindall; Ron Graham, Chris Carberry, Jake Howard, Stuart Gregory, Garrick Fay, Dick Cocks, Mark Loane, Peter Sullivan (captain).
Tries: Cole, Tindall
Penalties: McGill

Tonga: Valita Maʻake; ʻIsikeli Vave, Tali Kavapalu, Sione Foliaki, Sami Latu; Malakai ʻAlatini, Haʻunga Fonua; Eukaliti Hehepoto, Tevita Bloomfield, Ualeni Pahulu, Polutele Tuihalamaka, Faʻaleo Tupi, Siaosi Selupe, Sione Mafi (captain), Fakahau Valu.
Tries: Kavapalu, Latu, Mafi, Vave

TOUR DETAILS
Played: 10   **Won:** 4   **Lost:** 6
Points for: 125   **Points against:** 158

Results
South Australia 6 Tonga 29
Victoria 13 Tonga 10
Sydney 14 Tonga 19
New South Wales 18 Tonga 0
Australian Capital Territory 17 Tonga 6
Australia 30 Tonga 12
New South Wales Country 22 Tonga 11
Australia 11 Tonga 16
Queensland 18 Tonga 10
Darling Downs 9 Tonga 12

JONAH LOMU RUGBY

'It's the official Jonah Lomu rugby game: play hard
and fast with the world's most powerful winger
in the video game that he helped design!'
Back cover text from the *Jonah Lomu Rugby* box packaging

In 1997 New Zealand's Jonah Lomu was at the peak of his fame. Video game publishers Codemasters licensed his name for a video game that has become a cult classic in the rugby community and is one of the most important pieces of rugby union pop culture of all time.

Platforms: Sony Playstation, Sega Saturn, MS-DOS
Developer: Rage Software
Publishers: Codemasters
Release year: 1997

Jonah Lomu was one of the most important figures in the history of rugby. A genuine icon, his 'arrival' on the world stage in the 1995 World Cup with New Zealand was unlike anything else ever seen in the sport. His superhero-like exploits in that tournament, including his celebrated four-try effort against a helpless England, catapulted him to household-name status.

The 196cm (6ft 5in) and 120kg (18st 13lb) winger, was a revelation. Despite his bulk and size, he was faster off the mark than anyone in the All Blacks squad. Lomu was labelled a 'freak' by England captain Will Carling due to his combination of speed, size and raw power. Born in Auckland and of Tongan heritage, Lomu was the first global rugby superstar. At the peak of his fame, he appeared in everything from Pizza Hut commercials to McDonald's adverts and became an ambassador for Adidas, where he hung out with fellow brand stars such as Russian tennis star Anna Kournikova.

But one of the greatest and most fondly remembered aspects of his legacy wasn't what he achieved on the playing fields, as great as that was. Rather, it was a video game bearing his name. *Jonah Lomu Rugby* was released in 1997 for the Sony Playstation, Sega Saturn and MS-DOS. It remains one of the most significant moments in modern rugby popular culture and marked the first time a player's name was licensed for a rugby title. It was, quite simply, a phenomenon.

'Big Bloke. Big Game.'

In 2023, preparing for this book, I posted a tweet asking for other rugby fans on Twitter to share their memories of the game. The response was astonishing. The post was viewed over 250,000 times and received hundreds of passionate comments in a digital outpouring of joy and nostalgia.

Here are just a small sample of some of the tweets (edited for clarity) that came flooding in (note, at least a quarter of those I got quoted the game's 'digging like a demented mole' commentary audio):

- **From @chjones9:** *Knowing how to lift in the line-out and put up Garryowens (without turning around) separated the wheat from the chaff.*

- **From @jrodbourn:** *...I once played @paddyonsports in a best of 88 games series.*

- **From @SprtBookReviews:** *The best game ever. We used to have a mega tournament with all of my friends and brother's friends on Christmas eve for hours. Used to love the scenarios especially.*

- **From @scottemitchell:** *This game was a massive part of my life. Undisputed as the best rugby game ever. I can remember someone taking it, and the PlayStation to Argentina in 1999 for the U21 World Cup. And we (Wales u21 Squad) would sit around and play it. Obviously I smashed them all.*

- **From @johnnyisgreat:** *Bought this game a while back for the memories and found it really helped me feel calm whenever I felt stressed. Something about how simple it was just helped me to relax. That and the superb commentary.*

- **From @GuyHeveldt:** *Winning the World Cup with Japan. Genuinely the best game on any platform ever made. How there hasn't been a follow-up, with the same gameplay but better graphics is life's greatest mystery.*

- **From @Exploding_Heads:** *Just the pure joy at unlocking the team full of Jonah Lomus. Not a feeling in the world like it.*

- **From @ItsDTPT:** *I remember vividly that the last time I prayed to a deity was at 14; that my plane home from school wouldn't crash because my dad had bought me JLR for Christmas.*

- **From @wuggapowelll:** *I still have the original game for the ps1! Some of the commentary was classic! That's a big tackle enough to put him in ward 4 ! I hope not Bill that's a maternity ward ! Lol*

- **From @RugbyTimes:** *I recall furiously pressing the ruck button like you used to do on the Daley Thompson video arcade game if you wanted him to run faster. The commentary was good too.*

- **From@Sourdust:** *Working out how to win the NZvJAP "classic match" was an achievement so satisfying I considered putting it on my C.V.*

- **From @dominicj99uk:** *I once beat NZ playing as Japan. Still the single greatest achievement of my life.*

-From @jacquesvictor10: *We always had our own tournaments-used to write on a piece of paper all participants names with their team. Round robin until champion was declared. That person was too cool for school for the week, but rematched the next weekend, always same friends house used.*

- From @Patman1884: *Around 10 of us used to sneak out of school at lunchtime and play tournaments on a nearby mates PS1. The competition was fierce. Respect was earned, and lost. The catchphrases from the commentary was heard for years.*

- From @Bigchap27: *Laksanasompong, where is he now?*

- From @EvansLlywelyn: *Was bordering on a religion at our school. Simple gameplay done well. There were a hundred ways to absolutely cream the computer but once you got into multiplayer it was a whole different experience. I swear a couple of the boys at that school would be the best in the world!*

The making of a cult game

Created in the UK, *Jonah Lomu Rugby* was coded by Rage Software and published by Codemasters. The genius of it was that it avoided the trap so many other rugby games have fallen into. It did not try to make an accurate simulation of rugby, it rather went for arcade-style gameplay that captured the essence of the sport, but was easy to pick up and play. It smartly made up for its decision to 'simplify' the sport by being incredibly well executed, fast and unbelievably fun.

In 1997, Trevor Williams of Rage Software explained this concept in an interview with *Sega Saturn Magazine*: 'We wanted a game that stayed true to the rules, but was easy to pick up and play without a complete understanding of all [rugby's] ins and outs.'

This is something that Lee Mather, a 19 year old who was working at Rage at the time, agrees with. Mather helped compile the stats for the players in the game (showing the age of the game, books were the main reference sources for player info), but also worked as a general office administrator, doing everything from burning discs to game testing and IT tasks. He was not a rugby fan, but soon found himself enjoying it too. 'Yeah, it was that fact that anyone could sit down, pick it up and play it,' he says. 'And there were people that weren't rugby fans sitting down and playing it in our offices. It really was for anyone.'

The developers wisely decided to avoid using polygons or other memory-draining graphical techniques, and instead opted to use an engine that was sprite based. This both allowed for the game to perform well and at speed, while also giving it a unique, fun, almost cartoon-like visual appeal.

'If I remember correctly,' recalls Mather, 'all the animations were done on super high-end silicon graphic workstations and then brought down to a level that was usable on consoles with the memory that was then available.'

Rugby was, and remains, a notoriously difficult game to reproduce digitally due to its complicated laws and highly specialised positions and tactics. Yet the approach of Rage to the project was so brilliant that the game achieved such a cult status that a copy of it now sits in the Museum of New Zealand (Te Papa Tongarewa) as part of its Pacific Cultures Collection. The museum website states: 'As an artefact of popular culture, this video game helps us document the history of Pacific Islanders in sport but also how some became the marketing face of rugby both in New Zealand and internationally.'

It's in the game

Jonah Lomu Rugby (or *Great Rugby '98* as it was known in Japan) allowed players to play on their own against the computer or head-to-head with other human players (up to four people could play simultaneously). Gamers could choose from friendly mode, World Cup mode, Tournament mode, Territories Cup mode (this included tournaments such as the Five Nations, Tri Nations and Pacific Cup) and Classic Matches. The latter mode dropped players into a famous moment in a real historical rugby match and asked them to change the outcome. These challenges are a fondly remembered part of the Lomu formula. They ranged from the relatively simple (help New Zealand win the 1995 World Cup in extra time) to the insanely difficult (guide Japan back from 24–3 down against the All Blacks in the second half). Japan, of course, had lost to a second-string All Blacks 145–17 (see page 27). Completing these tasks would unlock special teams and modes, including the 'Extra Cup which featured the Codemasters, Rage All-Stars and Team Lomu sides.

The gameplay itself was a delight and a smart, intuitive control system meant that while new players could pick up the basics very quickly and start having fun, the more hardcore players who persevered would be rewarded by the depth of gameplay. A serious veteran of *Jonah Lomu Rugby* will always be happy to regale a captive audience with the strategies, tactics and techniques they developed to take their play to the next level.

Mather recalls how key it was that the developers nailed the flow and controls. 'The hardest part was to get a non-rugby person like me to enjoy it and give it a flow and that's what the coders managed to do,' he says. 'Unlike football, rugby has plenty of stops and starts and if you aren't familiar with rugby you need to understand why that is. Also, the coders focused on the fluidity of the passing and animations. Back then animation wasn't like it is today, so getting the players to look believable and have dynamism was important to the game's success.'

The Classic Matches also pitched the difficulty curve just right. Casual players may manage some of the early challenges, but only the dedicated would be able to pull off a Japan comeback against Lomu's inspired and relentless All Blacks.

The sound of tackles, moles and maternity wards
To get the basic sound effects and crowd noise for *Jonah Lomu*

Rugby, the developers acquired the audio rights to the 1995 Five Nations and used that to start building an ambient soundtrack that would be familiar to fans. Most famously of all, Rage pulled a blinder by getting the legendary 'voice of rugby', Bill McLaren, to supply the match commentary. The charismatic and beloved Scot was in the final years of his long and glorious career, so it was appropriate that the game arrived in time to capture his unique personality and make him a gaming as well as a broadcast immortal. Backing up McLaren was another Bill: ex-England captain and current World Rugby chair Bill Beaumont.

These were early days of responsive sporting commentary in video games. While by today's standards the vocabulary and phrases may seem limited and repetitive, at the time it was highly impressive. So critical was this audio track to the game's success, mention of the game in conversation today, over a quarter of a century later, is likely to send fans off into quote land, with the 'digging in like a demented mole' or the infamous 'maternity ward' phrases most likely to be the first ones lovingly imitated.

There is even a Twitter feed (now seemingly defunct) called *@Lomu_commentary* which used to throw out classic lines from the game's audio library along with the odd retweet of *Jonah Lomu Rugby* related features and articles.

The teams
There were 32 international teams included in *Jonah Lomu Rugby*. Alongside the main nations, more obscure national sides such as Chinese Taipei, Hong Kong, Sri Lanka, Singapore, Malaysia, Netherlands and Thailand were included. Indeed, one of the biggest memories many gamers had in the aforementioned Twitter discussion was of McLaren's energetically reciting the names of Thai players such as Laksanasompong and Rajangjongjitakorn.

As mentioned earlier, the best players were rewarded with special bonus teams that were unlocked upon completion of various challenges: Rage All-Stars, Codemasters and Team Lomu.

Rage All-Stars were made up of developers who worked on the game and they took advantage of their role in programming the game to give themselves some unique abilities. It was this team that made Lee Mather a video game legend. Playing on the left wing for the Rage team, he was both the smallest and fastest player in the entire game. In contrast, developer Trevor Williams at full-back was a huge unit (about four times the size of other players) and was about the only other in-game player who was a match for the feared Jonah Lomu in contact.

Mather smiles when asked about his iconic status among *Jonah Lomu Rugby* fans. 'I used to sit near Tony McCabe, one of the lead programmers,' he says. 'We had previously worked together on the stats for the football game *Striker* and we got on well. I don't remember when I found out that he had made me this super player in the game and it didn't really become a thing until way after when the internet arrived and people started talking about it. I didn't really consider it beyond thinking it was cool that I was on the team. For some reason, Tony made me really small and really quick for fun.'

When the internet arrived and provided a platform for nostalgic fans to reminisce over their love of the game, Mather couldn't avoid seeing how beloved his digital doppelganger had become. It seemed that his name was always among the first things discussed when hardcore fans got together and YouTube videos can even be found showing Mather at the peak of his digital rugby powers.

Codemasters too represented members of the company's staff, including the Darling twins who founded the company (Richard played on the wing and David at fly-half). Codemasters, incidentally, had a small history when it came to rugby, having also published *International Rugby Simulator* in 1988 for the Commodore, Spectrum, Amstrad and Atari.

The final team of the Extra Cup was Team Lomu which contained, as you may expect, 15 Jonah Lomus.

Licensing

Jonah Lomu Rugby was the first rugby game to have licences when it came to player names. Previous rugby games, such as EA Sports' *Rugby World Cup '95*, had lacked this touch, so fans appreciated finally being able to play 'puppet master' and control their favourite players in action.

In 2022, All Black winger Jeff Wilson told New Zealand journalist Jamie Wall that it was 'pretty funny' being in a video game. 'I was lightning quick in the game, but any time anyone got near me I bloody dropped the ball,' explained Wilson. 'I had to laugh, but I didn't take offence to it because I'm pretty sure I was the fastest player. No one could move as fast as me.'

Amusingly, the licence didn't extend to stadium names. Instead, gamers could choose from venues such as Tallfield, Aston Road, Hagley Road and Ballydown Park. The *Sydney Morning Herald* review of the game in 1997 praised almost everything about the game apart from the limited choice of 'English' stadiums.

While fans loved being able to control national teams with real player names and characteristics, it worked out better for some gamers than others. Kiwi gamers got to forever enjoy the thrill of playing with one of the great teams of all time, while Welsh fans were stuck with the haunted bones of the 1995 World Cup team which possessed all the cutting-edge of soft cheese.

The legacy

Despite being released in 1997, the game is still enjoyed by gamers and, incredibly, even professional rugby players. During the 2015 World Cup in England, Drew Mitchell of Australia put out a tweet asking if anyone could help him source a Playstation console and copy of *Jonah Lomu Rugby*. Sure enough, rugby Twitter quickly delivered. Not long after the request, fellow

Wallaby Matt Giteau shared a picture of a Playstation with a copy of the game that a follower had set him up with. The pair spent plenty of time between real-life matches and training on the console. A few days later, Giteau praised Mitchell as a wonderful rugby player who should be considered among the elite of the sport, but then added how since they had acquired the Playstation he had discovered how 'bad' his teammate was at *Jonah Lomu Rugby.*

BBC rugby presenter Gareth Rhys Owen is one of many in the broadcasting world to still hold a candle for *Jonah Lomu Rugby:* 'I used to play it religiously with my brother when I was about 15 or 16. I'm a video game nerd and a rugby nerd. Lomu's arcade quality was what made it so good. It captured the essence of rugby as it didn't try to mirror the sport exactly like more modern games have. It was about momentum and it didn't focus too much on the technical stuff. And rugby is all about momentum. The commentary was incredible and the jokes were lame. They were terrible, but the repetition and humour actually made it work.'

In late 2022, Squidge Rugby (see page 173), produced a video of Ospreys players Morgan Morris and Will Griffiths playing a few matches, which thrilled his older audience who remembered the game from first time around and no doubt intrigued those who had only heard of the fabled game but never seen it in action.

Journalist Jack Zorab looks back fondly upon mass competitions played in his school's common room, where the only rule was no one could be New Zealand due to the unfair advantage the digital Lomu gave people. In 2020, Zorab wrote a wonderful piece called 'Finding Mather' which dived into the making of the game and gave many fans a glimpse into the title that they had never had before.

Fans continually upload memories, articles or even game footage onto social media. One of the great finds came in 2023 when a Tom Davies on YouTube uploaded a video of every sprite and frame of animation for the players on *Jonah Lomu Rugby*. Amazingly, it showed that animations had even been made for the hooker hooking the ball in a scrum, even though the frames would never be visible to someone playing the game.

Jonah Lomu Rugby is regularly listed as the greatest rugby video game of all time, with newspapers such as the UK's *Daily Telegraph* and Ireland's *Irish Independent* bestowing that honour upon it.

What happened next?

Publisher Codemasters was acquired by gaming giants Electronic Arts (EA) for $1.2 billion in 2021. Sadly, there was not such a happy outcome for Rage Software. In 1996 it had been floated on the London Stock Exchange and seemed destined for great things. Unfortunately, an ill-advised venture into publishing proved costly and commercial failures (including a franchise based around football superstar David Beckham) led to the company winding up in 2003.

Several of the team that crafted *Jonah Lomu Rugby* went on to work on 2004's *World Championship Rugby* from Swordfish Studios and Acclaim Entertainment. It failed to recapture the magic.

Where is the true successor to *Jonah Lomu Rugby*? While a fair few argue that *Rugby 08* from EA Sports deserves to be talked about in the same conversation, the game never truly gained the cult following that Lomu's did.

In recent years, prominent figures in the sport have called for World Rugby to use an officially licensed and quality game to drive interest in youngsters who invest so much time and money in other sporting games. So far the appeal has fallen on deaf ears, which some consider ironic considering that Bill 'I hope not . . . that's a maternity ward' Beaumont has been chair of World Rugby since 2016. Hopefully, one day, a team of developers will emerge from a hole dug by a demented mole somewhere to produce a worthy successor.

Yet despite official involvement or movement on a new version, the game itself still evolves with a small community of modders adapting it to reflect the modern game. New Zealander Chris Chen, a software developer who describes himself as being at the centre of a Venn diagram featuring 'Rugby, Gaming, Software, and the 90s', has been working for over three years on building a mod that updates the game to include teams, kits and players from modern Super Rugby franchises and national teams.

'I had the idea to do it in 2015,' explains Chen. 'I was sick of waiting for a good rugby video game and wanted to play as the 2015 All Blacks. I was one of those people calling out for 'them' to remake JLR with new teams while keeping the same great gameplay. Then I realised I actually had both the skills and the passion to do it. I've spent somewhere between 500 and 1000 hours. It's hard to know. Many evenings and weekends have been spent on it and I'm still actively working on it and adding new features and new teams. My ultimate aim is to create the best rugby video game experience. Imagine the Lomu gameplay but with the game modes and breadth of teams of the top sports games like FIFA and NBA 2K.'

As for the fastest winger of all time? Lee Mather now works as senior creative director at EA. And while he may not have been a big rugby fan at the time, he admits that on occasion, he can be found standing on the sidelines at Gloucester or Coventry. The fans around him, however, have little idea they are in the presence of digital rugby greatness.

Rage All-Stars: T. Williams; S. Williams, O'Dowd, Cooper, Mather; McCabe, Bruce; Theobald, Taylor, Court, Clarke, Howard, A. Williams, Argentieri, Seabridge.

Codemasters: Gaffney; Cummins, Eddy, MacVarish, R. Darling; D. Darling, Smith; Regan, Holley, Osbourne, Bartlett, Walker, England, Gosbell, Urry.

Team Lomu: J. Lomu; J. Lomu, J. Lomu, J. Lomu, J. Lomu; J. Lomu, J. Lomu; J. Lomu, J. Lomu, J. Lomu, J. Lomu, J. Lomu, J. Lomu, J. Lomu, J. Lomu.

Game credits

Programming: Tony McCabe, Steve Williams and Antonio Argentieri

Commentary/audio programming: John O'Dowd

Game design: Tony McCabe, Andrew Hague and Richard Darling

Sound effects and music: Kevin Bruce

Artwork: Gordon Theobald, Lee Seabridge, Andrew Taylor, Claire Cooper, Michael Hanrahan

Motion capture: Rob Callaway

Team information: Lee Mather, Trevor Williams

Commentary: Bill McLaren and Bill Beaumont

Head of production: Steve Holley

Project management: Stewart Regan, Andy Williams and Tony McCabe

Quality assurance: Jason Walker

GIANT KILLERS
WALES WOMEN (2009)

*'I kicked it, and I did not even know if it went over because all the
girls jumped on me. It was the best moment of my life.'*
Non Evans, Wales full-back

**Wales and England had first met in women's rugby in 1987.
Ahead of the 2009 Six Nations clash, Wales had lost on all
24 occasions the rivals had met. And with the game clock
expired in 2009, Wales were trailing England once more and
looking at a 25th straight loss in the fixture. But then . . .**

Wales 16 England 15 (Maes Gwyn, Taffs Well)
14 February, 2009 – Six Nations
It's no secret that the country most Welsh athletes and sports
fans want to beat more than any other is England. It's the fixture
that fires up the hardcore supporters into a frenzy and even gets
the pulse racing above average for the casual fan. As anyone even
vaguely familiar with the social history of Wales and England
understands, the meaning and symbolism of the match goes well
beyond the accumulation of points on a scoreboard. It's sporting
and cultural warfare.

Wales first faced England in women's rugby at Pontypool Park
in 1987 in what was both countries' debut international game.
England triumphed 22–4 over Liza Burgess's team (see page

12 for more on Burgess). The sport was in its infancy in both nations, but England already had a significant lead in terms of both playing numbers and in quantity of teams. Over the years England would make that advantage count, even as the game in Wales grew.

In the 24 meetings between the sides prior to the 2009 Six Nations, England had won all 24. The aggregate score was England 927 Wales 146. At one point Wales went three consecutive games without scoring a single point. Below are the results from that period.

Bold indicates home game for England.

Year	Winner	Score
1987	England	22–4
1988	England	36–6
1989	**England**	38–4
1990	England	18–12
1991	**England**	24–13
1992	England	14–10
1993	**England**	23–5
1993 (Neutral venue)	England	38–0
1994	England	11–10
1995	**England**	25–0
1996	**England**	56–3
1997	England	24–22
1998	**England**	29–12
1999	England	83–11

2000	**England**	51–0
2001	England	18–0
2002	**England**	40–0
2003	England	69–7
2004	**England**	53–3
2004 (Neutral venue)	England	39–3
2005	England	81–0
2006	**England**	38–15
2007	England	30–0
2008	**England**	55–0
2008 (Neutral venue)	England	12–6

There had been a few agonisingly close contests over the years: 1992, the first time the women's team were allowed to play at the iconic National Stadium, Cardiff Arms Park, almost saw Wales claim a first win, but they ultimately came up four points short. The most frustrating result of all for Wales came in Bridgend two years later, when the Dragons were bested by a solitary point. The scorelines and performances of those early games in the decade gave hope that Wales would soon be able to claim a much sought-after first win over the Red Roses. Alas, they were instead the end of an era. In the coming years the gap didn't just widen between the two sides, an entire sporting chasm opened up. England exceeded 80 points on two occasions, over 60 points on another and went over 50 points in four other contests. For all intents and purposes, it had effectively stopped being a competitive fixture. As England challenged for world titles (and indeed won the 1994 World Cup), Wales struggled for consistency and progress.

In 2006, Wales didn't even manage to qualify for the World Cup. It was a dark time for the national side which was not helped by a decision not to pick non-Wales-based players between 2004-06. With top-level women's rugby in England far more suitable for developing players than Welsh club rugby at the time, the policy was hamstringing Wales. It was all the more ridiculous as players were amateur and often played in England to either make a living or to develop as players by being exposed to a higher level of club rugby. Yet the Welsh Rugby Union would penalise them for playing outside the borders of Wales.

Upon the reversal of the policy in 2006, Wales immediately improved. After a shock narrow win over France, Wales beat Scotland in two consecutive meetings – having not tasted success against them for the whole of the previous decade.

Getting closer

Although Wales had lost by a crushing 55–0 to England in the 2008 Six Nations, the women in red won all their other games in the tournament to finish a respectable second. The Dragons were steadily improving and took a new-found confidence into the 2008 European Championship in the Netherlands later that year. In the tournament, Wales dispatched Scotland (26–10) and France (18–10) before taking England to the wire. Leading 6–0 at half-time thanks to two penalties from Non Evans, Wales didn't concede until well into the second-half.

Then things turned sour quickly. Inspirational captain Mel Berry broke her collarbone and was forced to depart and, after 68 minutes, England finally pulled things level. Cruelly, it was not until two minutes from time that England's Katy Mclean kicked her third penalty to put England in the lead for the first time. To rub salt into the wounds, Mclean kicked another in the final play of the game to seal it.

After the game, England coach Gary Street said it was the first time his side had really been tested since the 2006 World

Cup final. Speaking for this book in 2023, he said: 'I was a big fan of Wales and good friends with several of their players. Their biggest issue was they would never play against anyone else with the ferocity they played against England. They hadn't been great earlier on in that European Championships, and as we had beaten them by big margins in recent years, I could see ahead of the game some of the England team couldn't quite believe Wales would challenge us. But that was a very good Wales team, especially their back row.'

While the result was tough to take for Wales, it did mean there now existed a core of players who knew they had the ability to compete with the Red Roses. And in a nation like Wales, where confidence is so critical to success and self-esteem, it was a vital moment in the side's development. Street also admits that the result knocked some of his team's confidence too and certainly played its part in what would unfold in the 2009 rematch.

The 2009 Six Nations

For the 2009 Six Nations, Wales were captained by Mel Berry and coached by Jason Lewis. Berry is one of the central figures in the history of the Wales team and came into the tournament with vast experience. Still only 27, she had already amassed 70 caps. Extraordinarily, for 50 of those games she had been captain too. Berry was first selected for the national squad aged 17, when she was too young to even get selected for an actual Test match. She was an inspirational, thoughtful and articulate leader and by the age of 18 was captaining Wasps. At the same age she made her full Test debut, but continued to represent Wales at age-group level. At 20 she captained Wales at the 2002 World Cup in Barcelona.

By 2009, Berry was turning out for Bristol, but had previously played with Wasps and Ponsonby in New Zealand. She had also tasted some success at the top-level in the red shirt of Wales against England, having captained both a Wales Sevens and under-19 side to victory over the white shirts, something that certainly helped Berry's mindset when it came to facing the formidable white wall of England. Speaking for this book, Berry said: 'I was fortunate at both age-group level and sevens to have a really good group of players around me and to be involved in those wins over England. And I was captaining Wasps playing in the Premiership. So I was used to playing against and beating these players regularly and realising that, yes, these players are good, but we have potential to be really good as well.'

For the 2009 tournament she lined up at number eight, but during her Test career she played across an incredible six positions in total, also lining up as blindside flanker, openside flanker, scrum-half and in both centre positions.

Wales launched their campaign with a comprehensive 31–10 win away to Scotland. Tries came from Berry, debutant winger Ali Wright and (full-back) Non Evans. The latter contributed 21 points in all, kicking two conversions and four penalties. The win was crucial as finishing in the top three in the final table meant Wales would automatically qualify for the upcoming World Cup. For most observers, France and England would likely secure the top spots so it was a scrap between the Celts and Italians for the coveted third-place spot.

Momentum is everything in a tournament like the Six Nations, and coming off the back of the Scottish win and the good results in the European Championship in 2008, Wales felt that in spite of the history of the fixture, they had a chance to topple England at Taffs Well on Valentine's Day in round two of the tournament.

Berry was set to win her 71st cap in the English game and genuinely believed that Wales had an opportunity to shock the world: 'That 2008 European Championship gave us a lot of confidence and made us realise that, yes, England were brilliant at playing a certain English way of playing, but that if you could understand what both their Plan A and Plan B was, you could disrupt that. Despite the score, we started to do that in the 2008 Six Nations and also the European Championship final later in the year. In the latter game, we did disrupt them and then we made some small errors later in the game. But we realised we had the potential to beat them.

'We thought about what we could do that they may not expect and how we could make decisions that were risky, but was what I call informed risk. We went into the game with players who had been together for a while and felt we had a chance. We didn't necessarily go in thinking we were going to win it, but we felt we had a chance.'

Wales were boosted by a great week of training and the camp had a positive attitude. Coaches and players had done extensive homework on England's patterns and took the attitude that they had nothing to lose as England were such red-hot favourites.

Non Evans, lining up at full-back, was one of Wales' most fascinating and impressive athletes. The Swansea born player finished her career with 489 international points, including an extraordinary tally of 64 tries – making her the highest try scorer for Wales for both the men's and women's sides. Her heroic sporting exploits weren't confined to the rugby field; she represented her nation at judo, weightlifting and wrestling and even appeared on the television show *Gladiators*.

Wales selected a matchday squad which featured 16 of the squad that had been humiliated by 55 unanswered points to England in 2008. As much as they would be thirsting for revenge and a famous first win over England, it must have been inevitable there were some serious mental scars from previous failures against the women in white that had to be dealt with.

In the starting backs, Non Evans, Rachel Poolman, Clare Flowers, Louise Rickard, Naomi Thomas and Amy Day survived from the previous year. While those that remained in the starting pack were Rhian Bowden, Jenny Davies, Louise Horgan, Catrina Nicholas and captain Mel Berry.

Among the Welsh matchday squad were several with vast experience. Heading into the 2009 Six Nations, flanker Jamie Kift had 63 caps, full-back Non Evans 71, centre Claire Donovan 66, second row Clare Flowers 58 and winger Louise Rickard 103. At the opposite end of the maturity scale, back Ali Wright was uncapped before the championship began, although she grabbed a debut try in the Scottish victory.

England, meanwhile, had not lost a match since defeat to New Zealand in the 2006 World Cup final and were looking for – and expecting – a 17th consecutive Test win and a fourth straight Grand Slam. They had blown Italy away 69–13 in their opening round and few expected them to struggle against Wales, a side they had not lost to in 24 games over a 22 year period.

The Red Roses contained some fantastic players, none more so than outside centre Emily Scarratt who was in just her second year of Test rugby. Born in Leicester, she was in the 'infant' days of a career that would see her earn 108 caps and win a World Cup (see page 16). Yet, even in 2009 she was already a major star. Her first year of international rugby saw her score a scarcely believable 12 tries in 12 games. Scarratt, playing with Lichfield at the time, had jumped into the latest campaign in fine fettle having already bagged two tries in the opening game against Italy.

England named an unchanged side from the one that swept the Italians aside and the matchday squad contained nine players from the 2008 version which handed Wales a 55–0 thrashing. In the forwards England included Rochelle Clark, Amy Garnett, Jo McGilchrist, Sophie Hemming and Catherine Spencer who had been involved the previous season. Behind the pack Amy Turner and Katy Mclean of 2008 again formed the half-backs. There were a couple of changes on the bench though, most notably winger Charlotte Barras was away on sevens duty.

Coach Gary Street was understandably in a positive mood ahead of the meeting, saying: 'We're looking forward to a tough game against Wales but are confident of producing another good performance with our rapidly improving young team. It's great to play two games back-to-back and have a real level of continuity. The team are in good spirits and are already looking forward to the weekend.'

His Welsh counterpart, Lewis, spoke of Wales hoping to make a long-held dream a reality, telling the BBC: 'It's an opportunity to have a go at the best team in the northern hemisphere and turn them over. That's our approach . . . long term our goal is to try to turn England over . . . We came close to them in the European Championship and want to build on that. [It's] understanding what we need to do well to counter the attacking threat they have throughout the team and capitalising on some of our strengths.'

Valentine's Day rugby romance for the Welsh

One of the most special results in Welsh international rugby history took place at Maes Gwyn, the home of Taffs Well RFC in Rhondda Cynon Taf. The sun was shining and the Wales team were boosted by the presence of a huge number of family and loved ones. While the weather was fair, the pitch wasn't. Graham Smith, assistant coach of England, speaking for this book, recalls it being 'heavy to the point of being muddy'.

They were pitch conditions that suited the home side who wanted to disrupt the well-oiled England machine. In her team talk, Berry stressed the need to enjoy things, even in the toughest moments that were to come: 'I said, we should play and focus on what we can do, rather than just focus on what the opponents could do, which was something that we were guilty of in the past.'

Wales drew first blood, with Non Evans kicking a penalty in the 13th minute to put the hosts ahead. It was just reward for a very good Welsh start which had seen hooker Rhian Bowden cross the English line but have the score disallowed as she didn't manage to ground the ball.

'It was so important we started well,' says Berry. 'We knew England traditionally started well and we did manage it this time. And we continued that for large periods of the first half.'

However, England got on the scoreboard just a few minutes later when Wales's captain Berry was dispossessed after a big hit from Scarratt. The ball popped out of the captain's hands as she was readying herself for a pass. A kind bounce put the ball up for England winger Fiona Pocock. A deadly finisher, Pocock gathered and zoomed over from 25 metres out. The conversion was added by Mclean.

If Berry felt she had let her side down, she helped to equal out the try-count in the 26th minute. England infringed just outside their own 22 in what was a very kickable position. As Wales were the underdogs, Berry felt that it was expected that they would take the conservative option and aim at the posts. Instead, she yelled at scrum-half Amy Day to take a quick tap penalty and attack – implementing the captain's philosophy of 'informed risk'. It paid off in spades as the visitors weren't ready and Berry took a pass and quickly beat the unprepared defence who were expecting a kick and went over for five precious points that put Wales back in the lead 8–5. Evans was unable to convert.

Before half time, Scarratt was again the thorn in the Dragons' side as she cut through the red shirts to rack up her third try of the campaign, cleverly finishing off a looping move she herself had initiated to glide over. Mclean was unable to add the extras this time and the sides went into the dressing rooms with England leading 12–8.

Although they were behind, Wales were having great success

when it came to frustrating England. Flanker Jamie Kift was a particular problem that England were struggling to answer.

'During that game Jamie killed us,' recalls Street. 'She was the best at slowing ball down and was unbelievable at falling on the wrong side and 'accidentally' slowing the ball down. I don't think she ever got pinged.'

All of this was said with genuine admiration, not bitterness.

'We always prepared for her before a Wales game and would have someone in a bib representing her in training. She was amazing.'

Early in the second half, Evans missed two penalty chances to pull Wales back, one of which hit the uprights. The full-back would be the first to admit she was not the most talented of kickers, but had worked hard to improve her technique over the years. But there was no hiding from it, she was having a bad day at the office when it came to goal kicks. Speaking to World Rugby in 2022 she spoke of her frustrations and successes with the boot and how she tried to be the best she could:

'I wasn't a particularly good kicker but it frustrated me for years that we'd lose games by one or two points because we didn't have a goalkicker so I thought, 'right, I'm going to practise'. My boyfriend at the time was Mark Perego, a flanker, he played for Llanelli and Wales, and he was so talented, he could kick off both feet, and we just used to go out in the field and kick and kick and kick.

'I wasn't the best in the world and didn't have any coaching but we did win quite a few games because I could kick, at least better than anyone in the past.'

The fact Evans was even playing at all was impressive enough. A nasty compound fracture playing against France in 2007 had looked so bad initially that she was told she wouldn't be able to run properly again, let alone play rugby. Yet she was back for the next game against France in 2008 and had stayed injury-free for the 2008/09 season.

But early in the second half at Taffs Well, it seemed Evans's boot wasn't going to rescue Wales this time. Then some good fortune, which had so often been a stranger in the previous 22 years of battle with England, made an appearance in red. Scarratt was sin-binned for a professional foul as the game entered its final quarter. Wales knew that their three-quarters, particularly the vastly experienced Rickard, could do some serious damage and they knew they needed to make the most of the extra attacker.

Up front, Bowden was having an extraordinary game, seemingly running off an inexhaustible supply of energy. Behind the scrum, to the delight of Welsh purists, fly-half Naomi Thomas was playing a fine game tactically and ensuring Wales remained in the contest and played in the right areas.

Wales made the most of the extra player, with replacement winger Aimee Young getting over in the corner to put Wales back in front 13–12.

'If you can score by going out wide it breeds confidence,' says Berry. 'And we did something that many teams hadn't done against this England side. It was a big moment.'

Evans was unable to convert. But this was serious now. Wales were actually in the lead as the game entered its grand finale and one of the biggest upsets in women's rugby history was an increasingly distinct possibility.

Yet, no side goes unbeaten for several years without being a damn fine team. England weren't going to kick a winning habit without a fight. Like all champions, they refused to believe they were beaten.

One of the most fascinating things in sport is when a giant-killing team is on the verge of being born, especially in a regular fixture. Games are never played in isolation and as the contest slowly ticked to its conclusion, every player wearing red would have been acutely aware that history was within touching distance. They knew that glory was calling and its call would go some way to energise tired limbs and burning lungs. And just as powerfully, every England player, during stoppages in the game, would have been considering the fact that they risked being the team that lost an undefeated record of 22 years against their fierce neighbours. And in turn, they too would find a bit more fire in their belly to keep slogging on, but with the confidence of winners.

And, yet, that pressure would just as likely make the potential giant-killer panic as it may make the potentially vanquished giant stutter. Pressure does funny things.

Every Wales fan screaming for their team to hang on that day would have been praying there was still romance in elite rugby. And what better day than Saint Valentines' Day to prove it?

And then, and then . . . England got a late penalty. In the final minute of the match, Wales infringed and England's Mclean coolly slotted over the three points to put the visitors back on track for a Grand Slam.

'We didn't even need to watch,' says Berry. 'Mclean wasn't going to miss it.'

Street meanwhile, admits to feeling huge relief that it seemed his side would 'scrape home'. Sport and romance can be cruel. With only injury time remaining, it would take something extraordinary to save Wales. A quick glance at the history books showed that extraordinary from Wales in this fixture was unlikely.

The home side kicked off as much in hope as expectation. But they threw everything that they had at one last shot. Most importantly of all, when they quickly regained the ball, they showed patience and composure, despite the nightmare result unfolding in front of them second by second. Slowly, they worked their way into the English 22 and got their reward with what to them was the beautiful sound and sight of a referee's whistle and the raised arm of a penalty in their favour.

One kick stood between them and history.

It was all down to Non Evans and her boot.

Or was it? Evans had not had a good afternoon with the boot. And while the kick was seemingly a relatively straightforward one, her low success rate for the afternoon and the immense pressure of it made it far from a sure thing.

Berry asked Evans if she felt she could do it. The captain was aware her team was tiring and knew that a kick to the corner or 'tap and go' may backfire. But she also knew that if her full-back said she could do it, she would back her.

Evans accepted the challenge and Berry signalled to the referee that she would go for the posts. By the time all preparations were made, the clock was up. It was all or nothing. One kick and either 22 years of pain was over and history was written, or England continued their incredible winning run in the series and their awesome unbeaten record since the 2006 World Cup.

Evans stepped up. Hit it. And hit it badly.

It wobbled. It was ugly.

And it went over.

And the game ended.

After the kick

In an interview in 2023, Non Evans remembers how the celebrations from teammates obscured her view of the kick: 'I kicked it, and I did not even know if it went over because all the girls jumped on me. It was the best moment of my life. I was asking if we won, and all my teammates were hugging me, crying and shouting, "We won, Non, we won!"'

The spell was broken. The Red Roses had finally been cut down by the women in scarlet.

Street, as devastated as he was by the loss as a rugby man and a professional coach, is philosophical about the result, saying: 'It was really weird, because I had been involved in the game for so long and I obviously wanted England to win for my job. But I also wanted women's rugby to grow and was desperate for women's rugby to be competitive. I knew how hard Welsh players like Jamie Kift and Clare Flowers worked. I was really pleased for them.'

Street admitted too that Wales's belief that England didn't have enough alternative ways to play if their primary plan was disrupted had been correct. The defeat was key in the development of expanding how they played and, ultimately, helping them on the road to their 2014 World Cup win. Street estimates that across sevens and all guises of the national team, he won 132 of 138 games he coached with England. Which is perhaps why he recalls the occasion so clearly.

Smith had no complaints about the defeat either: 'In the modern game, at all levels, people always look for referees, "they made bad decisions, this happened that happened". At the end of the day you aren't good enough. Are there other factors? Yes, of course, but at the end of the day generally you lose because you deserve to lose or win because you deserve to win.'

The exhausted Wales team celebrated with family and friends, but Berry admits the magnitude of the event didn't sink in immediately. The entire squad jumped on a bus to head to a private box at the Millennium Stadium in Cardiff to watch the men's team also triumph over England, but Berry, who doesn't drink, admits she couldn't have told you the result of that game. It was all about what her heroic team had achieved.

In contrast, the England squad, dressed in their tracksuits, had to sit in a bar to watch their male counterparts lose, with the locals revelling in the double defeat their nation had suffered in just a few hours.

Wales went on to win their first ever Six Nations Triple Crown, edging past Ireland 13–10 at the same venue they had beaten England. Italy too were defeated in Venice 29–7. Frustratingly, a chance for a Grand Slam had already been ended in round three when Wales, strangely flat, fell short to France 26–5 away from home. That one loss, cruelly meant England, who won all their other games, retained the title on superior points difference.

Nonetheless, the win and Triple Crown remain a high point in Welsh rugby history. Indeed, as of 2023, Wales have faced England on 40 occasions and have only two wins to their credit (the other win coming in 2015).

Non Evans, whose last-gasp kick is among the most important moments in Welsh rugby history, would go on to become an MBE in 2011. She was the first female rugby player to receive the award.

The victory was chosen as the subject for a commemorative stamp, one of just eight images picked to celebrate 150 years of the Rugby Football Union. Berry, who was represented in the image, bursting through an English tackle, likes to point out that her stamp was more expensive to purchase than the Jonny Wilkinson one.

Despite the historic significance of the moment, as of summer 2023, the match is unavailable to watch anywhere online, with neither the BBC, Six Nations nor World Rugby sharing the footage anywhere. A reminder, if it were needed, that so much of women's rugby history is at risk of being lost or forgotten. This chapter is an attempt, however small, to make sure these great moments are kept alive.

MATCH DETAILS

Wales: Non Evans; Ali Wright, Rachel Poolman, Clare Flowers, Louise Rickard; Naomi Thomas, Amy Day; Hannah Roberts, Rhian Bowden, Jenny Davies, Louise Horgan, Rachel Taylor, Catrina Nicholas, Mel Berry (captain), Jamie Kift.
Replacements: Claire Horgan, Gemma Hallett, Claire Donovan, Carys John, Laura Prosser, Awen Thomas, Aimee Young.
Tries: Berry, Young.
Penalties: Non Evans (2)

England: Victoria Massarella; Francesca Matthews, Emily Scarratt, Kimberley Oliver, Fiona Pocock; Katy Mclean, Amy Turner; Rochelle Clark, Amy Garnett, Sophie Hemming, Natalie Binstead, Joanna McGilchrist, Rebecca Essex, Catherine Spencer (captain), Lois Moulding.

Replacements: Ollie Poore, Claire Purdy, Gemma Sharples, Karen Jones, Georina Rozario, Tina Lee, Alice Richardson.

Tries: Pocock, Scaratt

Conversion: Mclean

Penalties: Mclean

KOJI TOKUMASU

'It wasn't the size of Wales that beat us, it was the skill, the flair, the beautiful running, the thinking. It was the most beautiful rugby I had ever seen. The All Blacks were said to be the strongest rugby team in the world at that time, but Welsh rugby was the most beautiful in the world.'
Koji Tokumasu

Thanks to a twist of fate when he was a young man, Koji Tokumasu was reluctantly persuaded to watch Wales play against Japan in Osaka in 1975. What he saw not only changed the course of his life, but would ultimately help revolutionise both Japanese rugby and the Rugby World Cup.

Main teams: Hoso Club (Japan), Cardiff College of Education, Meikei High School (coach), Shibuya International Rugby Club (founder/coach)
Key roles in rugby: Head of international relations (JRFU), board member of the Japan Rugby Football Union, board member of International Rugby Board (now World Rugby), president of Asia Rugby, general manager of Bid Committee for Japan 2019, senior director of the Rugby World Cup 2019 Organizing Committee.

In September 1975, Koji Tokumasu was a young journalist, not long out of university and utterly rugby mad. At the time he was playing regularly on weekends for Hoso Club, a social rugby club in Fukuoka, a city in the southern island of Japan, Kyusu.

Tokumasu wanted to play as often as he could, so when a friend suggested he join the club's short weekend tour to Osaka, he couldn't say 'yes' quickly enough. There was just one condition, though. If he played on the Saturday, he would have to go with them on the Sunday to watch Japan play a team called Wales. He reluctantly agreed.

'I had no interest in watching Wales at the time,' said Tokumasu in an interview for this book in 2023. 'I had never heard of Wales, I just wanted to play rugby on Saturday and so that was the only reason I agreed to go.'

As it turned out, his decision to attend that game would set in motion a series of events that would change his life and, ultimately, help bring the Rugby World Cup to Japan in 2019.

Falling in love with the game

Before Tokumasu went to university he had never played rugby. Indeed, in the 1970s in Japan rugby was very much a minority sport. While a respectable number of schools played it, it was largely a mystery to the average citizen. Tokumasu's high school had not offered the sport, but his chosen university – the International Christian University (ICU) in Tokyo – did play it. The fresher student soon found out that there was a tradition that the three dormitories at the university had an inter-dormitory rugby competition and he was recruited to play in it.

'I was forced to play,' Tokumasu recalls. 'But I loved it.'

One of the big things that appealed to the young student was the simplicity of what was at the essence of the sport. 'I'm not a great athlete to be honest,' admits Tokumasu. 'But in rugby, once you have a ball you go forward as hard as you can. You don't need much skill. Even someone like me, who didn't know much about rugby, could just pick up a ball and play. In that sense it is a very simple game. You go forward until you are hit and then you make the ball available to someone else. And when someone comes to you, you tackle them. It's very simple. The laws of the game are complicated, but what you need to do is simple. And when I was 18 and full of energy I found it beautiful. Afterwards you feel so happy as your energy is burnt up. There is the fulfilment and satisfaction that comes from physical contact. Everything is painful, but you are alive. You live.'

Tokumasu did enough to impress one of the senior players and he was soon recruited to play for a club team too. A love affair with the sport had begun. His university side was in anything but rude health though. When he first joined there were only a couple of other players and 'old boys' had to be recruited on weekends to make up the numbers so they could play matches.

While Tokumasu was a student, money was tight. His father had left the family when he was in his teens and there were always financial struggles. It made his dream of one day travelling abroad a very tough one to realise. During his studies, he even passed a test which made him eligible to spend time studying at UCLA in California. Sadly, successful students needed to pay 100,000 yen to attend and he simply wasn't able to afford it.

Despite the money troubles, Tokumasu still gave up some of his spare time to volunteer for a local children's home in Hachioji. After helping for a short while with tasks like painting walls at the home, he was asked to cover for a member of staff who was unable to work due to a physical problem. Wondering what he could do to occupy the students, it suddenly occurred to him that rugby could be an ideal activity.

'I felt rugby could be a good sport because everyone played together,' he reflects. 'There was a small space for us to play on and I brought a rugby ball along. All they had to do, I told them, was get the ball down in the other team's patch of ground. It was simple, fun and everyone could play together. Everyone was mad about it and loved it! It was great. It was a simple game and it didn't matter if they passed it forward, as long as they enjoyed it. And that was my first coaching experience.'

Not all Tokumasu's fellow staff were impressed and he did get warned about the small space being a bit dangerous and the risk of his players falling over the fence that surrounded the playing area.

Dragons inspire a new life

After graduating, Tokumasu worked as a journalist for the *Nishinippon Shimbun* newspaper in Fukouka. It was during these early years of his working career he made the fateful decision to go on that weekend tour and round it off by watching Wales play Japan at Osaka's Hanazono Rugby Stadium, in the first game of a two-match series (Wales did not award caps for Japan games until 1993). It was the first time the two sides had met in Japan and the tourists were overflowing with some of the game's all-time greats including Gareth Edwards, John Dawes, JPR Williams, Gerald Davies, Steve Fenwick, Mervyn Davies and Ray Gravell.

Although he hadn't been keen on attending the match, that all changed as soon as it started and the men in red from a faraway land started doing their thing.

'I had never seen anything like it,' he says. 'It was completely different rugby to anything I had seen before. I had always been told that foreign international teams were better than us due to their much bigger physical size. And remember, there was no way to watch things like the Five Nations, so we had no way of seeing them in action living in Japan. But, it wasn't the size of Wales that beat us, it was the skill, the flair, the beautiful running, the thinking. It was the most beautiful rugby I had ever seen. The All Blacks were said to be the strongest rugby team in the world at that time, but Welsh rugby was the most beautiful in the world. Wales played as individuals, but also as a team.'

The Wales XV crushed Japan 56–12 that day. Afterwards, Tokumasu was unable to stand up as he had been so physically moved by what he had seen and he lingered in the stadium long after most people had gone to allow himself to take it all in.

Around the same time as he had this transformative experience, Tokumasu also felt an urgent need to get involved in rugby more directly. Working as a journalist, he was able to observe rugby, but not really be part of it. One day he watched a high school team playing and was envious of how the coach (who was also their teacher) was able to be part of the experience and have a direct impact on the team. Even though the team he was watching was losing, he could see the coach was in it with his players. This inspired Tokumasu to become a teacher, rather than remain a journalist. And he wanted to be a teacher at an institution where he could coach rugby.

It was then he made his mind up to travel across the world to Wales to learn all he could about how the Welsh taught and played rugby. He quit his job and began working for a friend to earn some instant money so that he could gather enough cash to travel. For nearly a year he toiled delivering seafood such as fish, octopus and squid to local restaurants, driving around in a small lorry. By 1977 he had enough money for his adventure.

In those days, international travel was far more complicated, risky and expensive than it is now in the internet age. 'It was hard to find out much about Wales,' says Tokumasu. 'The exchange rate was terrible at the time. One pound was fixed as 500 yen and I knew even before I left that my money wouldn't go far and that I would somehow have to find work in Wales. I'd also heard that due to tough rules at places like Heathrow, there was a chance I either would only be allowed to stay a week or that they may even send me home straight away. So I needed to find a way to avoid Heathrow.'

Tokumasu certainly found it. He travelled with a Pakistan airline and went first from Tokyo to Beijing, then another five or six steps and changes to arrive in Copenhagen, Denmark. That first leg of the journey had taken him 32 hours. From there he jumped on a train to the west coast of Denmark, before sailing on to Harwich in Essex. When he arrived, his plan of avoiding Heathrow or a major travel port paid off and he was granted a six-month visa.

Not long after disembarking he travelled to London, where he wandered around hoping to find some rugby to play or watch. Alas, his trips to London parks, such as Regents Park, only resulted in him finding games of football. However, he did manage to get a ticket to see the British Lions play the Barbarians at Twickenham in a star-studded game to mark the Queen's Jubilee.

After that, Tokumasu boarded a train to Wales, clutching a book he had managed to purchase entitled: *Where to Stay in Wales*. The book revealed that the cheapest place he could find shelter was a dormitory at Cardiff University. He had to phone the receptionist from a phone box at Cardiff train station three times to persuade them to let him stay. Their policy was only to take people who had made reservations, but they soon realised he genuinely had nowhere else to stay and he got a room for £2 a night on the condition he could remain for just one week.

It's worth noting that Tokumasu had no contacts, that nobody knew he was coming and he had, quite frankly, no real plan. He had nothing more than a desire to learn about Wales and Welsh rugby.

After the first week, he managed to find a job as a cleaner that allowed him free board for cleaning the house and garden. The lady of the house gave him the job because of the five people who had been that day he looked the 'most serious'. Meanwhile, Lady Luck continued to smile upon him when it came to rugby. He came across a schoolboy game of rugby at Lady Mary High School in Cardiff and began taking photos to start building up his reference library. The team's coach, Leslie Gauntlet, wandered over and asked, quite understandably, what he was doing. When Tokumasu explained that he had come all the way from Japan to learn about rugby, the coach offered him a lift in his car and then took him to 'the best place in Wales' to learn about rugby: Cyncoed.

It was in Cyncoed, Cardiff, where the Cardiff College of Education was situated (now known as Cardiff Metropolitan University). Leslie soon introduced Tokumasu to the dean of the college, Mr. Aaron. It turned out that the dean had an interest in learning more about Japanese gymnastics and said that if Tokumasu would translate some Japanese literature on the sport into English for him, he would help him get permission to attend lectures at the college as an observer.

This was how Tokumasu ended up an 'unofficial student' and didn't have to pay any fees. He soon became more and more integrated with the renowned rugby set-up, made plenty of friends and even got to play rugby with them – making a name for himself as a strong tackling winger (they nicknamed him Kamikaze Koji).

It wasn't all plain sailing though. One day Tokumasu overslept and was fired from his cleaning job (he suspected later the woman was going to fire him anyway as autumn was over and he'd already cleaned up all the messy leaves in the garden). Desperate for money, he had to find a new place to live.

An unscrupulous estate agent offered him the cheapest property he could find. The poor student arrived late at night to a freezing cold house and had to sleep in multiple layers of clothing to stay warm. When he awoke in the morning he saw that the room he was sleeping in had a rectangular pile of snow on the floor! The main window was broken and it had quietly (and coldly) drifted in overnight. There were also a few rats scuttling around. In desperation he had to buy a portable bed from a second-hand shop and plead with his rugby teammates to stay with them until he could find somewhere a bit better.

Again, fortune dealt him a good hand when he randomly bumped into a Japanese woman in Cardiff while out walking. It turned out she was the wife of a Sony executive living in the country and they needed a tutor for their two young children. This gave him enough of an income to rent a small room in a flat. He worked for the family for a while before eventually losing that job too.

He laughs when he tells the story now. 'It turned out the woman's children had been back to visit Japan and they didn't like it and preferred it in the UK. They felt there were too many rules and too much social pressure in their homeland. The parents wanted me to convince them Japan was better, but I agreed too much with the children and so after about four months the parents fired me.'

Not long after this bit of luck, Tokumasu put 20 pence in a slot machine in the clubhouse of Cardiff Old Boys and won £150, an absolute fortune in the 1970s. He grabbed the cash and ran to the post office to give his mother a call and tell her that he was ok (he hadn't been able to make any international calls as they were so expensive at the time).

Tokumasu however, clearly proves the old maxim that you make your own luck. Soon after arriving in Cardiff he had taken himself to the Welsh Rugby Union offices and introduced himself to Ray Williams, the coaching organiser who helped revolutionise rugby and put Wales at the top of the world game at the time. Williams put Tokumasu on several coaching courses and also shared with him his book: *Rugby for Beginners*. The grateful student made the most of the opportunities and ended up translating the book into Japanese.

In the end, Tokumasu spent an incredible two years in Wales before finally returning home to become a teacher. He admits that he considered remaining in Wales forever as he was enjoying his life there so much with his rugby friends. But in the end, home was calling.

A new kind of rugby

Upon his return home in 1980, Tokumasu became a teacher and rugby coach at the newly opened Meikei Junior High School in Ibaraki, then an hour's train ride from Tokyo. He was determined to bring everything he learned about rugby in Wales to the students he coached.

'Japanese coaching culture was very traditional and old-fashioned at the time,' said Tokumasu. 'Schools would train around three or four hours a day, every day. They believed in long sessions. The coaches would dictate everything and players were not to think for themselves or question things.

'But I had seen first-hand in Wales that shorter, more focused sessions were better for learning. I encouraged the players to work as a team, but think for themselves, to show some individualism and to play with flair. I was lucky that the school I was coaching at was only a year old and there was no rugby tradition there. I could start afresh.'

As a coach, Tokumasu stressed the need for players to enjoy themselves while always giving their best. It may not seem revolutionary now, but it was almost an alien concept in Japanese coaching. It paid off handsomely. Tokumasu had players from the age of 12 to 18 years old under his wing and they lapped up his teachings. Less than a decade after his return from Wales, his unique approach brought Meikei High School a coveted national championship in 1989 at the Hanazono Rugby Stadium. In a poetic piece of sporting symmetry, it was won at the same stadium that Tokumasu had first watched Wales play 14 years earlier.

It was an extraordinary achievement. There was no other team playing the way his side did and no coaches operating how he was. Indeed, one journalist wrote how the 'glorious' Welsh style had been revived at the same stadium the real Welsh team had graced long before.

As is so often the case in sport, success built on new techniques is often dismissed as luck or a freak occurrence that cannot be sustained. Rather than learn from what he was doing, other coaches were outright dismissive. He would hear opposing coaches openly tell their players not to copy what Meikei were doing and that offloads and miss passes, for instance, were too risky and not to be imitated.

Tokumasu would show his players videos of Wales, the All Blacks and the Barbarians and how it was possible to play the game. His students made heroes of players like Gareth Edwards and Phil Bennett. 'I always told players to use their judgement,' says Tokumasu. 'Do what you like, as long as you make the ball available for your teammates.'

It took a long time, but eventually other coaches began to adopt some of his methods and, slowly, it helped change Japanese rugby for the better. But Tokumasu's greatest achievement was still to come.

Bringing the world to Japan

In 1994, a year before the game turned professional and Japan would be humbled 145–17 by a largely second string All Blacks team, Tokumasu joined the Japan Rugby Football Union (JRFU). His vision of change did not immediately come to fruition.

'I passionately wanted to make rugby a popular sport, but soon realised that I had no power or status to change this within JRFU,' he explains. 'Because in Japan it was a lot about the university you graduated from and I came from ICU, this unorthodox university where rugby status was regarded as 'nothing'. On top of that, football had exploded in popularity in the early 1990s and rugby seemed stuck. I felt like it was difficult to change the JRFU and I had very little influence. I got depressed, and I almost quit.'

Ironically, Tokumasu took inspiration from football, the sport that was racing ahead of rugby in Japan. In 2002, FIFA held the World Cup in Japan and Korea. It was a controversial move at the time as neither were 'traditional' footballing nations. However, it was a huge success. Tokumasu, working as a head of international relations persuaded the JRFU to make a bid for rugby's showpiece event.

Tokumasu had managed this almost by chance. In 2003 the JRFU chairman Nobby Mashimo wanted some input into what he should say for the union's New Year's message at a rugby forum organised by one of the major newspaper companies. 'I suggested that he should say Japan wants to hold a World Cup,' recalls Tokumasu. 'And he did. And that's how it started.

'The following morning, a newspaper wrote that the JRFU would like to host RWC in the near future. Some advertising agents then came to see the JRFU asking if this was the true story as it had not been discussed at a recent board meeting.'

Tokumasu was thrilled with the warm reception to the idea but had to pick up a phone to call the International Rugby Board (IRB) to see if it was really possible for Japan to host a World Cup.

Mike Miller, then CEO of the IRB, replied that it wasn't an impossible idea and that he thought it would help spread the game globally. Tokumasu jumped with delight upon hearing this and reported back to Mashimo and the JRFU board that the IRB was 'backing' their idea.

It's worth remembering that the concept of a rugby World Cup being held in Japan was a revolutionary one at the time. Many doubted the wisdom of it or thought there would simply not be enough fan interest and as a result games would end up being played in empty stadiums. Furthermore, Japan's tournament playing record, as can be seen on page 25, was dismal. Nobody wanted to see the hosts get humbled.

These attitudes, along with the archaic voting system of the IRB at the time meant that ultimately Japan lost the bid for the 2011 tournament to New Zealand. The major nations on the IRB had two votes each, compared to just one for 'Tier Two' nations like Japan. It's long been known in rugby circles that major unions often 'persuade' other member unions to vote for them by promising to play lucrative fixtures at the grounds of those who support them. The Japanese couldn't compete in that regard and it seemed impossible for the JRFU to overcome such numerical odds.

'We kind of gave up,' said Tokumasu. 'A month after the loss, I went to an Asia Rugby meeting and apologised for failing and said we had tried our best. But one delegate from Brunei said that we should not stop, that we were the only ones who could do it for Asia.'

Two years later, Tokumasu and the JRFU decided to build on what they had learned and to try again. 'We realised maybe we were not ready the first time,' he says. 'So we changed Asia Rugby to be more democratic and increased the number of staff in JRFU from 15 to 45. We looked at the weaknesses in our organisation and our first World Cup bid and tried to improve things.'

Tokumasu had noticed that the push from the IRB to include rugby sevens in the Olympics could be to Japan's advantage, especially as Bernard Lapasset, the French chairman of the IRB, was a keen believer that rugby should be included in Olympic Games. The JRFU and Lapasset felt that by hosting a tournament in Asia, it would help convince the International Olympic Committee that rugby wasn't just a sport played to an elite level in relatively few countries, but was a genuine global sport.

On top of that, it was decided by the IRB that the host countries of the 2015 and 2019 World Cups would be announced at the same time. England were the favourites for 2015 and organisers were confident that a tournament there would generate healthy profits. This allowed for a bit more 'risk' when it came to choosing a more unusual venue for 2019. The JRFU worked closely with the RFU to align their bids, with Tokumasu making daily calls to ensure the campaign ran smoothly.

It worked. In July 2009, Japan was chosen to host the 2019 event. Not only did this raise the profile of Japan in rugby terms, it also galvanised the national side. The famous win of 2015 over the Springboks (see page 23) and the subsequent triumphs over teams like Scotland and Ireland in the 2019 tournament, were connected to winning the hosting rights. Once the tournament was pencilled in for Japan, the JRFU threw more resources than ever into its national side so that it could compete with the best. And they succeeded.

For many, the 2019 World Cup was the best of all the tournaments to date. It confirmed Japan as a major rugby nation and helped massively to grow the sport within Japan too. It's remarkable to think that if a young and somewhat reluctant Tokumasu hadn't agreed to attend a rugby match between Wales and Japan in 1975, it might never even have happened.

When questioned about what his dream is for the future of the sport in Japan, Tokumasu's answer isn't what you may think it would be. For instance, it isn't that Japan win the World Cup. 'I think maybe I would look at everything in a different angle to others,' he says. 'Through the bidding process I saw how isolated Japan was in rugby terms. Japan was outside of the major forces. But through the bidding process we got into the footsteps of the major unions. My dream is not necessarily that Japan wins a World Cup, but that Japan makes more friends internationally and we are treated as equals and can compete as equals. We learn from abroad, but we can offer culture and hospitality to those that come and play here too. It doesn't really matter to me about Japan becoming the first or second best in the world. I want rugby to help our country make more friends. Japan 2019 was a success, but I don't want it to be seen as a one-off miraculous event.'

Tokumasu will always remain thankful to Wales, the country that helped shaped his life. He continues to be passionate about rugby and in 2017, two years ahead of the World Cup, set up the Shibuya International Rugby Club for local and international children. It now provides a place for over 260 multi-national children between four and 17 to enjoy rugby and make friends.

'I thank Welsh rugby for how it changed my life,' says Tokumasu. The rugby community should thank him too for changing the world of rugby in so many ways.

GIANT KILLERS
FIJI (1952)

'Rugby Union's new born baby of the Pacific, leapt to full-fledged maturity yesterday. Fifteen of her white-jerseyed dusky dynamos humbled the cream of Australia.'
The Truth

Fiji's extraordinary tour of Australia in 1952 is long forgotten to all but the most knowledgeable of rugby supporters. But the 'Flying Fijians" victory over the Wallabies and the rugby they played throughout the tour deserves to be remembered.

Australia 15 Fiji 17 (Sydney Cricket Ground, Sydney)
9 August, 1952
Few teams have conjured up as much magic and romance in sport as the Fijian rugby team. A small island nation in the Pacific with a population that doesn't even add up to a million, has consistently wowed opposing players and entranced global spectators despite limited resources and, often, a lack of support from other rugby nations.

Today, many think of Fiji primarily as a sevens powerhouse, thanks to a proud legacy of success in the Olympics, Sevens World Cup, World Rugby Sevens Series and Hong Kong Sevens. But over the years the Fiji international XV have contributed immensely to the senior game too. For modern rugby followers, their most famous moment was their 2007 elimination of Wales from the World Cup.

But one of Fiji's greatest victories came so long ago that few are aware of it now. Furthermore, many of those that may know about the result are unaware that the Fijians didn't just beat a major nation like Australia, they helped save them from rugby bankruptcy.

The tour that almost wasn't

Fiji had been invited to Australia by the Australian Rugby Union (ARU) after the Islanders had taken part in a successful visit to New Zealand in 1951. The impact of the Fijians on New Zealand was immense; they not only beat the New Zealand Maori team 21–14, three of their players made such a good impression that they were named in *The Rugby Almanack of New Zealand*'s list of players of the year. Only five players were listed each year, so it meant over half of those chosen were Fijian rather than locals.

The acclaimed players were captain George Cavalevu, Josefa V. Levula and Rusiate Vuruya. Levula was praised as 'a great wing-threequarter, we believe the world's best'. Vuruya 'demonstrated the true value of the number eight forward when the position was in the hand of a natural footballer . . . Our general fetish that the back-row forward should only know attack when the side is on attack, and that he should "make for the corner post" when on defence, and stand up and wide when opponents are getting the ball, was annulled by watching Rusiate Vuruya in action. The genial Fijian proved that the success of the number eight game lay in that player being at all times where the ball was, and in Rusiate the Fijians had a man who possessed the speed and intelligence to carry out his duties in the manner . . . [he] was everywhere during a game – a veritable Jack-in-the-box, and it was no uncommon sight to see him up with his three-quarters, to squatting behind a loose scrummage if his half-back was late arriving on the spot.'

The *Almanack* went as far to ask if Vuruya was the best in his position in the world and proclaimed that he made the New Zealand number eights look third rate. However, he was to be a late addition to the Fijian tour party to Australia in 1952 due to injury, joining his countrymen for the fifth game against Queensland.

The third name on the list, Cavalevu, was a second five-eighth (inside centre) who received praise for his willingness to retain possession, rather than kick it away as his Kiwi counterparts were liable to. The *Almanack* said he was the 'mainstay' of the side and 'possessor of sound knowledge of the game'. Cavalevu played in all 15 matches on the tour (as did Levula), a remarkable feat in a trip plagued by injury that often saw backs having to slot into the forwards and all manner of players playing out of position just to ensure a full team could be fielded.

With such an impression having been left on their neighbours across the Tasman Sea, and with Australia in need of attractive opponents to raise income and stave off a financial crisis, the ARU extended an offer to the Islanders to tour in 1952.

Fiji had been playing Test rugby since 1924 (the sport had first been played between Fijian and European soldiers in 1884). In 1939 they had managed an unbeaten tour of New Zealand where, it is claimed, some players still preferred to play barefoot. Fiji's history and reputation for unorthodox and exciting rugby made them a natural choice for a touring invitation. The stumbling block though had always been money. It was estimated that the cost of bringing Fiji over for the ARU was cheaper than inviting a European side, but would still see them need an outlay of between 5,000 to 6,500 Australian pounds and they risked losing almost a third of that.

The worry of not covering costs was a legitimate one. When the All Blacks played three Tests in Australia in 1951, a mere 40,000 fans attended the three-match series. Panic about pennies briefly won out too. By February of 1952, just months before the Fijian tour was to begin, it was cancelled on financial grounds.

But pressure soon came back for it to go ahead and former Wallaby Bryan Palmer pushed for tour support, telling newspapers: 'The Fijians will stagger Rugby Union supporters with their speed. The tour will give the code a great boost.' Alan Sylvester, an Australian who coached in Fiji, wrote a letter complaining of the tour cancellation; attempting to stir up interest he declared that the Fijian forwards averaged 6ft 6in (a slight exaggeration) and that 'each of the backs could cover 100 yards in even time'.

The touring party is announced

By March the tour was back on and soon a touring party of 22 was announced. Fifteen of the squad were veterans of the expedition to New Zealand the year before. The captain was named as 35-year-old Apakuki Tuitavua, a back row and lock whose international career spanned from 1938 to 1954. A veterinary assistant in the Department of Agriculture, he was listed as 85.73kg (13st 7lb) and 182.88m (6ft) tall. This was not an insignificant size for the time.

Fiji's squad included their national 100-yard champion (Kalivate Cavulati), their 220-yard champion (Josefa Levula) and a sprinter from the 1950 Empire Games (Manasa Nukuvou). All but seven of the group had represented Fiji previously. Several players from the 1951 tour were unavailable due to military service. One newspaper raved about how, 'New Zealand critics last year were amazed by the risks taken by the backs in throwing the ball all over the field, even when pressed on their own line. They were also amazed by the way they recovered from their mistakes and got away with them, due to an ability to throw long passes almost across the field and take difficult passes.'

The tour wasn't just attractive to rugby fans either. The *Methodist*, a religious Sydney newspaper, previewed the tour and revealed that on 6 July the touring party (which consisted of 'several teachers, a policeman, a veterinary assistant, a laboratory assistant, an assistant medical practitioner, and a boiler maker') would 'visit Churches at Beecroft, Roseville, Five Dock, Balgowlah and Manly. In the afternoon they will attend the Pleasant Sunday Afternoon at the Lyceum and take part in the proceedings.'

The paper, which proclaimed 21 of the 22 Fijian players as being Methodists, also laid out the venues that readers could attend to see the team in action.

Upon arrival on Australian soil, the players were given coats and tracksuits by the locals to help them adjust to the 'cold' weather. The overcoats were delivered to the team by Wallaby Nick Shehadie who ran a dry-cleaning business. Much was also made of the fact the team said grace before meals and prayed in the mornings.

The *Daily Telegraph* warned local girls that 'they shouldn't feel upset if the Fijians are backwards in asking them for a dance. In Fiji the girls ask the boys to dance.' It was also noted their choice of refreshing beverage was lemonade and that beer would not be consumed.

One New South Wales newspaper condescendingly declared: 'The Fijian footballers provide perhaps the most striking evidence of the widespread appeal of Rugby football. The race of islanders, who less than 100 years ago were primitive and uncivilised, now possess a remarkable grasp of the game.'

Flying start

Fiji were an immediate hit with locals. After the opening 21–9 win over South Harbor, *The Sun* (a Sydney newspaper) related how the crowd that witnessed the clash 'laughed and roared excitedly in turns at the rollicking play of the giant visitors' and that Sydney had 'never had such hilarious football entertainment'. It also noted that four players were knocked out by the visitors and much was made of the physical approach of the tourists. It was claimed that local fans enjoyed seeing their players manhandled. *The Sun* declared how the 'crowd enjoyed the discomfiture of the local players as the Fijians hurled themselves at their necks to throw them around spinning.'

The islanders didn't just hit the ground running, they set off at 100 miles an hour and simply kept going. Wins followed over City of Sydney (28–9), New England (30–18), Queensland (24–17) and Australian Services (33–14). The only minor blot was a 14–14 draw with New South Wales, which was hardly a poor result. It meant the tourists headed into the Test match undefeated.

First Test
The Fijians had brought a 'silver mounted, polished, turtle shield' called the Noel Levy Shield for the teams to compete for in what originally was to be the only Test match of the tour. Despite their rugby bringing smiles to the faces of tens of thousands of spectators on the tour, the weather gods did not smile upon Fiji and the first Test match between the nations was played in a soaking wet Sydney Cricket Ground. It was hoped the contest would bring the largest union crowd in Australian Test history, but 'one of the wettest days Sydney had ever seen' put paid to that dream and a disappointing 13,457 fans attended.

Interestingly, this was the first time Fiji had played a full International Rugby Board member. Rugby historian Richard Steele notes that their previous 28 international matches since 1924 (of which they had won 16) had come against Tonga, Western Samoa and the New Zealand Maoris.

Fiji were captained by Tuitavua and Australia by centre John Solomon. Star winger Josefa Levula played despite badly injuring his wrist against the Australia Combined Services the week before (he had returned to the field with a bandaged wrist after possibly breaking it).

Fiji's unbeaten run crashed to an end in 15–9 defeat as they were outscored four tries to two in torrid conditions that saw large sections of the field underwater. The *Truth* newspaper proudly proclaimed that 'Australia burst the Fijian bubble with a brand of football which ranks the Test as probably the greatest exhibition of wet weather play at the famous ground. There was no doubting Australia's superiority.' The Wallabies were praised for their handling ability in the wet – all the more remarkable when one considers the smooth leather balls used at the time. Fijian coach Pat Raddock also complimented the play of Australia and admitted their back play 'was too good on the day for our fellows'.

Fiji still delivered thrills, however, and their opening try from prop Sailosi Valewai came straight from the kick off after just 15 or 20 seconds (reports vary). But in the end the home side settled down in the dire conditions better and their tries came from captain Solomon, flanker Brian Johnson and wingers Garth Jones and Eddie Stapleton. Centre Herb Barker added a penalty. Fiji's other points came via a try and penalty from full-back Taniela Ranavue.

It was noted that the Fijian players would signal a successful kick at goal from their opponents by raising their arms 'excitedly into the air'. At one point in the game, the referee's whistle was so full of mud he was unable to use it and had to find a new one.

The Australians immediately offered the tourists a second match. The tour had already grossed 13,000 Australian pounds and the Test, which had only a fraction of the attendance they hoped for due to the biblical rain, added another A£1,281. After Fiji consulted with 'people at home' it was eventually agreed a rematch would take place on 9 August.

Second Test
Fiji got back to winning ways after the Test defeat, beating Central Western (50–8) and Newcastle (28–24). Concern about further

bad weather had prompted the ARU to take out insurance worth A£3,000 ahead of the Test rematch in case Mother Nature stopped the game going ahead or once more severely limited attendance.

Australia named an unchanged team for the encounter, but full-back Peter Rothwell had to pull out with injury and was replaced by Ray Colbert. Fiji made three changes, intended to tighten up their defence as well as replace the injured star Vuruya. A further change in the second row was forced on them not long before kick-off. Impressively, five of the Fiji team had played in every single game of the tour: captain Apakuki Tuitavu, Joeli Susa (hooker), Taniela Ranavue (full-back), Semi Ralagi (prop), and Waine Salabogi (fly-half).

The gamble to hold a second Test paid off quite literally for the ARU as 42,004 spectators turned up to the Sydney Cricket Ground (at the time a post-war record for Australia) to see a thriller. This time conditions were ideal.

Refereed by Australian referee Donald Furness, who had taken control of the first Test as well, Fiji recovered from a poor kick-off to clear their lines and then settled down into their 'usual startling' way of playing. Some clever interplay sent prop Semisi Ralagi over early on, but the try was disallowed for an infringement in the build-up. Journalist E.W. Kann wrote that the 'Fijians' long passing nonplussed the Australians and thrilled the crowd'. Shortly after the disallowed try, Fiji butchered another with the tryline unguarded.

To prevent a bright start by the home side, Fiji coach Pat Raddock played full-back Taniela Ranavue at centre, switching Navitalai Taga to cover at the back. This was to keep powerful Australian centre Herbert Barker under wraps in the early sorties.

One Australian attack was thwarted by fierce Fijian defence that saw Australia's winger Garth Jones thrown around by the jersey 'like a sack of potatoes'. The home crowd apparently found it most entertaining. Yet despite the early probing of Australia's defence by Fiji, the Wallabies struck first, scoring a try after 13 minutes after smart and sharp play from the backs sent right wing Eddie Stapleton over to give them a 3–0 lead. The conversion was unsuccessful.

Fiji levelled soon after with a penalty from scrum-half Suliasi Vatubua. While Fiji were showing plenty of their usual flair in the open, the home side were getting the upper hands in the scrums and causing the tourists plenty of problems in the pack. But after 27 minutes, Fiji took the lead. After a 'brilliant passing burst', Ralagi made up for the disappointment of having his early try disallowed and stepped his way over to make it 6–3.

The lead was short-lived: five minutes later Australia captain and centre John Solomon knocked over a drop goal from about 35 metres out. 6–6.

Fiji came straight back though and Kann summed up the Fijian exploits, writing: 'The Fijians raked in passes from all angles with their magnetic fingers. As half-time approached they were racing the ball everywhere and had Australia in trouble.' Before the interval Australia conceded another penalty and full-back Taniela Ranavue put his side ahead 9–6 at the break. Fiji had won 12 line-outs to Australia's seven, but had won just five of the 25 scrums.

The second half

The Wallabies came out of the gate like banshees after the restart and scored through lock Nick Shehadie, who had gathered a cross-kick from fly-half Murray Tate. Again, Australia failed to add the conversion (using their third kicker of the match). 9–9.

Not much later, after passing that seemed like 'juggling', Ranavue kicked a drop goal to put his side back ahead at 12–9.

The Australians hit back by punishing Fiji for some loose passing. Winger Josefa Levula threw a wild pass that didn't come off after being tackled and Wallaby flanker Col Windon seized the ball and galloped off. Support was on hand by the faster Stapleton who carried it on before scrum-half Brian Cox went over for the three points. 12–12. And, yes, Australia missed the conversion.

The game continued to thrill and Fiji kept serving up some special moments, even if they didn't always end with points being added to the scoreboard. It wasn't all glamour though, at one point fisticuffs ended with Wallaby full-back Windon getting laid out and needing treatment.

Not only were the home crowd amused to see their own players manhandled (as they had been when Jones had been swung around by the collar), they booed their own referee when he disallowed a try from Vatubua for a forward pass. The half-back questioned the Australian referee's call too, which was not the done thing in the more strict days of the 1950s. But Vatubua was not down-hearted and was key to Fiji's relentless attacking game. The scrum-half even carried on after being knocked out cold in one collision. Not only were there no HIA replacements then, there were no replacements at all. In those days, players usually carried on as long as they could retain their balance to stay upright.

With five minutes remaining, and shaking off the blow he had suffered earlier, Vatubua converted a try from his half-back partner Wame Salabogi who had combined excellently with winger Samuela Domoni and second row Isikeli Cawa. The late score meant it was 16–12 to Fiji. History was within touching distance.

But just as modern Australian teams are known for never giving up, neither were their 1952 counterparts. With the full-time bell ringing out over the packed stadium, the Wallabies came at the tourists one last time. Starting from their own 22, Barker made a vital breakthrough and then fed Solomon who carried it further upfield. Windon was on his captain's shoulder to keep the attack alive and squeezed in at the corner just as the Fijian cover arrived for a dramatic long-range team score. It made it 16–15 to Fiji with the equalising kick to come.

The score was Australia's fourth try and they had failed to convert the previous three. Could they manage the kick from the touchline to save the day? Did Fiji deserve to have glory taken from them at this moment? Stapleton stepped up . . . and his failed kick sent Fiji into rugby folklore. They had done it.

The victorious islanders 'whooped with joy, embraced each other and their Australian rivals, and gaily swapped jerseys'. To the backdrop of a local band playing 'Auld Lang Syne', the victors made a circle with their opponents and linked arms – a far cry from how a similar result today would pan out on the field between professional players.

The aftermath

Fiji's win had come despite being outscored four tries to two, losing the scrum count 26–14 and the line-out battle 22–17. The *Truth* newspaper declared: 'Rugby Union's new born baby of the Pacific, leapt to full-fledged maturity yesterday. Fifteen of her white-jerseyed dusky dynamos humbled the cream of Australia.'

Alongside comments on the native referee not helping the tourists at all, the paper also stated: 'The Fijians have proved that there is nothing wrong with Rugby Union . . . All the code has been suffering from is the palsied, patterned, stereotyped stuff which has been served up as football Saturday after Saturday.'

Several papers pointed out the home crowd's seeming support, or at least encouragement of the Fijian team and noted the abuse given to referee Don Furness.

But while their team may have lost, the ARU won in another way. The tour saved the union financially and left them with a tidy A£7,000 profit, boosted massively by the extra Test which alone had a record gate income of A£5,190. Fiji too benefited to the tune of A£2,000.

The *Daily Telegraph* praised the visitors and marvelled at how the locals had taken to their style: 'The Fijians have emphasised that the Australian public demands bright, entertaining touring teams and football. The grim, steam-roller All Blacks and Springboks may get the cold-shoulder for future tours.' The paper even proposed that tour invitations would be extended to the likes of America, the Maoris, Italy and France.

Before all that though, the Wallaby players had a tour of their own and actually flew that night to New Zealand. Showing just how well the Fiji team had done, the Australians won eight of their ten tour matches in the Land of the Long White Cloud and drew the Test series 1–1.

Fiji returned to Australia in 1954 for another tour, but this one was marred by a more hostile atmosphere and, many claim, rough tactics by home sides who wanted to disrupt the Fijian play and frustrate their ability to play the magic rugby that everyone loved. The Test series was also a 1–1 tie with Fiji once more taking a tense second Test. As of 2022, Fiji have not yet beaten the Australians again. The series stands at 19 wins to Australia, two wins for Fiji and one drawn match (1961).

MATCH DETAILS

Australia: Ray Colbert; Eddie Stapleton, John Solomon (captain), Herb Barker, Garth Jones; Murray Tate, Brian Cox; Lou Hatherall, Nev Cottrell, Bob Davidson, Nick Shehadie, Alan Cameron, Brian Johnson, Tony Miller, Col Windon.
Replacement (used): Ray Colbert
Tries: Cox, Shehadie, Stapleton, Windon
Drop goal: Solomon

Fiji: Taniela Ranavue; Samuela Domoni, Navitalai Taga, George Cavalevu, Josefa Levula; Wame Salabogi, Suliasi Vatubua; Sailosi Valewai, Joeli Susu, Semisi Ralagi, Semesa Seruvatu, Isikeli Cawa, Semisi Baleca, Manasa Nukuvou, Apakuki Tuitavua (captain).

Tries: Ralagi, Salabogi
Conversion: Vatubua
Penalties: Ranavue, Vatubua
Drop goal: Ranavue
Referee: Donald Furness (Australia)

TOUR DETAILS

Played: 10   **Won:** 8   **Lost:** 1
Drawn: 1
Points for: 254   **Points against:** 153

RESULTS

South Harbor 9 Fiji 21 (5 July)
City of Sydney 19 Fiji 28 (9 July)
New South Wales 14 Fiji 14 (12 July)
New England 18 Fiji 30 (16 July)
Queensland 17 Fiji 24 (19 July)
Australian Services 14 Fiji 33 (23 July)
Australia 15 Fiji 9 (26 July)
Central Western 8 Fiji 50 (28 July)
Newcastle 24 Fiji 28 (2 August)
Australia 15 Fiji 17 (9 August)

DAVE GALLAHER

*'Enough was seen of Gallaher's methods to convince the most
latitudinarian that the 'winger' is not a person to be encouraged,
but to be vigorously penalised, for he was offside most of the game,
and is almost amusing, so frank is his disregard to the rules as to
passive and active obstruction.'*
Daily Express, 1905

**Dave Gallaher captained the 1905 New Zealand side and
played a critical role in developing the reputation and
philosophy of the famed team. A national icon, he still
remains one of the most important figures in All Blacks and
rugby history.**

Main teams: Parnell, Ponsonby, North Island, Auckland, New
Zealand
Position: Rover/wing forward
International caps: 6 (1903-1906)

Dave Gallaher sits at the top table of New Zealand sporting
deities. He played his last game for the All Blacks in 1906, but
almost every New Zealand fan today would still be able to tell
you the basics of his life. And what a life it was.

Gallaher was born in Ramelton in County Donegal, Ireland,
in 1873. His father, who was 69 at the time, worked as a

shopkeeper. Gallaher senior had been widowed and had two children from his first wife. His second wife Maria Hardy, was 29 years old when Dave was born and she gave her mature husband seven children in all. Tragically three of them died in infancy. Financial hardship led the family to emigrate to New Zealand, a route taken by so many of their fellow countrymen and women at that time. Upon arrival in New Zealand, they simplified their name, dropping the second 'g' from what had been 'Gallagher'.

It was a three-month voyage to New Zealand and the Gallahers left their sickly eight-week old boy, James Patrick, in the care of another family. It had been intended that, at a future date when his health recovered, he would also join them. Alas, he never did and he was to become one of the aforementioned three children that died in infancy.

The family's dream of a better life did not live up to expectations. The farm they had been allocated as part of a settlement scheme to encourage new arrivals to the 'colony' of the British Empire (for this was what many back in the 'motherland' viewed it as) was not quite in the condition that had been promised and was unsuitable for their needs.

Things got worse: promised jobs never materialised, the father was too old to find suitable work and the young Dave Gallaher suffered muscle problems in one of his legs which required surgery to address the condition which had led to a curvature of the spine. Maria ended up the main wage earner in the early years, working as a teacher, but she succumbed to cancer in 1887. This fresh tragedy forced several of the older Gallaher children to find work to prevent their younger siblings being forced into adoption by local authorities.

By the age of 13, Dave had quit school so that he too could earn a much-needed wage to share with the family. Away from his harsh working life, the young Gallaher displayed a natural instinct for sports, with his talents at cricket and rugby coming to the fore. In his later teen years, Gallaher began working in an abattoir in Auckland. Author Matt Elliott has pointed out how the backbreaking work he did here, such as shifting heavy animal carcasses around, helped build stamina and strength. He would remain in the industry for the rest of his life, ultimately rising to the position of foreman.

Gallaher, who would later become the grandfather of the grand Kiwi tradition of great flankers and wing forwards, played some of his early first-class rugby as hooker. It was in this position that he broke through to the Auckland province. His debut for the senior Auckland side came in the 1896 win over Queensland. At club level, he tasted success with Ponsonby, helping the side to the 1897 Auckland club championship.

War interrupts

In 1901, the shadow of war first cast itself over Gallaher's life. Patriotic and with a sense of duty to the British Empire, Gallaher joined the army to fight in the Anglo-Boer War. To join the New Zealand Mounted Rifles he gave a date of birth that made him appear three years older than he was. There is no exact agreement on why he did this, but it does mean that when reading contemporary sources, his age is almost always listed incorrectly.

Gallaher saw plenty of action and had several close shaves – admitting in one letter home he thought his time was up. He fought with a sense of natural justice, once deciding against firing on enemy soldiers as they were collecting their wounded.

During his war service, Gallaher still won rugby honours. He led a military team representing New Zealand to success in a tournament held among various British forces. Upon his return to New Zealand in the late summer of 1902 he was decorated with several medals in recognition of this service and was given the rank of Regimental Sergeant Major.

The 1905 Originals and the Irish-Kiwi rover

Gallaher's eternal rugby fame rests on his leadership of the 1905 All Blacks on their epic tour of Europe and North America. Christened 'The Originals', New Zealand played 35 games across England, Scotland, Wales, Ireland, France and the USA. Leaving home and setting sail on 30 July 1905 they arrived, after two short stops, in the UK on 8 September 1905. They eventually returned home to Auckland on 5 March, 1906.

Gallaher was 29 when he embarked on this rugby odyssey. He was listed in tour publicity as 1.83m (6ft) and 82.6 kg (13st). Not much in today's money, but hefty enough in 1905.

He had first captained New Zealand back in 1903 during their tour to Australia. The squad won all ten games in Australia (they did lose a warm-up to Wellington, however) and Gallaher was captain in the first ever All Black Test match as his side eased home 22–3 in Sydney.

Gallaher next won a cap against Great Britain in Wellington in 1904 in a 9–3 victory. The wing forward was a hugely respected figure in the Kiwi rugby community. His All Black teammate and utility back Billy Wallace once said: 'Dave was a wonderful captain, immensely popular with the team and the officials wherever he went. Always the welfare of his team and the honour of the country he represented were the first considerations. He was a very shrewd judge of a player and always endeavoured to be fair and just to every member of the team.'

The 1905 tour helped to forge the identity of modern New Zealand. It's worth noting that in the early 20th century, many British people considered places like New Zealand and Australia as, first and foremost, colonies of the British Empire. They did not see them as unique, vibrant countries in their own right with their own history and culture.

The All Blacks would be so dominant over the teams of the 'Mother Country' on the 1905 tour – and the visiting players seemed so athletic, healthy and muscular compared to locals –

that many believed it demonstrated a decline in the masculinity of men of all classes in Britain. Arguments were made that the fresh air and honest toil in the colonies had allowed the men in the faraway corners of the Empire to become physical superiors. It was, in modern parlance, fantastic PR for New Zealand.

Indeed, several of the match programmes for this tour contained advertisements proclaiming New Zealand as the 'Land for Settlers' and boasted of it being a 'Country with a fertile soil, well-watered. and a temperate climate. No extremes of heat and cold.' Application forms for interested parties could be gotten through the High Commissioner of New Zealand in London and the advertisements listed all relevant details.

At the start of the tour though, many in Britain and Ireland, full of smug superiority, had thought the visitors would struggle. When they crushed Devon by 55 to 4 in the opening game people were astonished. Rugby scribe E.D.H. Sewell wrote: 'You will, I doubt not, observe the almost uncanny silence in which [New Zealand] play . . . The men do not need to be told where the ball is, for the simple reason that each is watching it . . . I saw several movements in the New Zealanders' play which I do not believe it possible for human agency to improve.'

Next up they dismantled Cornwall and Bristol by the same score of 41–0. Every match seemed to bring a fresh massacre. And remember, this was the era of a three-point try. Rugby in the home unions had seen nothing like it. They were extraordinary scorelines and they just kept coming.

In those early games the British rugby community got a good glimpse of Dave Gallaher. There was no doubting his leadership qualities, his athleticism or his footballing skills. But there was great consternation at the position he played and what it meant for the 'spirit' of the sport.

Gallaher played as a wing-forward or 'rover'. This position was revolutionary to the Home Unions and almost none of the teams the All Blacks faced had any answer to it. The rover placed the ball in the scrum, rather than the scrum-half as was traditional. The actual All Black scrum-half could then wait at the back of the scrum, ready to cleanly and quickly whip the ball out to his backs, giving his side vital extra seconds to attack and with much cleaner ball. This was also aided by the rover 'obstructing' the opposing scrum-half, who was now effectively unable to pressurise his opposite number.

Making this even more effective, the Kiwis packed down with seven forwards in the scrum in a 2–3–2 formation, deploying two hookers, three players in the middle row and two in the back. This formation allowed for quicker ball than most of the home packs could muster themselves, once again giving Gallaher's men a huge offensive advantage. The sheer size and fitness of the All Blacks meant the lack of an extra man in the scrum made little difference.

The rover position made Gallaher a controversial figure among home players, administrators and supporters who often disapproved of such 'obstructive' methods. After the victory over Cornwall, one newspaper wrote: 'The great innovation in the New Zealanders' game is the winging forward. As a matter of fact, he is not a forward, and is a wolf in sheep's clothing. He makes no pretence to do scrimmage work but claims the privilege of a forward. Apparently, his position has been invented to obstruct the opposing half . . .'

On similar lines the *Daily Express* wrote: 'Enough was seen of Gallaher's methods to convince the most latitudinarian that the "winger" is not a person to be encouraged, but to be vigorously penalised, for he was offside most of the game, and is almost amusing, so frank is his disregard for the rules as to passive and active obstruction'.

As the black wave swept across the Home Unions, washing away each team they met, this outrage concerning Gallaher only increased.

What made Gallaher's 'Originals' so good?

The 1905 All Blacks brought a potent mix of fitness, physicality, size, skills and sporting intelligence. They utilised ideas, tactics, formations and strategies that were alien to the European community (barring, perhaps, the select few that had toured there with the likes of the 1903 British Isles team).

Some of the tactics they employed were so different to what rugby sides in the 'Mother Country' did that the Kiwis were accused of being unsporting or cheating.

One major example of the unique New Zealand approach was that at scrum time each player had a specific role, whereas the British and Irish teams would generally pack down in a scrum in the order they arrived. Specialisation had not yet become the norm. This gave the All Blacks a major advantage as they all knew exactly what was expected of them and understood what each man around them would do and how they all fitted together.

Alongside their use of the seven-man scrummage formation and deployment of a rover as mentioned earlier, the tourists also obsessively practised their line-out, giving them a cohesion many other teams lacked. The backs too were different to the European teams, where they deployed two five-eighths (instead of a traditional fly-half and centre).

The New Zealand players were also able to draw upon their stamina, forged from domestic games that involved two halves of 45 minutes, unlike the 35 minutes a half often played in the British Isles.

One blemish on the 'perfect' team

Gallaher led New Zealand into the Test in Cardiff with his side boasting a perfect record. It was to be not only one of the most famous matches in the game's history, but helped secure the sport's cultural place in both New Zealand and Wales. Even today, most Kiwi fans can tell you about the famous disallowed try from All Black Bob Deans that supposedly robbed the visitors. New Zealand rugby writer Terry McLean has claimed that the game was the greatest moment in his nation's rugby history and provided the starting point for what the game is today.

New Zealand had won all their 27 previous tour games before this encounter, a run which included wins over Scotland, Ireland and England. The All Blacks were in good form: no team had scored against them for seven games. They had scored 801 points to 22 during the tour to date. Wales, meanwhile, were holders of the Triple Crown and the best side in Europe (there was no Grand Slam on offer in those days as France had not joined the championship). Adding extra spice to the clash, on the eve of their departure from New Zealand, the prime minister had specifically spoken of the importance of beating Wales, who were seen as the European rugby elite.

In an age before world cups, the Test with Wales in Cardiff was therefore regarded as an unofficial world championship. Excitement was at fever pitch and the All Blacks needed a police escort to get through the 'dense mass of humanity' and into the ground on time.

The tradition of singing national anthems before international sporting occasions is often traced back to this game. Wales wanted a way to combat the haka before the teams kicked off. The Welsh team decided to respond by singing 'Hen Wlad Fy Nhadau' (Land of my Fathers) which was fast becoming the 'unofficial anthem' of Wales.

When the haka finished, Wales winger Teddy Morgan led his team in singing and, when they realised what was happening, the crowd of 47,000 soon joined in. Gallaher said he had never been more impressed in his life than hearing the singing that day and a newspaper in New Zealand said the anthem gave a 'semi-religious' feel to the contest.

Alas, for Gallaher, his team fell 3–0. Wales had done their homework and decided to mirror the controversial 'rover' position that Gallaher occupied. They also found a cunning way to counter the unusual scrum formation of the visitors. Wales lined up with four men in the front row. When the New Zealand pair lined up and packed down, Wales would remove one prop – leaving them with what is now known as a 'loosehead'. The extra man was then moved to the back row to add weight. It was smart and played a major role in the game.

Wales scored the only try of the match through Teddy Morgan ten minutes from the interval. But later came the most famous disallowed try of all time. Bob Deans' non-try is a subject that still comes up every time the two nations meet. After the game itself, it is claimed by some that the players themselves seemed to have said nothing about it at the post-match dinner. It was only the next day when a mischievous *Daily Mail* reporter, looking for a scoop, suggested to Deans he may have scored. Deans laughed and said: 'I thought I did!'. The pressman jumped on it, got Deans to wire a telegram to their offices, and the paper ran the story: 'Deans says he scored'.

From there, the legend only grew. Rhys Gabe, the man who to his 'immortal glory' tackled Deans, was in no doubt there was no try. He later said that 'as [Deans] kept struggling to go forward, I knew he had not reached his objective. Other players joined the maul from outside the Welsh line'.

Different New Zealanders and officials put forward their own thoughts on the matter. Later, the match official John Dallas, who was criticised for being unfit and behind play by the losers, was even moved to publish a letter defending his decision. A recent international himself, he would not have been as unfit as legend has frequently portrayed him.

A romantic, but likely nonsensical, myth sprang up years

later that Deans claimed once more he had scored while on his deathbed.

As for Gallaher, he was not only an excellent leader in victory, but also in defeat. After the match, while wearing the red jersey of Welsh captain Gwyn Nicholls, with whom he had exchanged shirts, he was interviewed by the *Athletic News*.

> Gallaher: *'It was a rattling good game, played out to the bitter end, with the result the best team won.'*
> Athletic News: *'Is there any point about the defeat which you regard as unsatisfactory?'*
> Gallaher: *'No, the better team won, and I am content.'*
> Athletic News: *'What of the refereeing? Have you any opinion favourable or otherwise to express?'*
> Gallaher: *'I have always made it a point to never express a view regarding the referee in any match in which I have played, so you must excuse me now.'*

After the sickening loss, Gallaher guided his men to seven more victories before they returned home, hailed by tens of thousands of their fellow countrymen and women as conquering heroes. It had been an extraordinary achievement and Gallaher had played a key part in defining his nation's national sport and in setting the high standards still expected today of those wearing the silver fern.

Tour statistics and results
Played: 35   **Won:** 34   **Lost:** 1
Points for: 976   **Points against:** 59
Average score: New Zealand 28 Opponents 2

OPPONENT	RESULT	SCORE
Devon	WON	55–4
Cornwall	WON	41–0
Bristol	WON	41–0
Northampton	WON	32–0
Leicester	WON	28–0
Middlesex	WON	34–0
Durham County	WON	16–3
Hartlepool Clubs	WON	63–0
Northumberland	WON	31–0
Gloucester	WON	44–0
Somerset County	WON	23–0
Devonport Albion	WON	21–3
Midland Counties	WON	21–5
Surrey	WON	11–0
Blackheath	WON	32–0
Oxford University	WON	46–0
Cambridge University	WON	14–0
Richmond	WON	16–0
Bedford	WON	41–0
Scotland	WON	12–7
West of Scotland	WON	22–0
Ireland	WON	15–0
Munster	WON	33–0
England	WON	15–0

Cheltenham	WON	18–0
Cheshire	WON	34–0
Yorkshire	WON	40–0
Wales	LOST	0–3
Glamorgan County	WON	9–0
Newport	WON	6–3
Cardiff	WON	10–8
Swansea	WON	4–3
France	WON	38–8
British Columbia	WON	43–6
British Columbia	WON	65–6

Gallaher played in 26 of the tour matches, scoring one try and one conversion. Unfortunately, he missed the game against Ireland, the nation of his birth, due to injury. However, he did visit the area he hailed from and met relations of his.

Retirement from the field and a return to war

Gallaher hung up his boots after returning home, but remained involved as a selector for the All Blacks and often helped coach. He put his boots back on occasionally to assist old teams in need, most notably turning out twice in 1909 for Auckland after an injury crisis as the province successfully defended the Ranfurly Shield.

With teammate Billy Stead, Gallaher published *'The Complete Rugby Footballer'* which detailed the approach to rugby the All Blacks believed in and was packed full of insight and tactics. It is considered one of the great books of rugby literature.

When the horrors of the First World War came, Gallaher was above the age to be conscripted. Never shirking his duty, he enlisted himself. One of his younger brothers, Douglas, was killed in 1916, before he himself was deployed. Another brother, Henry, would also die in the war and yet another, Charles, would be severely wounded.

Gallaher trained in Britain before being deployed, as a sergeant, in 1917. On 4 October, at the Battle of Broodseinde near Ypres in Belgium, the brave soldier was killed by a shrapnel wound to the head. He was 43 and survived by a wife, Nellie, and a daughter, Nora. In later life Nora said she remembered her father as a 'jolly man'.

Gallaher was one of 13 All Blacks who died in the conflict.

Lasting legacy

Gallaher is one of the key figures in New Zealand rugby. On several occasions touring All Blacks sides or representatives have made a pilgrimage to Gallaher's grave in Belgium. Since 1922 he has been remembered through the Gallaher Shield, awarded to the winners of the Auckland Rugby Football Union's senior premier competition. Fittingly, Gallaher's old club Ponsonby have laid claim to the trophy more than any other side.

In 2005, several members of the All Blacks visited his birthplace and unveiled a plaque, marking his old home's historic importance. The All Blacks also opened the new rugby pitch at Letterkenny Rugby Club and celebrated the naming of their ground as the Dave Gallaher Memorial Park. His name is also included on the club crest.

Since 2000, New Zealand and France have competed for the Dave Gallaher Cup when they meet. Of all the giants who strode across the fields of Test rugby before the advent of television cameras, perhaps none can claim such a lasting legacy on the popular imagination of 21st century followers as Dave Gallaher.

MARK ELLA

*'The greatest player I have ever seen, or
had the pleasure of playing alongside.'*
David Campese

**Without doubt one of the finest Australian players of all
time, Mark Ella retired from Test rugby aged just 25. Yet in
his short top-flight career, he wowed the rugby world, helped
redefine outside-half play and secured his place in rugby
folklore.**

Main teams: Randwick, New South Wales, Amatori Milano,
Australia 7s, Australia
Position: Fly-half, centre
International caps: 25 (1980-1984)
Points: 78 (6 tries, 3 conversions, 8 penalties, 8 drop goals)
Honours: World Rugby Hall of Fame, Australian Rugby Union
Hall of Fame, second-ever indigenous Australian athlete to
captain a national team, Member of the Order of Australia,
Young Australian of the Year (1982), Hong Kong Sevens winner
(three times), Five Premiership titles with Randwick.

Australia are one of the three major southern hemisphere
powerhouses of rugby and one of the 'traditional eight' nations

that, for most of the 20th century, made up the top tier of Test rugby.

Winners of the 1991 and 1999 World Cups, the Wallabies have contributed much to rugby union and are arguably one of the great innovating nations in the sport, often having to overcome a relatively small playing base by smartly making the very most of what they have.

Yet younger rugby fans may be surprised to learn that despite the fact they first toured the Home Unions in 1908 (hot on the heels of the 1905 All Blacks and 1906 Springboks), until the 1980s Australia were not quite regarded with the same awe and wonder as New Zealand and South Africa. It was only in the 1990s that Australia truly forged a reputation as consistently one of the game's great international teams and it was the two world titles in 1991 and 1999 that cemented their elite status.

Mark Ella, along with his two brothers Gary and Glen, was pivotal to the changing of the world order. And Mark, playing at fly-half (or five-eighth as the locals call it) was key to helping reimagine what could be done in attack in rugby and as a result is rightly considered one of the most important players in rugby union history. If that isn't impressive enough, Mark achieved all he did in the game as an Indigenous player at a time when it was incredibly hard for people of Aboriginal origin to break through social and economic barriers in Australia. He reached the peak of the sport in just a few short years; the rugby genius chose to hang up his boots aged just 25.

Overcoming history

In 1984, Australian journalist Bret Harris released a book about the three Ella brothers. Entitled simply, *'Ella, Ella, Ella'* it told the remarkable story of three exceptional rugby union players who had captured the imagination of the rugby world. In the book's foreword, Nicholas Shehadie, an ex-international and a former Lord Mayor of Sydney, gave some context to just how incredible their ascent to the top was: 'This book attempts to capture the plight and the struggles of a disadvantaged Australian family who rise to achieve considerable success . . . The matriarch of this remarkable family, May Ella, set her family a very high standard in an environment beset with poverty, in a home where the roof leaked and in which most modern conveniences were absent. There was, however, the greater compensations of abundant love, emotional security and fun . . . Mark, Glen and Gary were fortunate to have experienced the warm and understanding teachers who guided, encouraged and inspired these boys to develop their confidence and skills . . . This family has proven to all that given the opportunity, Aboriginal people can aspire and achieve to the highest.'

Mark was born in June, 1959, in La Perouse, in the Eastern Suburbs of Sydney. He was one of 12 children born of May and Gordon Ella. They lived in a leaky old house built by their grandfather that had no hot water or modern plumbing. The 14 occupants shared just three bedrooms. In *Ella, Ella, Ella,* Glen said: 'We didn't bring many friends home from school because we were too embarrassed. The house was falling to pieces.'

It was a loving and supportive family though and the parents, May and Gordon, had a passion for sport. They encouraged their children to play and, May in particular, made sure they stayed on the straight and narrow and always looked to be the best at what they did. It wasn't just Mark, Glen and Gary that would go on to taste sporting success at the top level, one of their sisters, Marcia, went on to become the first Indigenous netballers to represent Australia.

It was far from easy for Indigenous people in Australia in the 1980s and members of that community were at a huge disadvantage economically and socially. Mark was born just before the 1960s arrived, a time in which not all Indigenous Australians even had the right to vote. In 1901, the Commonwealth Franchise Act granted voting rights to all men and women, with the exception of 'any Aboriginal native of Australia, Asia, Africa or Pacific Island, except New Zealand'.

Slowly and painfully, certain concessions were granted over the decades. For instance, in 1949 Aboriginal people who had served in the army were permitted to vote in federal elections. But shamefully it was not until 1984 that all Indigenous people were entitled to vote.

Also in the infamous 1901 Franchise Act, Indigenous people were barred from working in post offices, enlistment in the armed forces, or claiming maternity allowance and pensions. It was not until 1967 that Aboriginal Australians were counted in the national census.

For two centuries, Indigenous people had either seen their land seized from them by force, or had been battling to recover their rights to the land their ancestors had lost. No real progress was made on this issue until 1976, when the Aboriginal Land Rights Act was passed in the Northern Territory. This was the first piece of legislation that enabled First Nations people to 'claim land rights for Country where traditional ownership could be proven'.

Perhaps most horrifically of all, between 1910 and 1970, it is estimated that in some parts of Australia, anything between one in ten and one in three Indigenous children were forcibly removed from communities and families by government agencies and religious institutions. This drastic and cruel initiative was driven by the belief that mixed-race children should be removed from Aboriginal families due to fears of the race 'dying off' and the need to assimilate these children into white society.

Against this cultural backdrop and under the heavy clouds of history, Mark, Glen and Gary Ella still managed to succeed in sport and life.

Early promise

The three Ella brothers were sporting naturals. Mark and Glen were identical twins and everyone, including members of their own family, had trouble telling them apart when they were young. Indeed, the pair admit themselves that when they look at old photos they sometimes aren't sure who is who either. Mark wasn't a great fan of being a twin, but he and Glen did have fun with it growing up. They often pretended to be one another – even on the rugby field to the despair of their coaches. To ease confusion, the twins eventually agreed to have different hairstyles.

In their early lives, rugby league was their main sport and all three siblings excelled at it and they played at the local La Perouse club. The trio also had an older brother, Rodney, who had a short spell as a pro league player. League was the sport the family loved and union was not really on their radar. Cricket was another passion for the trio. It was a childhood of almost non-stop sport and it didn't take long for the family house to get even more crammed as all sorts of trophies, medals and awards started being accumulated.

Gary was soon recognised by regional selection for rugby league teams. Mark and Glen, who were not the quickest developers physically, had to wait longer than their talents should have made them wait to get representative honours. Selectors all too often went with size over skill and it led to plenty of frustration for the dynamic twins.

The fateful moment in the boys' lives (and a fateful moment in the course of Australian rugby) came when they began attending Matraville High School in South Sydney. A tough school in a tough area, the school took sport seriously and the rugby code it favoured was union, not league. The boys didn't stop playing league outside of school, but their exposure to union would ultimately set them on a new sporting path. At Matraville, the Ellas played with a certain Eddie Jones too.

Even at high school, the Ellas loved dreaming up and executing intricate back moves. Not only did these moves cut their opponents to shreds, some of them eventually ended up being used years later for the Wallabies. Representative honours in union came thick and fast for the three youngsters, while league selectors often continued to ignore their talents. As a result of their consistent performances for many years for Matraville, international schoolboy honours came their way.

Brilliant schoolboys

In the era that the Ella brothers were coming of age, international school rugby was a critical element of the player pathway, with tours by schoolboy teams being major events reported on by national newspapers and recorded in popular rugby annuals and almanacs. The Australian Schools side that toured Britain and Ireland in December 1977 and January 1978 were so spectacular they still get mentioned in discussions about the evolution of attacking rugby. All three Ella brothers made the tour party and the Australians won each one of their 16 matches on the expedition (this includes one game in Japan and one in the Netherlands) and scored 110 tries while conceding a mere six. The fixtures included successful Tests against their Welsh, Irish and English counterparts. In the 25–6 win over Wales in front of 20,000 fans at Cardiff Arms Park, each of the Ella brothers scored a try.

The squad contained future league star Wally Lewis, and six other players who would go on to achieve full international honours: Tony Melrose, Dominic Vaughan, Shane Nightingale, Chris Roche, Tony D'Arcy and Michael O'Connor.

The team's coach, Geoff Mould, insisted on running rugby and players were firmly told to keep kicking to the absolute minimum. If any player kicked excessively, they risked being dropped. Forwards were expected to play like backs as well and it all came together beautifully. The UK's *Daily Telegraph* gushed: 'They make overlaps from close quarters as naturally as they breathe, and undoubtedly the stars of the team are the three Ella brothers.'

Amusingly, in one match, Glen was told to come off at half-time in a game the Australians were winning 18–0. He didn't want to leave. So, when Mould was otherwise distracted, Glen and Mark switched jerseys and the 'subbed' player remained on the field and had a stormer of a game.

The three brothers were a constant source of media interest, to the point where it made them uncomfortable and coach Mould complained they had been turned into 'side-show freaks'.

The 1978/79 *Rothmans Rugby Yearbook* similarly got in a flutter over the touring schoolboys:

> *It must be many years since a touring party of any kind won such widespread acclaim throughout the British Isles . . . The facts of their unbeaten tour speak eloquently for themselves, but the figures, impressive though they are, are unimportant compared with the manner in which they were achieved.*
>
> *Brimming with talent, the Australians had such confidence in their attacking powers that they were able to introduce into their play a spirit of adventure all too rarely seen here, even among the schools. Kicking to touch was reduced to a minimum and they attacked consistently from positions deep in their own territory. Tactically they presented a new-old concept of back play in their short, quick passing along the line to give space for the wings or for players looping outside them. Not for the Australians the long pass from the base of the scrum. At times the fly-half stood off no more than two or three yards and transferred the ball with lightning rapidity to his inside centre.*
>
> *The three Ella brothers, extraordinarily gifted players, provided some of the most exciting moments. With their instinctive sense of position and elusive running they formed the spearhead of the attack, with G J Ella at full-back making an especially notable contribution.*
>
> *Mr Douglas Harrison, President of the Rugby Football Schools' Union said, 'If these players were typical, Australia had the material to become the greatest Rugby Union country in the world.*

The tour helped give Australian rugby a vital jolt of life. In the late 1970s the Australian Rugby Union (ARU) was almost bankrupt and it couldn't afford to even play any Test games in 1977. The tour revitalised interest in the sport and showed that the Wallabies could find a way to win and entertain their demanding fanbase at the same time.

Randwick and Australia

Not only did the Australia Schoolboys help 'save' rugby in the country, it helped keep the Ellas in rugby union. Many feared the trio would head to league, but speaking for the *Ella, Ella, Ella* book, Mark said: 'We had to give rugby something in return for sending us on the tour. It was designed to build Australian rugby and we felt committed. At that stage there was no way we would play league after what rugby had done for us.'

The three brothers went on to play club rugby for Randwick, a Sydney club nicknamed the Galloping Greens. Their coach was Bob Dwyer, who would go on to lead the Wallabies to the 1991 World Cup win. Dwyer didn't want to waste the youngsters in youth rugby for too long and soon fast-tracked them into the senior team where they would go on to be club legends.

Within just a few games they had made such an impact league clubs began offering serious money for them. Randwick would eventually win five consecutive Premiership titles with the Ellas and they were a huge part of that incredible success. Eddie Jones also played in that side and would later write that Mark was 'God'.

In 1979, still only 20, Mark was selected to travel with Australia for their tour of Argentina. He had impressed at state level for New South Wales that year, shining as they beat a touring Ireland side. He played in three of the non-capped games of the Argentina tour and bagged a try.

In 1979, Mark then helped Australia win the Hong Kong Sevens for the first time. He was, naturally, a huge success in the shortened code as a player and, later, a coach. He was adored in Fiji for his abilities in sevens and was mobbed when touring there with the Wallabies.

By 1980, Mark was a full international, making his debut against New Zealand at the Sydney Cricket Ground in the first of a three-match Bledisloe Cup series (Glen and Gary would win their first caps in 1982, winning four and six respectively). His mother fainted upon hearing of his selection.

Mark admitted he shook with nerves for the opening quarter of the game, but he still performed and it was to be a winning start for his international career as the All Blacks were overcome 13–9. Mark kicked a key drop goal using his 'weaker' right foot and, employing his trademark loop, set up the winning try for Mick Martin when the scores had been tied at 9–9. Ella combined beautifully throughout the game with his centres Mike Hawker and Michael O'Connor and later reflected it was the best combination he ever got to be part of.

Australia lost the second Test 12–9 in Brisbane, but bounced back to claim the series with a 26–10 victory in Sydney, with Mark again landing a drop goal in a game he said he knew they would win. It was an extraordinary start to his Test career and he was soon called up to play at Cardiff Arms Park for a World XV to face Wales in a special match celebrating their centenary. In those days, these invitation games were huge honours and his selection showed just how highly he was regarded around the world.

Mark was praised for the way he played so close and tight to the scrum. This was unusual for the era, especially as opposition backs did not need to retreat five metres in defence. By standing so close, and at a carefully chosen angle, he would tempt and draw the opposing openside in such a way that when Mark gave a pass, the flanker would be unable to drift and cover the inside centre, thereby freeing up his midfield. His incredible workrate as a loop, link and support player caused havoc with defences and made it so hard to defend against.

Years later, World Cup winner Michael Lynagh, who combined so well at centre with Mark in the celebrated 1984 side, would admit to being hugely influenced by the way Ella played. He said: 'Mark would say that if he touched the ball twice the team tended to score and if he touched it three times he himself tended to score. His sleight of hand, his decoys and so forth, were mesmeric, and he was also a lovely communicator. He was great fun to play with.'

An historic captain

In July 1982, to the surprise of many, Mark was named captain of the Wallabies for their tour of New Zealand. He would lead an understrength squad as nine capped players had made themselves unavailable for the tour due to business commitments. But there was plenty of talent in the squad that did travel. Among the 12 uncapped players called up was a certain David Campese, already being hailed as a 'one of the most brilliant newcomers in Australian rugby' as far away as England. It was an incredibly proud moment for the Ella family as all three brothers made the squad and it marked only the second occasion an Indigenous Australian had ever captained a national sports team (rugby league legend Arthur Beetson was the first).

Incredibly, Mark, still only 23 at the time, claims if he had known he was going to be given the captaincy he would have rejected it. He appreciated it was a great honour and gave the role his all, but he said later that he would have preferred to have focused on establishing himself as the team's five-eight and not have to worry about the stresses that come with leadership.

Australia won 10 of their 14 games on the tour of the Land of the Long White Cloud. While they lost the Test series and, therefore, the Bledisloe Cup, they did win the second of the three-match series – a 19–16 win in Wellington in which Gary

Ella, playing at outside centre, became the first Ella to score a Test try.

The 'Grand Slam'

The 1984 tour of Britain and Ireland is one of the most treasured and significant moments in Australian rugby history and a personal highlight for Mark Ella. Coached by Alan Jones and captained by three-quarter Andrew Slack, the Wallabies achieved their first clean sweep of the Home Unions, winning each of their international clashes.

Outside of the international arena, the tourists weren't perfect. The squad won 13 games, drew one and lost four (losing to Cardiff, Ulster, Llanelli and the South of Scotland). Unlike the Springboks and All Blacks, the Wallabies were traditionally always hampered by a far shallower talent pool. It meant the tour was more fairly judged on success in the capped matches than on what happened on the club fields.

Spearheaded by the supreme gifts of backs like Mark Ella, Roger Gould, David Campese, Michael Lynagh and Nick Farr-Jones, and backed up by tough, uncompromising forwards like Simon Poidevin, Tom Lawton, Enrique Rodriguez and Steve Cutler, the men in gold presented an Australia that the Home Union sides had never seen the like of.

Sadly, Gary Ella was unavailable due to business commitments and Glen was not included, leaving Mark the only one of the siblings to be part of this historic expedition.

England were brushed aside 19–3, Ireland beaten 16–9, Wales crushed 28–9 and Scotland drubbed 36–12. Like the schoolboy team Ella had been a part of just a few years earlier, the Wallabies were praised for their exquisite tactical play, commitment to attack and incredible skill set. Even in the rain of Edinburgh, in the match that sealed their historic 'Grand Slam', they remained committed to attacking rugby and were duly rewarded with four tries. Australia had only beaten the Scots three times in their previous nine meetings, so this was a significant win over the side that had claimed the 1984 Five Nations Grand Slam.

Ella scored a try in every one of the four Test matches. His effort in the opening international at Twickenham was classic Ella and typical 1984 Wallabies. The Aussies had a five-metre scrum, five metres in from the left touchline. Ella, standing wider than was often the case, softly passed to Michael Lynagh after taking just a couple of sideways steps. The centre straightened, and almost instantly popped it back inside to a fast-moving and looping Ella. The fly-half offered the hint of a pass to outside centre and captain Andrew Slack, who smartly drew and obstructed his man. Meanwhile the England backs were also being checked by fullback Roger Gould who was steaming up on a line outside the still looping Ella who, suddenly, stepped hard off his right foot and shot through the gap and the desperately flailing English hands to accelerate over the line. It was beautiful. And, according to local interpretation, made by illegal blocking. Either way, it was a thing of perfection and helped Australia to a convincing 19–3 win.

Ella scored a try and two drop goals in a tight win over the Irish in Dublin (16–9). Australia have rarely produced prolific drop goal experts, so his ability and willingness with the boot were another mark of just how important he was to the team. Ireland had led 9–6 in the second-half before Ella helped steer his team to safety. His second drop goal levelled the scores in the final quarter. Then he broke Irish hearts with one of the greatest pieces of support running you'll ever see. After helping launch a move from a line-out (he took the ball at speed two metres inside his own half), he expertly put Lynagh into space. If you watch Ella off the ball on the videos you can still find on YouTube, you'll see him work hard in support, then suddenly burst into a sprint and change his line as he sees the attack develop through Matthew Burke and Campese. The way Ella slows down and goes outside Campese to put himself in a position to score out on the far left is as gorgeous as support play gets in rugby. The ever-alert Campese gave the perfect soft pass and glory was secured with just seven minutes left on the clock.

At Cardiff, Ella scored another kind of try with a late interception of a desperate pass from Welsh number eight Eddie Butler, sprinting over from over 40 metres out. It gave the Wallabies a record-breaking 28–9 win in Cardiff, which at the time was the biggest losing margin Wales had suffered at home.

When Ella crossed for his historic try against Scotland in the final match, sealing his personal Grand Slam, you could probably have seen his smile from space. It was joyous. The 36–12 win was also a record and rounded off a glorious Grand Slam. In later years, the tour was looked back on as a key part of Australia's rise to the top of the sport in the 1990s. Ella's four tries in four consecutive games were all the more extraordinary as in his prior 21 Tests he had scored just two in total.

Rothmans summed up their summary of the tour saying that: 'Britain was a less entertaining place in rugby terms when Australia left.'

After rugby

And then it was all over. At 25, Mark amazed the sporting world by retiring from the sport. He had announced his intention to step away from the game on 22 August ahead of the tour of UK and Ireland, although it seemed many had refused to believe it. Several teams, from league and union, tried to change his mind. The offers were varied, but serious. The Monday after the final tour match of 1984 against the Barbarians, even saw English rugby league club Fulham announce a failed bid to attract Ella. He was also linked earlier in the tour with CIYMS of Northern Ireland, who seemed confident of securing his services.

But Ella turned all the money and incentives down. He spoke of the need to secure a job and start the next stage of his life and to 'blossom in a new world rather than being stuck at something that came naturally'.

Ella did have a short spell in Milan, Italy, between 1988-1990 alongside David Campese before coaching the side to national silverware. He also made a few appearances around this time for Randwick to 'lose weight', scoring in his final game against a touring Bath side in 1990.

Decades later, writing for *Athletes Voice* he said: 'Why did I retire? I had better things to do. I never wanted to play forever. I'd told my wife and friends and most of the people at Randwick knew that win, lose or draw I was going to retire.'

Mark has had success in a number of fields from broadcasting and journalism to PR. One of his great achievements has been the Mark Ella Foundation, which aims to help improve the 'health and happiness of First Nations children and youths through behavioural change that will improve their chances of a better life and enhance their chances of employment in future life'.

In 1988 he managed the Aboriginal Cricket Association tour of England. He also coached the Australian Sevens team and helped lead them to a bronze in the 1998 Commonwealth Games.

In 2022, the Cook Cup – which is competed for each time England and Australia meet outside of a World Cup – was renamed the Ella-Mobbs cup. The new name combined Mark's with that of Edgar Mobbs, an English war hero and Test winger. Upon the announcement of the renaming, Mark spoke of the racism that he and his brothers had encountered at times in their career:

When we started out we used to get the crowds because people would come out of curiosity to see these Aboriginals play, thinking 'can they play rugby?' In the early days there was a bit of a novelty. We'd play and be called 'black this, black that' from all of our opposition. After three or four months we realised that instead of belting them, literally, and trying to fight them because of what they were calling us, we'd actually beat them on the scoreboard. That meant a lot more to us because we were actually winning.

There are not a lot of Aboriginals to have played for Australia, but hopefully this trophy will be the start of the end of that. Kurtley Beale is the most current Aboriginal Wallaby, but there aren't too many who even play the game. In Australian rugby, if we want to use the natural talents of the Indigenous community we need to work a lot harder. In Australian Indigenous communities this trophy means a lot. It also means a lot when the Wallabies wear the Indigenous jersey because it shows we've come a long way in supporting the Indigenous as players and acknowledge their presence.

Glen Ella would go on to a successful coaching career, often working with Eddie Jones at Test level. Gary too would go into coaching and work with Randwick, New South Wales, Leinster, Parramatta and the Australian U19s side.

Few families have ever had such an impact on a nation's rugby history as the Ella family. Their period at the top of the game may have been a short one, but it was one of the most exciting and romantic of all.

SELECT BIBLIOGRAPHY

An extensive array of books, autobiographies, audiobooks, match programmes, video cassettes, DVDs, online videos, newspapers, television programmes, match programmes and blogs have been referenced for this book. Below is a short select bibliography only.

The Oval World: A Global History of Rugby (2015) – Tony Collins (Bloomsbury)
Cardiff Rugby Club – History and Statistics 1876–1975 (1975) – D.E. Davies (Cardiff Athletic Club)
Scrum Queens: The Story of Women's Rugby (2022) – Ali Donnelly (Pitch Publishing)
The International Rugby Championship 1883–1983 (1984) – Terry Godwin (Willow Books)
The Book of English International Rugby 1871–1982 (1982) – John Griffiths (Willow Books)
The Phoenix Book of International Rugby (1987) – John Griffiths (Phoenix House)
1905 Originals (2005) – Bob Howitt and Dianne Haworth (Harper Sports)
Ella, Ella, Ella (1984) – Brett Harris (Springwood Books)
World in Their Hands: The Story of the First Women's Rugby World Cup (2022) – Martyn Thomas (Polaris Publishing)

Second Sight: Rugby and Redemption (2022) – Ian McKinley with Gerry Thornley (Reach Sport)
A Game for Hooligans – The History of Rugby Union (2006) – Huw Richards (Mainstream Publishing)
'James Peters: The Man They Wouldn't Play' *(2015)* – Tom Weir (De Montfort University, Leicester)
Shane: My Story (2009) – Shane Williams and Delme Parfitt (Mainstream Publishing)

Annuals

Rothmans Rugby Union Yearbook (Multiple editions referenced) (Queen Anne Press)
Welsh Brewers Rugby Annual for Wales/Worthington Rugby Annual for Wales/Buy as You View Rugby Annual for Wales (Multiple editions referenced from 1969 to 2003)

Websites and online materials

Asia Rugby, Athletes Voice, BBC, Bleacher Report, British Library, Cardiff Rugby Museum, Classic Wallabies, *The Daily Telegraph*, *Economist*, ESPN Scrum.com, *Fiji Times*, Fiji Rugby, Fox Sports, Gamespot, Gloucester Rugby Heritage, *The Guardian*, *The Herald*, *The Independent*, *Irish Independent*, *Irish Times*, National Library of Australia, Moby Games, Museum of New Zealand, National Library of Wales, *New York Times*, Pathe, Premiership Rugby, Reuters, RFU official site, The Roar, The Rugby Archive, Rugby History Society, *Rugby Journal*, *Rugby World*, Rugby 365, *The Times*, Scrum Queens, Six Nations, Sky Sports, *South Wales Echo*, Squidge Rugby, Swansea RFC, *Sydney Morning Herald*, Twitter, U.S. Women's Rugby Foundation, Wales Online, Wikipedia, World Rugby Museum, WRU official website, Yahoo! Sport, YouTube (various).

ACKNOWLEDGEMENTS

I am grateful for the help I've had from across the rugby community in preparing this book. Countless people have helped with filling in the gaps when I've been researching a story or have supplied links, contact numbers, video footage or old newspaper clips. It is all appreciated.

As always, thank you to Peter Burns and all at Polaris Publishing for believing in this series enough to make it a trilogy. It's been an honour to make them with you.

Huge love to Raluca Moldovan for the art. Raluca has been the main artist in both the previous books, but this time also stepped up to do the cover art. It is a thing of beauty. Raluca, the late nights were more than worth it. Enjoy the well-earned break!

Plenty of people were kind enough to speak with me for this book and I thank you all. In particular, I would like to express my gratitude to: Mel Berry, Sara Cox, Tara Flanagan, Gheorghe Ion (and his son, Adrian), Noriko Kishida, Lee Mather, Rob Owen, Will Owen, Jillion Potter, Gareth Rhys Owen, Graham Smith, Gary Street, Koji Tokumasu, Fakahau Valu, Ian Watkins and Jack Zorab.

The list of others who have helped in some way or other is very long and it isn't possible to mention them all, but I would in particular like to send thanks to Riccardo Ball, Aled Betts,

Chris Chen, Steve Coombs, Alice Cooper, Richard De Jager, John Dennison, Richard Diplock, Ali Donnelly, Laura Eddie, Katie Field, Niva Valu Filise, Kerri Heffernan, Fredric Humbert, Sam Larner, Amber Lewis, Justin Middleton, Jon Newcombe, Sian Prescott, Huw Richards, Alberto Pico Sánchez, Hendrik Snyders, Alice Soper, Paul Williams and Jamie Wall.

As ever, huge thanks to Marc Stafford for keeping my website *The East Terrace* up and running, which helps me to get the word out about my books. Thanks to my amazing mother for still storing so many of my rugby books and programmes in her attic back in Wales (they will be gone soon, I promise!).

Finally, unending love and gratitude to my wife Helena and my wonderful children Michael and Helena for letting me spend so much time writing about men and women running around a grass field.

James Stafford

ABOUT THE AUTHOR AND ILLUSTRATOR

James Stafford

James is founder of cult rugby website *The East Terrace* and has written on sport for a wide range of newspapers, websites and magazines. In 2017 his collection of short webcomics, *The Sorrowful Putto of Prague*, was published to critical acclaim in the Czech Republic. In 2021 he released *An Illustrated History of Welsh Rugby* with Polaris Publishing and a children's book, *How Wales Beat the Mighty All Blacks*, with Y Lolfa. Both titles quickly sold out and were reprinted, with the former title also being expanded and updated. In 2023 he released *An Illustrated History of English Rugby*.

James broke various limbs and ruined multiple muscles, ligaments and nerves playing rugby for Barry Plastics, Old Belvedere, London Japanese and Nyrsko. Born in Cardiff and raised in Barry, he now lives in Prague.

Twitter/Instagram: *@jpstafford* *Website:* *www.theeastterrace.com*

Raluca Moldovan

Raluca is a book, comics and commercial illustrator based in Constanța, Romania. Her previous published work includes *The Sorrowful Putto of Prague*, *An Illustrated History of Welsh Rugby* and *An Illustrated History of English Rugby*.

Instagram: *@_raloux*

AN ILLUSTRATED HISTORY OF
ENGLISH RUGBY
FUN, FACTS AND STORIES FROM OVER 150 YEARS
OF MEN'S INTERNATIONAL RUGBY

JAMES STAFFORD
Art by Raluca Moldovan
with Carys Feehan, Josel Nicolas, Anne Cakebread and Ched De Gala

REVISED AND UPDATED EDITION

'A big achievement and will frame the game for
young readers and curious grown-ups alike.'
CAROLYN HITT, *THE WESTERN MAIL*

AN ILLUSTRATED HISTORY OF
WELSH RUGBY

FUN, FACTS AND STORIES FROM 140 YEARS
OF INTERNATIONAL RUGBY

JAMES STAFFORD

Art by Raluca Moldovan

with Carys Feehan, Josel Nicolas, Anne Cakebread and Ched De Gala

RUGBY HAS F***ING LAWS *NOT RULES*

PAUL WILLIAMS

A GUIDED TOUR THROUGH RUGBY'S BIZARRE LAW BOOK

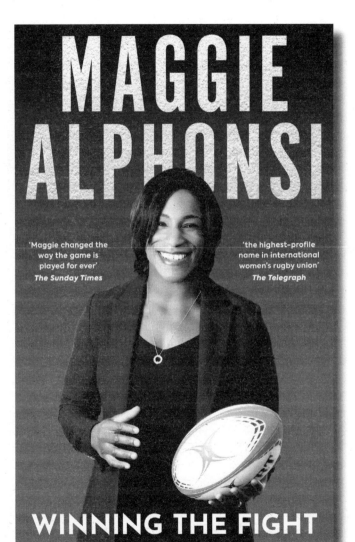

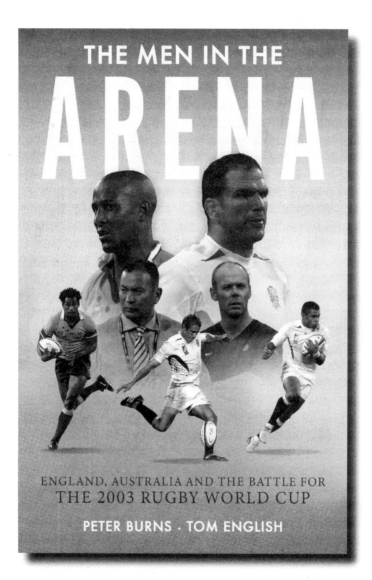

THE MEN IN THE

ARENA

ENGLAND, AUSTRALIA AND THE BATTLE FOR
THE 2003 RUGBY WORLD CUP

PETER BURNS · TOM ENGLISH

'A remarkable and inspirational story'
SARAH MOCKFORD, *RUGBY WORLD*

'A hilarious, thoroughly interesting and endearing read about
those who paved the way for women's rugby today. One of the
best rugby stories in history — men's or women's — told perfectly'
JESSICA HAYDEN, *THE TIMES*

WORLD IN
THEIR HANDS

THE STORY OF
THE FIRST WOMEN'S RUGBY WORLD CUP

FOREWORD BY SARAH HUNTER

MARTYN THOMAS

'James Hook has nailed it. A book packed with positive messages – what young rugby fans have been waiting for'
Alan Pearey, *Rugby World*

JAMES HOOK

CHASING A RUGBY DREAM

BOOK ONE

KICK-OFF

with **DAVID BRAYLEY**